# THE KITCHEN PARAPHERNALIA HANDBOOK

### HUNDREDS OF SUBSTITUTIONS FOR COMMON AND UNCOMMON UTENSILS, GADGETS, TOOLS, AND TECHNIQUES

*Jean B. MacLeod*

MacLeod How-To Books
The Kitchen Paraphernalia Handbook
Hundreds of Substitutions for Common and Uncommon Utensils, Gadgets, Tools, and Techniques

ISBN: 0997446439
ISBN-13: 9780997446432
Library of Congress Control Number: 2017916267
Jean B. MacLeod, Torrance, CA

*To all waste-wise practitioners.*
*And to you, dear reader, thank you.*

Also by Jean B. MacLeod

*If I'd Only Listened to My Mom, I'd Know How to Do This: Hundreds of Household Remedies*

*The Waste-Wise Kitchen Companion: Hundreds of Practical Tips for Repairing, Reusing, and Repurposing Food*

*The Waste-Wise Gardener: Tips and Techniques to Save Time, Money, and Energy While Creating the Garden of Your Dreams*

*The Food Substitution Handbook: Hundreds of Stand-ins for Familiar and Not-So-Familiar Ingredients*
(Coming April, 2018)

# Contents

# A

**ADJUSTABLE BLADE SLICER/BENRINER CUTTER/MINI MANDOLINE**
**(ultra-sharp handheld cutter; used for cutting firm fruits and vegetables into uniform slices)**
- Food processor with the slicer blade
- Y-shaped vegetable peeler
- Slicing slot of a box or sheet grater
- Sharp cheese plane/slicer with a 2- to 3-inch slot
- **For the julienne feature:** julienne peeler; food processor using the julienne blade; or swivel vegetable peeler with a serrated blade

**ADJUSTABLE RING;** *see CAKE RING/ENTREMETS RING, EXPANDABLE*

**AEBLESKIVER PAN (7-hole metal pan for cooking sphere-shaped Danish pancakes)**
- Electric doughnut cooker

**AIRLOCK (sealing device that prevents air from entering a vessel while allowing gas from the vessel to escape; used for alcohol ferments)**
- Balloon or latex glove (poke one or two holes in the balloon or glove; then place it over the mouth of the vessel and secure with a rubber band)
- Folded piece of cheesecloth (place it over the mouth of the vessel and firmly secure with a rubber band)

**ALUMINUM FOIL, HEAVY-DUTY**
- Two layers of regular foil

### ALUMINUM FOIL, NON-STICK HEAVY DUTY
* Heavy-duty regular foil (or two layers of regular foil) coated lightly with cooking spray, shortening, or oil

### ALUMINUM FOIL, REGULAR
* **For holding pie weights in a blind-baked pie:** disposable aluminum pie plate (can be used numerous times)
* **For covering a large casserole dish:** cookie sheet or baking sheet
* **For covering refrigerated foods:** large plastic food lids
* **For lining a baking sheet or baking dish:** parchment paper

### APÉRITIF GLASS; *see* CORDIAL GLASSES

### APPETIZER SERVING DISHES; *see* CONDIMENT BOWLS/SMALL SAUCE DISHES

### APPLE CORER (*tubed-shaped tool for removing cores from fruit or vegetables*)
* **For whole fruit or vegetable:** paring knife or short, thin-bladed knife
* **For fruit or vegetable cut in half:** melon baller; grapefruit spoon, or sturdy metal measuring spoon

### ASADOR; *see* PEPPER AND TORTILLA ROASTER, STOVETOP/ASADOR

### ASIAN ROLLING PIN (*thin, lightweight wooden pin for rolling out dumpling or wrapper dough*)
* 12-inch piece of wooden dowel, 3/4-inch in diameter (lightly sand and then rub with food-grade mineral oil; let dry before using)

### ASPARAGUS GRILL COOKER (*narrow mesh basket; used for grilling asparagus*)
* Two skewers (line the spears up; then thread the skewers close to the top and bottom ends of the line)

### ASPARAGUS PAN (*tall narrow pan for steaming asparagus vertically*)
- Double boiler with top portion inverted as a lid, or two tall pans of the same diameter (bundle the spears together, secure loosely with kitchen twine, and then stand the stalks upright in the pot)
- Electric kettle
- Coffee percolator with basket and stem removed

### ASPARAGUS PEELER (*long-bladed tool for removing thin layers from the base of asparagus stalks*)
- Cheese plane
- Y-shaped peeler

### ASPIC/JELLY CUTTER, 1-INCH ROUND (*implement for cutting out aspic, canapés, or truffles*)
- Large end of a 1-inch decorating tip
- End of a large-size apple corer
- Screw top from a sauce bottle, soft-drink bottle, or milk or juice carton
- Small/regular thimble, preferably metal

# B

**BABA MOLDS/BABAS AU RHUM MOLDS (2 1/2-x-2 1/2-inch metal molds for baking babas, individual brioches mousselines, or bouchons)**
- Dariole molds
- Jumbo muffin cups

**BACON COOKER, MICROWAVE (dish for microwaving bacon vertically)**
- Large paper plate folded in half and set on a microwave-safe plate as an inverted V (drape the bacon strips over the top)
- Microwave-safe bowl or Pyrex measuring jug set on a microwave-safe rimmed plate (drape the bacon strips over the rim of the bowl or jug)

**BACON COOKER, OVEN (pan with rack for cooking bacon in the oven)**
- Inverted V-shaped roasting rack or collapsible rib rack set on a rimmed baking sheet (drape the bacon strips over the rack)
- Piece of foil crimped diagonally at 1-inch intervals and set on a rimmed baking sheet (lay the bacon strips horizontally over the top)

**BACON FAT CONTAINER; see COOKING FAT/BACON GREASE CONTAINER**

**BACON PRESS (cast-iron block for holding bacon flat so strips cook evenly without curling)**
- Cast-iron skillet or other heavy pan, weighted if necessary
- Universal lid or other flat saucepan lid with a knob (for reducing splatters)

**BAG CLIP/BAG SEALER, REUSABLE (spring-loaded plastic clip for keeping food packages sealed)**
- Clothespin
- Paper binder clip

- Small spring clamp
- Plastic barrette
- Large paper clip

**BAGGY RACK/BAG CADDY (10-inch tall device for holding a food storage bag while being filled)**
- One- or two-quart Pyrex jug; wide-mouth jar; or tall drinking glass (turn the top of the bag over the rim of the support and hold in place with a rubber band, if necessary)

**BAGUETTE PROOFING PAN; see** COUCHE, BAKER'S

**BAKER'S FLIPPING BOARD (16-inch narrow board; used for transferring baguettes from the proofing cloth to the oven)**
- 16-x-4-inch piece of plywood

**BAKER'S PEEL/PIZZA PEEL/PADDLE (long-handled metal or hardwood paddle; used for transferring pizzas and yeast breads to and from a heated oven)**
- Large grill spatula
- Lightweight wooden cutting board
- Rimless cookie sheet
- Piece of heavy, stiff cardboard; or thin piece of plywood cut into a 14-inch square
- Pair of tongs, or long-handled fork for pulling pizza from the oven (to make it easier, remove the other oven rack before preheating the oven)

**BAKING MAT (reusable, nonstick silicone mat; used for lining a baking sheet)**
- Non-stick foil or regular foil misted with cooking spray
- Parchment paper (to keep parchment flat for cookies, place a small dab of dough on the underside of each corner of the paper, or clip the paper in place with clothespins or food bag clips and then remove them before baking)

**BAKING MAT WITH MARKINGS (*reusable, nonstick silicone mat with marked circles; used for baking cookies the appropriate distance apart*)**
- Parchment paper (draw circles on the paper, using a small upturned glass as a guide; then turn the paper over for baking)

**BAKING SHEET, HEAVY OR INSULATED (*heavy-duty rectangular rimmed sheet*)**
- Regular baking sheet lined with parchment paper or a double layer of heavy-duty foil
- Two regular baking sheets nestled together

**BAKING SHEET RACK, SPACE-SAVING (*four-tiered steel rack for holding baking sheets ready for the oven or right from the oven*)**
- Sturdy metal organizer turned on its side (for extra stability, anchor it from the back or at the base)

**BAKING SPATULA/OFFSET SPATULA (*narrow, angle-bladed spatula for spreading frostings and batters evenly*)**
- **For spreading and smoothing frosting:** sandwich spreader, fish knife, pastry server, palette knife, putty knife, non-serrated butter knife, clean metal ruler, or back of an oval serving spoon
- **For spreading and leveling dough or crumb crust:** pastry roller, bottom of a drinking glass or measuring cup, loaf pan, flat-bottomed meat pounder, or clean hands (cover dough with plastic wrap or waxed paper if necessary)

**BAKING SPRAY/BAKER'S SPRAY, NONSTICK (*aerosol oil-flour mixture for coating baking pans*)**
- Two parts non-hydrogenated vegetable shortening (or half shortening and half vegetable oil) to one part all-purpose flour; mix to a paste and then store in a small jar (use a pastry brush to brush it lightly onto the cake pans)

- One part melted butter or coconut oil to one part all-purpose flour or rice flour (use right away; or for a Bundt pan, brush the pan with soft butter or coconut oil, freeze it, and then sprinkle on the flour)

### BAKING STONE/PIZZA STONE (flat piece of unglazed clay or terra-cotta; used in the oven for producing a crustier finish on pizzas and free-form breads)

- Large steel slab (heavier; cooks and browns quicker)
- Unglazed quarry tiles, preferably high-fired and at least 1/2-inch thick; 12-x-12-inch ceramic floor tiles; or unglazed terra-cotta paving tiles fitted close together or placed on a baking sheet. (Make sure baking stone does not cover any of the vents in a gas oven and that there is a 2-inch space between it and oven walls.)
- Inverted 10-inch terra-cotta plant saucer
- Cast-iron griddle or pizza pan
- Heavy-gauge cookie sheet or inverted baking sheet (not nonstick or insulated)

### BAMBOO STEAMER (stacked steamer for cooking food over boiling water; the lid controls the steam so it does not drip onto ingredients); see also STEAMER

- Pasta cooker/pot (line the bottom of the insert with perforated parchment paper, and cover the pot with a cotton napkin or paper towels before putting on the lid)

### BANANA TREE/HOOK/HANGER (small plastic or metal column topped with a hook; used for hanging a bunch of bananas to prevent bruising and promote even ripening)

- Large hook (attach under an upper cabinet or shelf)
- Long hat or coat hook (attach to the wall or side of a cabinet)
- Free standing paper towel holder (from a dollar store)

**BANNETON (bentwood willow basket; used for the final proofing of bread dough)**

- Seven- to nine-inch-wide wicker basket, medium colander, stainless-steel or glass mixing bowl, or wooden fruit bowl (line with a linen dish-towel, coarse-weave cloth napkin, or piece of canvas liberally dusted with flour)

**BARBECUE BASTING BRUSH/MOP; see** GRILL BASTING BRUSH/MOP

**BARBECUE CLEANING BRUSH; see** GRILL CLEANING BRUSH

**BARBECUE COOKER; see** GRILL, CHARCOAL

**BARBECUE FORK; see** GRILL FORK

**BARBECUE TONGS; see** GRILL TONGS/BARBECUE TONGS

**BAR SPOON (long-stemmed, stainless-steel spoon for mixing/stirring cocktails)**

- Stainless-steel iced-tea spoon
- Sundae spoon
- Long swizzle stick
- Chopstick
- Sturdy drinking straw

**BASTER, BULB (long, hollow cylinder with a squeezable rubber top; used for siphoning cooking juices to baste the food)**

- Squeeze bottle
- **For swabbing on the juices:** pastry brush or new paint brush
- **For spooning on the juices:** small ladle or large spoon

**BASTING BRUSH, BARBECUE; see** GRILL BASTING BRUSH/MOP

**BASTING BRUSH HOLDER** *(receptacle to hold the brush while it's being used in cooking)*
- Tall, heavy-bottomed drinking glass

**BATTENBERG PAN/RUSSIAN SLICE PAN** *(8-x-6-inch aluminum pan with removable partitions; used to make Battenberg cake)*
- 8-inch square pan, or 9-x-5-inch loaf pan, divided in half with parchment paper (after baking, slice each section in half, then cut each half lengthwise into two equal pieces; arrange the strips so the squares alternate, and then sandwich together with jam or frosting)

**BATTER BOWL** *(container for measuring, mixing, and pouring batter)*
- Two-quart glass measuring jug
- Flexible plastic bowl (coat the container's edge with cooking spray; the batter slides more easily over a slippery edge)

**BATTER DISPENSER/PANCAKE PEN** *(device for making funnel cakes or designer-shaped pancakes)*
- Medium-size funnel (hold your finger over the hole while filling it with batter)
- Fat separator, preferably depositor-style, bottom-opening type
- Pastry bag fitted with a 1/2-inch round decorating tip
- Freezer bag with a bottom corner snipped off
- Bulb baster
- Clean plastic squeeze bottle
- Clean, empty 1-quart milk carton

**BENCH SCRAPER/DOUGH SCRAPER/PASTRY SCRAPER** *(metal rectangle with a beveled edge and rolled or textured handle; used for scraping dough from a work surface)*
- Inverted, square-edged, thin metal spatula/pancake turner
- Blunt edge of a cleaver or long straight knife
- New sheetrock taping knife, spackle knife, or putty knife

- 4-x-3-inch piece of plastic cut from an old flexible cutting mat
- Old or unsolicited credit/discount card
- Sturdy plastic ruler

**BENRINER (Japanese-style mandoline); see** *ADJUSTABLE BLADE SLICER/BENRINER*

**BEVERAGE COVERS, OUTDOOR; see** *DRINKING GLASS COVERS, OUTDOOR*

**BEVERAGE HOLDER, COLD; see** *ICE COOLER, LARGE*

**BISCUIT CUTTER, 1 1/2-INCH ROUND (metal or plastic cylinder for cutting biscuit dough)**
- Gently form biscuit dough into a 1 1/2-inch log; then slice it into 1/2-inch segments for biscuits, 3/4-inch for scones, or 1-inch for shortcakes
- Pat biscuit dough to flatten it slightly; then cut into squares
- Spoon biscuit dough onto an ungreased baking sheet
- Drop biscuit dough into a muffin pan (increase liquid in recipe to make drop biscuits; for same-shape biscuits, use an ice-cream scoop)

**BISCUIT CUTTER, 2-INCH ROUND**
- Clean, empty 6-ounce tomato sauce can (not pop-top) with both ends removed
- Nonstick cooking spray cap
- Inverted fine-edged juice glass (cut by pressing straight down without twisting the glass)

**BISCUIT CUTTER, 2 1/2-INCH ROUND**
- Clean, empty 8-ounce tomato sauce can (not pop-top) with both ends removed
- Inverted fine-edged drinking glass (cut by pressing straight down without twisting the glass)

### BISCUIT CUTTER, 3-INCH ROUND
- Clean, empty 15-ounce vegetable or fruit can, or 10 3/4-ounce condensed soup can (not pop-top), with both ends removed
- Doughnut cutter with the inner circle disengaged
- Inverted fine-edged drinking glass (cut by pressing straight down without twisting the glass)

### BISMARCK PIPING TIP (decorating tip used for piping filling into the interior of a pastry)
- Section of a fat plastic drinking straw

### BLADE GUARD/EDGE GUARD, PLASTIC; see KNIFE HOLDER/GUARD/ PICNIC KNIFE HOLDER

### BLENDER, IMMERSION/STICK BLENDER (handheld blender with small blade or interchangeable attachments; used for blending directly in the pot)
- Handheld/portable electric mixer using one beater only
- Rotary beater/egg beater
- **For small amounts:** battery-powered cappuccino whisk, handheld beverage frother, whisk, or muddle.
- **For emulsifying soup in the pot:** potato masher

### BLENDER, IMMERSION/STICK BLENDER, BEAKER (tall narrow mixing "bowl" used with an immersion/stick blender)
- Wide-mouth, quart-size Mason jar
- 32-ounce yogurt container
- 13- or 14-ounce coffee tin
- Take-out "big-gulp" soft-drink cup

### BLENDER, IMMERSION/STICK BLENDER, SPLATTER SHIELD (protective cover used for avoiding splatters)
- Large plastic food lid cut to fit around the beater stem and suspended over the bowl or beaker

**BLENDER SPATULA** (*narrow flexible tool for guiding ingredients into the blender blades*)

- Rubber spatula
- Bamboo skewer
- Chopstick, preferably Chinese-type with a blunt edge
- Trimmed celery stalk

**BLENDER/STAND BLENDER** (*small electric appliance for aerating, emulsifying, blending, pureeing, and liquefying*); see also *BLENDER, IMMERSION/STICK BLENDER; ICE CRUSHER, MANUAL*

- **For pureeing, blending, and pulverizing most ingredients:** food processor with the metal blade (drain off and reserve most of the cooking liquid, and then process the solids before adding back the liquid and processing to a smooth puree)
- **For blending soft, semisoft, and liquid ingredients:** electric mixer
- **For chopping hard ingredients in small batches:** nut chopper, rotary grinder/cheese grater, spice/coffee grinder
- **For pulverizing and blending soft and semisoft ingredients:** perforated potato masher
- **For pureeing soft ingredients:** sieve and large spoon (push the ingredients through the sieve with the back of the spoon, and then mix in the liquid last)
- **For emulsifying liquid ingredients:** jar with a screw-top lid (shake the jar vigorously)
- **For crushing ice, spices, and hard ingredients:** heavy-duty plastic bag and mallet or rolling pin
- **For crushing and blending small amounts of most ingredients:** mortar and pestle

**BLINI PAN** (*flat pan with seven indentations for cooking yeast-raised mini pancakes*)

- Silver dollar pan
- Swedish plätt pan/*plättlagg*
- Large frying pan (add the batter in teaspoons)

**BLOWTORCH, BUTANE KITCHEN/CHEF'S TORCH/CRÈME BRÛLÉE TORCH** *(hand-held tool for browning gratins and caramelizing desserts)*
- Propane welder's torch
- Gas oven broiler (for caramelizing tops of *crème brûlée* and *crema catalana* place chilled ramekins in a baking pan containing crushed ice and broil 5 inches from the heat until sugar has caramelized, three to four minutes)
- Hair dryer set on low heat (for unmolding terrines or creamy or frozen desserts, softening frosting on cakes, reviving shines to cake glazes, or melting a surface coating of cheese or chocolate)

**BOARD OIL; see** *CUTTING-BOARD OIL*

**BOTTLE CLEANER; see** *SPORTS BOTTLE CLEANER*

**BOTTLE, OPAQUE** *(amber or other dark-colored glass bottle, used for storing extract, tincture, olive oil, or other light-sensitive liquid)*
- Metal bottle/can
- Clean, empty, dark glass olive oil, vinegar, wine, or soda bottle
- Regular bottle wrapped in brown paper or folded cloth
- **For small bottle:** clean, empty, dark glass pill or vitamin bottle, essential oil bottle, or extract or essence bottle (to remove any lingering odor, let the bottle sit 8 to 12 hours filled with water and dry mustard, then rinse and dry)

**BOTTLE OPENER** *(small gadget for prying off bottle caps)*
- Tab/screwdriver feature on all-purpose kitchen shears or all-purpose penknife
- Hooked cap lifter on a rotary can opener
- Belt buckle
- Stubby, flat-head screwdriver
- Old house key
- Grill tongs

**BOUQUET GARNI BAG/SPICE BAG/CHEESECLOTH SACHET/SACHET D'ESPICES** *(small drawstring bag for holding herbs or spices; used in flavoring soups, stews, and stocks)*
- Metal tea ball or infuser (if it has a chain, hook the end over the rim of the pot)
- Tea filter bag made for loose tea, or tea bag with tea leaves removed and then closed with the tea bag string
- Opened-up square gauze pad or double thickness of cheesecloth, tied at the top with a piece of kitchen twine or leftover tea bag string
- Small paper coffee filter tied at the top with a long piece of kitchen twine
- Soft lettuce leaf secured with a wooden toothpick

**BOWL ANCHOR/STABILIZER** *(two-sided silicone appliance that anchors a mixing bowl in place while using)*
- Dampened, folded tea towel

**BOWL/BOWLS; see** *CHILL BOWL; CONDIMENT BOWLS/SMALL SAUCE DISHES; COPPER BOWL, UNLINED; DIP BOWL; FRUIT SALAD SERVING BOWL(S); ICE-CREAM BOWLS; MIXING BOWL, LARGE; MIXING BOWL, NONSLIP; PAPER BOWLS/BOXES; PUNCH BOWL; SOUP BOWL; STAINLESS-STEEL BOWL, LARGE*

**BOWL SCRAPER, PLASTIC** *(curved rectangle of flexible plastic; used for efficiently scraping batter from bowls)*
- Rubber spatula
- Piece of plastic measuring 4 x 3 inches cut from the lid of a wide food or coffee container, including the rim

**BRAISING PAN/BRAISER/BRAZIER/RONDEAU** *(heavy, shallow, two-handled pot with tight-fitting flat or domed lid; used for stovetop or oven slow-cooked food)*
- Dutch or French oven
- Heavy sauté pan with a tight-fitting lid

⊕ Ovenproof skillet with high sides and a tight-fitting lid (or parchment-lined, heavy-duty foil to serve as a lid)

**BREAD BAKER/DOMED BAKER;** *see CLOCHE/LA CLOCHE/BREAD DOME/ COVERED BAKER*

**BREAD BASKET (woven wicker basket for holding bread and rolls at the table)**
⊕ Banneton, fruit basket, pasta dish, cazuela, or shallow casserole dish, lined with a cloth napkin
⊕ Breadboard, cheese board, rectangular platter, or small serving tray

**BREAD BOX/BIN/CROCK (well-ventilated container for keeping yeast bread fresh and crusty)**
⊕ New paper bag
⊕ Vented bread bag
⊕ Linen napkin or clean linen dishtowel (wrap bread loosely)
⊕ Breadboard, cutting board, or clean countertop (place bread cut side down)

**BREAD/BUN WARMER (terra-cotta disk for keeping contents of a bread basket warm)**
⊕ Sterilized flat stone or rock (heat in the oven)
⊕ Small pie pan containing sterilized pebbles or river stones (heat in the oven)
⊕ Small quarry tile, paving stone, or terra-cotta flowerpot saucer (soak in water 10 to 20 minutes; then microwave on High 2 minutes)
⊕ Raw rice or beans enclosed in a pouch made from a cloth napkin or several layers of cheesecloth (close securely and microwave on High three minutes)
⊕ Piece of heavy-duty foil (place under the napkin lining the bread basket)

**BREAD KNEADING MAT (silicone mat for kneading and rolling dough)**
⊕ Flexible plastic cutting board/sheet

* Large wooden chopping board
* Clean countertop (wood, stone, or non-porous)

## BREAD LAME/FRENCH LAME (knife with an extra-sharp blade for scoring loaf tops before baking)

* Single-edge razor blade
* X-Acto/craft knife
* Box cutter
* Sharp, thin-bladed knife
* Metal blade of a food processor
* Kitchen shears or scissors (best for very wet dough; for very sticky dough, spray the shears/scissors with cooking spray)

## BREAD PAN (plain aluminum pan for baking yeast bread); see also BREAD BAKING CROCK; FLATBREAD PAN; LOAF PAN, DISPOSABLE ALUMINUM; LOAF PAN, DOUBLE; LOAF PAN, GLUTEN-FREE; LOAF PAN, SMALL PULLMAN/PAN DE MIE; LOAF PAN, THREE-PIECE/TRIO/THREE-IN-ONE/LINKED

* Casserole dish
* Regular stainless-steel mixing bowl (not nonslip) or other ovenproof mixing bowl
* Plain aluminum gelatin mold
* Deep round cake pan
* Long sheet of foil folded lengthwise into thirds, greased, loosely wrapped around formed bread dough, and then placed on a baking sheet (join foil ends by folding them together, or wrap the foil-wrapped loaf loosely with kitchen twine)
* Small, food-safe paper bag folded down 3 or 4 inches, greased inside and out, and placed on a baking sheet (bread dough should half fill the bag before final rise)
* **For high-moisture/wet dough:** loaf pan with a nonstick coating
* **For sandwich-style bread and sweet yeast bread such as babka, panettone, and kulich:** large, empty, clean coffee can; or PBA-free

food or juice can (place parchment in the bottom, and if necessary, a greased collar of folded foil around the can, extending 2 or 3 inches above the rim and held in place with kitchen twine

* **For whole-grain bread:** deep-sided skillet (not nonstick) with ovenproof or detachable handle(s)

**BREAD PEEL; see** BAKER'S PEEL/PIZZA PEEL/PADDLE

**BREAD PROOFING BASKET; see** BANNETON

**BREAD PROOFING BOARD/BAGEL BOARD (18-x-26-inch wooden board for holding proofing bagels or baguettes)**
* Large inverted sheet pan
* 18-x-12-inch flexible plastic cutting mat
* Large piece of stiff cardboard or thin plywood

**BREAD PROOFING BOX (heat and humidity controlled dough rising box)**
* Large lidless cardboard box enclosed in a large plastic bag and tied closed
* Heavy stoneware covered bowl set on a heating tray turned to medium
* Heavy bowl positioned below a long-corded heat lamp
* Inverted Styrofoam chest or corrugated box set over a seed-starting mat
* Insulated cooler containing a jug or large mug of hot water
* Microwave oven containing a jug of hot water
* Slow cooker on warm setting
* Oven with the oven light turned on and door slightly ajar (not for an oven with a pilot light)
* Oven containing a skillet (or pan) of boiling water (place the skillet on the oven floor, and then add the boiling water)
* Gas oven with a pilot light
* Electric oven heated for three minutes at the lowest setting and then turned off

- Large bowl or pan containing slightly warm water that comes halfway up the sides of the proofing bowl
- Clothes dryer run for one or two minutes with a clean bath towel (rest the bowl on top of the warm folded towel inside the turned-off dryer)
- Dishwasher just turned off but still warm (wipe out condensation if necessary)
- Microwavable neck wrap heated in the microwave for one or two minutes and wrapped around the bowl of dough.

### BRICK OVEN/HEARTH OVEN/BREAD OVEN/PIZZA OVEN (wood-fired, high temperature unglazed clay oven)

- Two baking/pizza stones, unglazed quarry tiles (or FebraMental slabs): one on the upper rack and one on the oven floor (or lower rack for an electric oven); make sure there is a 2-inch clearance between the stones and oven walls
- Three-piece ceramic oven insert (such as HearthKit)
- Stoneware or cast-iron domed baker/bread cloche (for baking bread)
- KettlePizza (for fitting over the top of a charcoal or gas grill to bake pizza)
- Ceramic grill such as the Big Green Egg
- Charcoal or gas grill plus a pizza stone or unglazed quarry tiles

### BRINE TESTER; see SALOMETER/BRINE TESTER

### BROILER (stove compartment for cooking food by direct exposure to radiant heat; or self-contained broiler unit used to finish or brown dishes)

- Top shelf of a preheated 500°F oven with the door propped open and the lower shelf covered in heavy-duty foil
- Toaster oven
- Outdoor grill
- Kitchen blowtorch (for searing and charring)

**BROILER PAN** *(two-part metal pan with a shallow base and ridged, perforated top; used for holding food cooked under the broiler)*
- Metal cooling rack placed inside a rimmed baking sheet (adjust oven rack accordingly, or elevate baking sheet by resting it on an upturned cast-iron pan)
- Nonstick, heavy-duty foil placed over a stainless-steel or disposable roasting pan (crimp the foil at the pan rim, then make holes or cuts in the foil using the tip of a sharp knife)

**BROILER PAN, PETITE** *(small broiler pan for one or two servings)*
- Wire cake rack set on a broiler-proof cake, pie, or pizza pan (adjust oven rack accordingly)
- Broiler-proof pie or cake pan with metal skewers placed over the surface
- Nonstick, heavy-duty foil placed over a cast-iron skillet (crimp the foil at the pan rim; then make holes or cuts in the foil using the tip of a sharp knife)

**BROTFORM** *(coiled cane proofing basket); see BANNETON*

**BROTFORM LINER** *(knit cotton liner shaped to fit a brotform)*
- Linen dishtowel, coarse-weave cloth napkin, or piece of canvas (dust liberally with flour)

**BROWN SUGAR SAVER/SUGAR BEAR** *(small ceramic disk for keeping brown sugar moist)*
- Small piece of broken terra-cotta planter (soak it in warm water 20 minutes; then store in a sealed container with the brown sugar). Alternatively, enclose the inside bag of boxed brown sugar in a sealable plastic bag

**BUBBLE REMOVER SPATULA** *(heat-resistant, flat-edged plastic tool; used for releasing air bubbles from canning jars)*
- Chopstick, preferably Chinese with a flat edge
- Thin-bladed plastic knife

* Narrow offset spatula
* Wooden skewer

**BUDARE (Venezuelan arepas griddle); see** COMAL

**BURGER PRESS, ADJUSTABLE (handheld tool for dispensing uniform-size hamburger patties or sliders)**
* Adjustable measuring cup (set to desired weight or size, lightly grease, fill with meat mixture, and then press it out)
* Clean, empty tuna can with both ends removed (lightly grease, fill with meat mixture, and then press it out with one of the can ends)
* Small cazuela, ramekin, or high-rimmed jar lid (line with plastic wrap, fill with meat mixture, and then unmold)

**BUTTER CHURN (handheld gadget with a crank for churning milk into butter)**
* Sturdy lidded jar (fill 1/3 full and shake the jar vigorously for 15 or more minutes)
* Deep, narrow bowl and an immersion blender (beat for 10 minutes)
* Stand mixer with a whisk attachment (whisk on medium speed for 10 minutes)

**BUTTER KEEPER/SAVER (water-sealed stoneware container; used for keeping butter fresh and spreadable without refrigeration)**
* Clean, empty cheese crock or mini cocotte (for filling with butter) nested inside a larger container holding cold water (replace the water every three days)
* Small footed dessert bowl (for half filling with butter) placed upside down in a larger container filled with cold water (the water will create an airtight seal; replace water every three days)

**BUTTER MUSLIN; see** CHEESECLOTH/TAMMY CLOTH/ÈTAMINE

**BUTTER PADDLE (small, grooved wooden board; used for rolling butter balls for decorative serving)**
* Melon baller (warm it first in hot water; then drop the butter balls into iced water)

**BUTTER WARMER (small container set over a heat source; used at the table for keeping butter warm);** see also *GRAVY WARMER*
* Cup warmer with matching mug
* One- or two-cup crock (or glass measuring jug) set on a drip coffee-maker base plate

# C

**CAKE BASE/BOARD** *(corrugated cardboard disk; used for supporting a cake while decorating or transporting)*
- Removable base of an 8- or 9-inch tart or springform pan
- Clean cardboard lid saved from a round (8-inch) take-out container
- Inverted base of a large cake carrier
- Clean top from a pizza box, the side of a corrugated cardboard box, or other sturdy cardboard, cut to size and then covered tightly with plastic wrap or foil

**CAKE COLLAR** *(acetate strip for extending the height of a cake or to hold filling in)*
- 36-x-12-inch strip of foil or parchment paper folded in half twice length-wise (to extend the height of a pan)

**CAKE COMB/DECORATING COMB/ICING COMB** *(metal or plastic scraper with a serrated edge; used for making a ridged design in cake frosting)*
- Wedge cut from the plastic lid of a food or coffee container using pinking shears
- Old credit or discount card, washed thoroughly and then trimmed on the long side with pinking shears
- New comb
- Plain fork
- Knife with a serrated or scalloped edge

**CAKE COOLING RACK; *see* COOLING RACK**

**CAKE COVER/CAKE KEEPER (*large plastic dome for placing over a cake to keep it fresh, usually accompanied with a base*)**
* Large inverted mixing bowl, grill dome, cake pan, pot, or outer bowl of a salad spinner (mostly for round cakes)
* Large microwave steamer top or inverted storage container (mostly for square cakes)
* Clean domed cover saved from a store-bought cake
* Large cookie tin (use the lid for the base and the inverted tin for the cover)
* Plastic wrap spritzed with cooking spray

**CAKE CUTTER/DIVIDER (*comb-like tool for cutting soft cakes such as angel food*)**
* Serrated skeleton knife or sharp serrated knife, using a gentle sawing motion
* Two forks inserted back-to-back
* Unflavored dental floss, using a sawing motion

**CAKE DECORATING STAND/TURNTABLE (*rotating disk on a pedestal; used when applying frosting or decorations to a cake*)**
* Banding wheel
* Small Lazy Susan
* Inverted deep cake pan or wide-based bowl (anchor the cake with a dab of frosting on the bottom, and rotate the pan or bowl as needed)

**CAKE DOME; *see* CAKE COVER/CAKE KEEPER**

**CAKE INSULATING STRIP (*aluminized fabric strip for wrapping around a cake pan to promote an even rise to the batter*)**
* Several sheets of dampened newspaper, a cut-up brown paper bag, or paper towels, folded lengthwise and wrapped in a long length of foil (wrap around the outside of the cake pan and join overlapping strips with a staple or clip)

* Double thickness of dampened cotton terrycloth or an old dishtowel (wrap around the outside of the cake pan and join overlapping strips with a clip or pin, or tie it in place with kitchen twine)

**CAKE LIFTER (10-inch stainless steel disk with a beveled edge and long handle; used for moving cake layers)**
* Pizza peel
* Large grill spatula
* Rigid prep board
* Rimless cookie sheet

**CAKE PAN (round or square metal pan, preferably dull finish for even heating; or ovenproof glass with oven heat reduced 25°F);** see also *CAKE RING/ENTREMETS RING, EXPANDABLE; CAKE PANS, MINI PAPER*
* Casserole dish or ovenproof serving dish
* Sauté pan or saucepan with ovenproof or detachable handles (not nonstick)
* Shallow porcelain or stainless-steel mixing bowl (regular, not nonslip)
* Metal gelatin mold
* Foil take-out container
* Clean, empty 11- to 13-ounce coffee can or 28- to 32-ounce BPA-free food can (grease and flour substitute pans thoroughly or line with parchment paper, fill no more than half to two-thirds full, set on a baking sheet if necessary, and adjust baking times accordingly)

**CAKE PAN, BATTENBERG; see BATTENBERG CAKE PAN/RUSSIAN SLICE PAN**

**CAKE PAN, CHRISTMAS TREE–SHAPED**
* Double thickness of heavy-duty foil formed into a five- or seven-point mold, then set on a parchment-lined (or greased and floured) baking sheet

### CAKE PAN, HEART-SHAPED

* 8-inch round pan plus 8-inch square pan (cut the round layer in half; position the square layer with its corner pointing up so it looks like a diamond, and then place each cut half on either side of the top point (the frosting will conceal the seams)

### CAKE PAN, LIGHT

* Dark-colored pan (reduce the baking time, or wrap the exterior of the pan snugly with foil; do not fold the foil over onto the interior)

### CAKE PAN, PUMPKIN-SHAPED

* Two Bundt pans or 32-ounce pudding bowls (join the two baked cakes, base to base, to resemble a pumpkin)

### CAKE PAN, SMALL

* Regular large cake pan lined with heavy-duty foil folded into a 1 1/2- or 2-inch high peak/pleat where the smaller pan edges are to be; if necessary, fill the space between the foil peak and pan edge with pie weights

### CAKE PAN, TALL

* Regular cake pan fitted with a store-bought cake collar or a homemade collar (36-x-12-inch strip of foil or parchment folded in half twice lengthwise with ends overlapping, and then stapled or pinned together; for a sturdier arrangement, wrap the foil or parchment around a cardboard strip and secure the top with kitchen twine)

### CAKE PAN, TUBE (cake pan with a center tube); see also RING MOLD/ SAVARIN MOLD

* Springform pan plus a container to set in the center (ovenproof beaker, tempered drinking glass, or clean, empty (PBA-free) food can filled with pie weights)

### CAKE PANS, MINI/INDIVIDUAL *(small-size pans for two servings)*
* Eight-ounce ovenproof bowls or soup mugs
* Eight- to ten-ounce custard cups or ramekins
* Half-pint canning jars
  (Fill two-thirds full and bake on a baking sheet; for cheesecake, fill containers three-quarters full and bake, uncovered, in a large baking dish with enough hot water to reach half to three-quarters of the way up the cups/jars)

### CAKE PANS, MINI PAPER *(small, single-use, bake-and-give pans)*
* Strips of heavy card stock (1 1/2- or 2-inch wide) formed into rings, ovals, rectangles, or squares (overlap the ends, staple closed, and then set the mini pans on a parchment-lined baking sheet; best for spoonable/heavy batter)

### CAKE PILLARS *(cake supports for wedding cake layers)*
* 1/4-inch dowel rods
* Thick plastic milkshake straws

### CAKE PLATE, DISPOSABLE *(small picnic serving plate)*
* Lid from a plastic ice-cream pail or other large, food-safe container
* Sturdy piece of cardboard cut into a square or rectangular shape and covered with foil

### CAKE PLATTER *(large presentation serving plate)*
* Cardboard cake base
* Cutting board or inverted rimmed baking sheet tightly covered in foil
* Removable turntable/carousel plate from a microwave oven

### CAKE RING/ENTREMETS RING, EXPANDABLE *(bottomless, adjustable frame for baking thick batters directly on a baking sheet)*
* Piece of heavy-duty foil folded lengthwise into a thick, 2-inch-wide strip and formed into the desired-size ring; overlap the ends and then staple,

pin, or clip them together (set the ring on a parchment-lined baking sheet)

**CAKE ROUNDS, CARDBOARD; see** *CAKE BASE/BOARD*

**CAKE SAVER (adjustable plastic wedge; used for preventing leftover layer cake from drying out)**
* Folded parchment (press it into the cut edges); for a loaf cake, affix a thin slice of white bread to the cut surface and wrap in foil

**CAKE SERVER; see** *PIE SERVER/PIE KNIFE*

**CAKE STAND/FOOTED CAKE STAND (round presentation cake plate)**
* Large inverted salad bowl, soup plate, or shallow serving bowl, topped with a heavy, flat plate (affix plate with double-sided tape or Play-Doh, if necessary)

**CAKE STAND, TIERED; see** *TIERED SERVER*

**CAKE STENCIL (perforated plastic disk; used for creating patterns with confectioners' sugar or cocoa)**
* Paper doilies
* Piece of heavyweight paper with designs traced on and then cut out with an x-Acto/craft knife or tip of a box cutter

**CAKE TESTER (long metal wire or thin wooden skewer; used for testing the doneness of a cake)**
* Strand of spaghetti
* Poultry skewer/turkey lacer
* Wooden toothpick
* Straw broom bristle
* Straightened out metal paper clip
* Instant-read thermometer (will register 190°F to 205°F)

**CALDERO** *(Latin American cast-aluminum, two-handled cooking pot; used for all-purpose stovetop and oven cooking)*
- **For large caldero used in stovetop and oven cooking:** Dutch oven; or heavy, lidded braising pan
- **For small caldero used in oven cooking:** ten-ounce custard cup

**CAMP DUTCH OVEN/BASTABLE** *(deep, heavy, cast-iron or aluminum pot with a tight-fitting flanged lid and three small legs; used for cooking over hot coals or briquettes)*
- Four- or five-quart cast-iron Dutch oven with a flat lid

**CAMP DUTCH OVEN LID LIFTER/POT HOOK** *(T-shaped crossbar or metal bar bent into a hook)*
- Grill grid lifter/grate grabber
- Fireplace poker or fire iron
- Long, heavy tongs
- Pair of big pliers; vice grips; or hammer hook

**CAMP DUTCH OVEN LID STAND** *(steel trivet; used for resting a hot Dutch oven lid when not in use)*
- Sheet tray
- Large, flat stone
- Piece of heavy-duty foil

**CAMP DUTCH OVEN STAND** *(triangular piece of metal; used for elevating the oven above the coals)*
- Three parallel bricks set in a triangle
- Three 2- to 3-inch-high paving stones set a little apart

**CANDLE HOLDERS, CAKE** *(small holders for birthday candles)*
- Miniature marshmallows or small gumdrops
- Life Savers candies
- Drinking straw(s) cut into pieces

**CANDY/DEEP FRY THERMOMETER; see** *THERMOMETER, CANDY/DEEP FRY*

**CANNED DRINK COOLER (insulated holder for keeping a chilled canned drink cold)**
* Bubble wrap or small folded towel (wrap it around the can and secure with tape or a rubber band)

**CANNELÉ/CANELÉ MOLDS (small, tightly fluted molds for baking cannelés)**
* Small silicone or nonstick baba or bouchon molds set on a baking sheet (larger; increase baking time)
* Mini muffin pan (smaller; reduce baking time)

**CANNING BUBBLE REMOVER SPATULA; see** *BUBBLE REMOVER SPATULA*

**CANNING FUNNEL; see** *FUNNEL, CANNING*

**CANNING JAR CLEANING BRUSH (long-handled, soft-bristled brush for cleaning Canning jars)**
* Bottle brush or baby bottle cleaning brush

**CANNING KETTLE/WATER BATH CANNER (large, straight-sided, lidded pot containing a sectioned rack with handles; used for preserving high-acid foods)**
* Large pasta pot with perforated insert
* Large stockpot with rack (deep enough so water will cover canning jars by at least 1 inch)
* Electric pressure cooker, such as the Instant Pot (for small batches)

**CANNING LID WAND/LID LIFTER (long plastic stick with a magnetic base; used for retrieving Canning lids from hot water)**
* Canning tongs (for easier retrieval, keep the lids and bands together, with bands facing up)
* Kitchen tongs, preferably with silicone tips

**CANNING RACK/JAR RACK** *(sectioned wire rack with handles; used in a canning kettle to raise the jars from the bottom of the pot)*
- Round metal cake cooling rack that fits inside the pot
- Canning jar rings (top side up) joined together with twist ties to form a circle
- Crumpled heavy-duty foil
- Folded kitchen towel

**CANNING TONGS/JAR LIFTER** *(wide, rubber-lined tongs with plastic handles; used to lift and lower canning jars into the water)*
- **For regular jars:** spring-loaded tongs with heavy rubber bands wrapped around the gripping ends
- **For small jars:** metal kitchen tongs

**CANNOLI CUTTER** *(diamond-shaped metal cutter for cutting cannoli pastry dough)*
- 4-inch square pastry cutter (roll the cut-out squares into 4-x-5-inch diamonds; or use a 8cm cutter for square cannoli forms)

**CANNOLI FORMS** *(tin or stainless-steel tubular molds; used for frying cannoli shells)*
- 6-inch lengths of stainless steel tubing, 1/2 inch in diameter
- Giant bamboo/reed cane/*Arundo donax* cut between the ridges into 6-inch pieces
- 1-inch-thick dowel or broom handle sawed into 6-inch segments
- Strips of heavy-duty foil (12 x 6 inches) loosely rolled lengthwise to form 6-inch-long hollow cylinders, 3/4- to 1-inch in diameter

**CAN OPENER, BEVERAGE** *(device for punching triangular holes in beverage or other pouring cans)*
- Hammer and screwdriver (punch a hole in each side of the can's top)

*CAPPUCCINO FROTHER/ESPRESSO MACHINE STEAMING WAND;* see also *FROTHER, BEVERAGE/HOT CHOCOLATE SWIZZLE/MOLINILLO*

* Glass container from a plunge-filter coffee maker/French press (fill no more than one-third full and then pump the plunger until milk doubles in volume, about 20 seconds; remove plunger and microwave container on High until froth rises almost to the top, 30 to 45 seconds)
* Tightly closed jar (fill no more than half full; shake the jar vigorously 20 to 30 seconds and then microwave, uncovered, 30 seconds on High)
* Inversion blender (beat heated nonfat milk, up and down and in circles, until foamy)

*CARAFE (bottle with flared top; used for holding wine or water)*

* **For wine or water:** tall, narrow drinking glass topped with an inverted shorter wider glass
* **For a bedside water glass:** drinking glass covered with a plastic jar or canister lid, washed lid from a food container, or a silicon suction lid

*CARTOUCHE (parchment paper circle with a small ventilation hole in the center; used for controlling moisture evaporation in braised dishes)*

* Parchment cake-pan liner or parchment paper cut to size (make a hole in the center)
* Pot lid (leave it slightly askew to allow for ventilation)

*CARVING BOARD (ridged wooden board for resting and carving meat or poultry)*

* Flat cutting board placed inside a rimmed baking sheet

*CASING PRICKER (small three-pronged tool; used for removing air pockets in filled sausage casings)*

* Pin or needle (sterilize over a flame)
* Toothpick/cocktail stick

**CASSEROLE DISH/COCOTTE (round or oval lidded baking dish for oven cooking)**
- Small Dutch or French oven
- Ceramic insert from a crock pot (for temperatures up to 400°F)
- Deep-sided cast-iron or enamel-coated lidded skillet
- Regular stainless-steel mixing bowl plus a double layer of foil for the lid
- Ovenproof bowl or serving dish with a tight-fitting lid (or crimped foil)

**CASSEROLE LID**
- Ovenproof plate, inverted if necessary
- Pan lid with a stainless-steel knob (or black phenolic knob protected with foil)
- Inverted baking sheet (for square or rectangular dishes)

**CAST-IRON CLEANER (chain-mail square for cleaning cast-iron skillets);** *see* PAN/POT SCRAPER/SCRUBBER

**CAST-IRON SEASONING (formula for seasoning, or reseasoning, cast-iron skillets)**
- Kosher salt and vegetable oil (spread the salt in a thick layer in the skillet, add 1/2 inch of oil, and heat over high stovetop heat until smoking; let cool and then remove salt and oil and rub the inside of the pan with paper towels or a clean rag until smooth and glossy
- Vegetable oil (coat the pan with oil and bake it upside down in a preheated 350°F oven for one hour; let pan cool in the turned-off oven (line the oven floor with foil to avoid a mess)

**CAST-IRON SKILLET, SEASONED (heavy iron pan for cooking non-acidic ingredients)**
- Cast-iron griddle
- Heavy-duty carbon steel skillet
- Hard, anodized aluminum skillet
- Enamelware cast-iron skillet

**CATAPLANA** *(clam-shaped, hinged copper vessel with two handles; used for steaming and serving seafood and vegetables)*
- Two thin sauté pans (one as the base and one, inverted, as the lid)
- Metal marmite, brazier, or other large pan with a tight-fitting lid (or use two pieces of foil for the lid)

**CAVIAR SPOON** *(small serving spoon made of gold, glass, mother of pearl, or tortoise shell)*
- Very small spoon, such as a salt spoon made of ivory, bone, glass, wood, or other non-metal material
- Plastic ice-cream or gelato tasting spoon (such as Baskin Robbins), or other tasting/sample spoon

**CAZUELA, LARGE** *(Spanish, round, glazed terra-cotta dish; used for oven cooking or stovetop cooking with a heat diffuser)*
- Turkish earthenware *tavia/tespsi*
- Shallow stoneware or earthenware baking dish
- 10- to 12-inch straight-sided skillet with ovenproof handles (will not provide the same earthy flavor)

**CAZUELA, SMALL/CAZUELITA** *(Spanish, round, glazed terra-cotta dish; used for oven cooking)*
- **For 1/2-cup (4 1/2-inch size):** small ramekin
- **For 1-cup (6-inch size):** ovenproof soup plate or bowl
- **For 3-cup (8-inch size):** gratin dish

**CHAFING DISH/RÉCHAUD** *(metal container set in a water basin with a source of heat directly beneath it; mostly used for keeping food hot)*
- Electric wok or skillet set to very low
- Slow cooker or electric roaster set to warm
- Earthenware dish, cast-iron pot, or heavy granite bowl set atop two parallel bricks with a votive candle or canned fuel set between the bricks

* Heavy covered saucepan set on a single-burner electric hotplate or table-top butane burner
* Large fondue pot and heated stand
* Covered casserole or baking dish set on a warming tray
* Double boiler containing very hot water
* Lidded earthenware dish set in a larger dish containing hot water

**CHAMPAGNE SAVER (*flattened stainless-steel rod for inserting into an opened champagne bottle to keep it bubbly another day or two*)**
* Narrow, stainless-steel knife or other stainless-steel utensil

**CHAMPAGNE-STYLE BOTTLES (*thick bottles with matching corks and bottle wires; used for bottling sparkling wines and effervescent beverages*)**
* New or used sanitized beer bottles with crimped caps (use a capping device to seal the lids)

**CHAMPIGNON (*drum- or flat-headed wooden tool; used for pressing food through a tamis or reducing food to a pulp*)**
* Wooden meat mallet, or back of a large wooden spoon

**CHAPATI PRESS; *see* TORTILLA PRESS/TORTILLERA**

**CHARCOAL STARTER/CHIMNEY STARTER/CHARCOAL CHIMNEY (*small metal cylinder with holes near the bottom; used as a charcoal fire starter*)**
* Empty cardboard milk carton (make large holes near the base, fill with crumpled newspaper, put charcoal on top, and then light the newspaper through the holes)
* Cardboard (not Styrofoam) egg carton (put one charcoal lump in each section; then light the carton)
* Empty paper-towel roll stuffed with crumpled newspaper (place under the charcoal; then light the cardboard roll)

- Empty toilet-paper tubes stuffed with dryer lint and wrapped in newspaper (twist the ends of the newspaper, place the tubes under the charcoal, and then light the ends of the newspaper
- Dry pinecones wrapped in a used paper bag (place under the charcoal and then light the bag)
- Sheets of folded newspaper twisted into cylinders (dip one end of each cylinder in used cooking grease or oil, place the oiled end under the charcoal, and light the dry end)
- Paraffin or sawdust cubes (arrange charcoal, teepee-fashion, over the cubes; then light the cubes)

### CHECKERBOARD CAKE PAN/BATTENBERG PAN/RUSSIAN SLICE PAN;
*see* BATTENBERG PAN/RUSSIAN SLICE PLAN

### CHEESE BAG (cotton bag for draining homemade cheese)
- Large piece of nylon muslin, unbleached cotton, or a scalded cotton dishtowel, draped in a colander. Alternatively, place ingredients in the material and tie the ends; hang it from the kitchen faucet or from a wooden spoon suspended over a bowl in the refrigerator.

### CHEESE BELL/GLASS CLOCHE (wooden base with tall glass cover; used for serving and storing cheese)
- Inverted glass bowl or small cake dome set on a plate or cheese board
- Covered rectangular or oval butter dish (for storing an opened goat-cheese log)

### CHEESE BOARD (wooden board for serving and cutting cheese)
- Small cutting board, carving board, or bread board
- Lazy Susan base, preferably wood
- Pizza/bread peel
- Wooden plate (bamboo or mango)
- Plate or platter (ceramic, earthenware, or soapstone)
- Footed cake stand (china or glass)

- Large slate or granite floor tile, ceramic tile/trivet, mirror tile, or piece of marble
- Piece of 3/4-inch plywood painted on one side with two coats of chalkboard paint
- Straw tray or mat lined with clean, nontoxic, pesticide-free leaves (bamboo, banana, berry, lemon, rose, vine, etc.), leaf-shaped cheese paper, or reusable artificial leaves made specifically for food

**CHEESECAKE KNIFE (*nonstick knife with a tiered 3 3/4-inch blade; used for cutting cheesecake into smooth slices*)**
- Cheese knife/serrated skeleton knife (the kind with holes to prevent cheese from sticking)
- Waxed, unflavored dental floss, fishing wire, or kitchen twine, held taut
- Long, sharp knife dipped in very hot water and then wiped dry

**CHEESECLOTH/MUSLIN (*Two- or three-ply coarse, loosely woven, white cotton gauze; used for wrapping and straining ingredients*)**
- Unbleached muslin
- Ultra-fine nylon curtain netting or nylon tricot
- Large, white, cotton handkerchief
- Thin, white, not-terry tea towel
- Piece of clean nylon hose
  (Sanitize item by running it through the dishwasher, or hand wash with unscented soap or detergent; then scald with boiling water or iron)
- One or two basket-type paper coffee filters (preferably oxygen bleached); or two or three pieces of plain paper towels

**CHEESECLOTH SACHET/BAG; see *BOUQUET GARNI BAG/SPICE BAG/ CHEESECLOTH SACHET/SACHET D'ESPICES***

**CHEESECLOTH/TAMMY CLOTH/ÈTAMINE (*double-thickness, fine-weave cotton gauze; used for wrapping and straining ingredients*)**
- Butter muslin
- Triple layer of regular cheesecloth

* Tightly woven unbleached muslin
* White cotton or linen napkin
* White, non-terry cotton dishtowel or flour sack towel
* Piece of old cotton pillowcase or sheeting (freshly washed with unscented soap or detergent and ironed or scalded)

### CHEESE CUTTER/CHEESE WIRE (long, thin wire with handles; used for cutting soft and semi-firm cheese)

* Girolle or thin-bladed knife (brush it with a little oil, or heat it in a glass of hot water and then wipe dry. Freezing soft cheese for 30 minutes also makes it easier to slice; bring to room temperature after slicing)
* Unflavored dental floss (place floss underneath the cheese, cross both ends over each other, and pull; this cuts the cheese into neat slices)
* Food mill (for shredding fresh mozzarella)
* Pizza cutter (for cutting thin-sliced cheese into strips)

### CHEESE FORM; see CHEESE MOLD/FORM/FAISELLE

### CHEESE KNIFE, HARD/PARMESAN KNIFE/GOUGER (small wedge- or oval-bladed knife for cutting chunks out of hard cheese)

* Oyster or clam knife
* Stubby flat-head screwdriver
* Small mortar trowel
* Two forks
* Truffle shaver/slicer or Y-shaped vegetable peeler (for slicing off thin shards)

### CHEESE MARKERS (signage used for identifying cheeses on a cheese board)

* Manilla tags, Rolodex cards, or cut-up card stock skewered on a toothpick/cocktail stick
* Rice paper Washi tape wrapped around a toothpick/cocktail stick

- White-ink calligraphy pen, or chalk-ink marker (for writing cheese names on a slate cheese board, large slate tile, or 3-x-2-inch erasable chalkboard labels)
- Fine marking pens (for writing cheese names on a cheese platter covered with parchment paper)
- Small picture frame with photo and cheese name (for a large cheese display)

## CHEESE MATTING (open-weave stiff plastic mesh mat; used for supporting drying or aging cheese)

- Bamboo sushi mat
- New, undyed bamboo placemat

## CHEESE MOLD/FORM/FAISELLE (perforated stainless-steel or plastic container; used for draining and shaping fresh curds)

- Clean, empty plastic milk container with the top half cut off and holes poked from the inside into the bottom and sides (use a hot nail or small pointed knife blade to make the holes)
- Clean, empty plastic food container or large plastic cup with holes punched from the inside into the bottom and sides
- Clean, empty coffee can, or 28- to 32-ounce BPA-free food can, with both ends removed and lined with muslin or a few layers of cheesecloth
- **For a small amount or a goat-cheese mold:** small plastic colander/sieve; plastic berry basket; or perforated insert from a 10-ounce ricotta container, such as Angelo & Franco

## CHEESE PAPER (two-ply coated wrapping paper; used to extend the life of artisanal cheese)

- Foil or plastic wrap lined with parchment or waxed paper (or place the cheese, wrapped in parchment or waxed paper, in an unsealed plastic bag)
- Covered rectangular butter dish (for fresh chèvre/goat-cheese log)

**CHEESE PLANE/SLICER** *(small spade-like utensil with a single 2- to 3-inch cutting slot; used for cutting cheese slices evenly)*
- Slicing slot of a box or sheet grater
- Vegetable peeler (chill soft cheese in the freezer 10 to 30 minutes to make it easier to slice)

**CHEESE PLATTER;** *see CHEESE BOARD*

**CHEESE THERMOMETER;** *see THERMOMETER, CHEESE*

**CHEF'S KNIFE/COOK'S KNIFE/FRENCH KNIFE** *(8- to 12-inch carbon or stainless-steel knife with a wide, tapered blade; used for chopping and mincing)*
- Japanese-style all-purpose knife/*gyuto* or *santoku* (both a little lighter in weight)
- Chinese 8-inch lightweight vegetable cleaver size 2
- Sharp, all-purpose utility knife

**CHEF'S PAN/MULTI-FUNCTION PAN/FAIT-TOUT PAN** *(large, flared saucepan with a wide base and rounded sides; used for sauces, soups, and sautéing*
- Sauté pan
- Flat-bottomed wok
- Braising pan
- Chicken fryer

**CHEF'S RING MOLD;** *see FOOD MOLDS/CHEF'S RING MOLDS/ PRESENTATION MOLDS*

**CHERRY PITTER/STONER** *(handheld, punch-type tool for pitting sweet cherries)*
- Clean, needle-nose pliers (twist around the pit to loosen it and then pull out the pit)

- Sturdy plastic drinking straw; end of a clean pencil (without an eraser); metal pastry tip; paper clip opened into an S shape; or fat end of a chopstick (push the pit from the bottom end and out through the stem end; alternatively, set the cherry on the mouth of a wine or beer bottle and push the pit through)
- Rolling pin or mallet (roll or tap several cherries at a time to expose the pits and then pick out the pits individually; place the cherries in a plastic bag to save any juice)

### CHESTNUT ROASTER/CHESTNUT ROASTING PAN (large, shallow iron pan with holes in the bottom and a long handle; used for roasting chestnuts over a gas or wood flame)
- Large cast-iron skillet or other heavy-duty metal skillet (pierce chestnut skins with a sharp knife to prevent exploding, shake the pan frequently to prevent scorching, and use long-sleeved oven or grill gloves)

### CHICKEN FRYER (10- to 12-inch heavy pan with slightly sloping sides, pouring lip, small handle, and domed lid)
- Heavy sauté pan or large cast-iron skillet, plus high-domed lid (or piece of heavy-duty foil to act as a lid)

### CHICKEN ROASTER, VERTICAL (pan with a central post for cooking chicken upright)
- Tall, narrow can (such as a 7 1/2-inch beverage or 12-ounce beer can) half filled with liquid or pie weights and placed in a shallow baking or cake pan
- Angel food pan or insert from a two-piece tube pan, placed in a round baking or cake pan
- Wire coat hanger fashioned into an 8-inch spiral and wedged in a baking or cake pan
- Large Bundt pan

**CHILE ROASTING RACK (adjustable portable grill for roasting chiles)**
  ✤ Wire rack placed atop a gas stovetop burner

**CHILL BOWL (insulated polypropylene serving bowl for keeping ingredients cold)**
  ✤ Heavy earthenware bowl chilled in the freezer 60 minutes

**CHIMNEY STARTER, CHARCOAL; see** CHARCOAL STARTER/CHIMNEY STARTER/CHARCOAL CHIMNEY

**CHINESE SAND POT/SAH BO (lidded, earthenware, bowl-shaped pot, glazed on the inside and sometimes reinforced with wire on the outside; used for stovetop or oven one-pot meals)**
  ✤ Japanese clay pot/donabe
  ✤ Three-quart covered cast-iron pot
  ✤ Three- or four-quart Dutch oven
  ✤ Three-quart ovenproof and flameproof covered casserole

**CHINESE SPIDER STRAINER; see** SIEVE, FINE-MESH/STRAINER

**CHINOIS/CHINA CAP/BOUILLON STRAINER (one-handled, ultra-fine conical sieve; used for straining purees, sauces, and stocks)**
  ✤ Fine-mesh sieve lined with several layers of ultra-fine cheesecloth

**CHOCOLATE CHOPPER (wide metal fork with heavy prongs; used for breaking up chocolate)**
  ✤ Heavy serrated bread knife (use both hands to apply pressure to the edges of the chocolate, or hit the back of the knife with a mallet)
  ✤ **For breaking up paper-wrapped chocolate bars:** flat side of a cleaver, small hammer, chisel, ice pick, or edge of a counter

- **For cutting chocolate into tissue-thin shards:** truffle shaver/slicer, mini mandoline, or Y-shaped vegetable peeler
- **For creating thin chocolate curls from melted and then firmed chocolate:** channel knife
- **For grating chocolate:** largest holes on a box grater (pre-freeze the grater to prevent the chocolate from melting)

## CHOCOLATE COMB (small utensil for giving chocolate a wavy texture)
- New plastic comb
- Notched trowel/spreader with rectangular teeth

## CHOCOLATE DIPPING FORK; see DIPPING FORK/CANDY DIPPING FORK

## CHOCOLATE DRYING RACK (board used for drying chocolate-dipped fruit or other skewed food items)
- Piece of foam (floral or heavy Styrofoam) or other rigid polystyrene plastic, wrapped in foil
- Large grapefruit or pomelo, anchored for stability (for a small amount)

## CHOPPER, GROUND MEAT (heat-resistant, stick-type tool for breaking apart   ground meat during cooking)
- **For use with cast-iron and stainless-steel pans:** stainless-steel potato masher, dough whisk, bench scraper, pastry blender with parallel blades, or spatula end
- **For use with nonstick pans:** bamboo or heavy plastic spatula-spoons

## CHOPPER, SPRING ACTION/SPRING LOADED (open plastic cylinder with a plunger-type handle; used for chopping nuts and small pieces of food)
- Food processor with the metal blade (for nuts, add a little granulated sugar from the recipe)
- Blender
- Two heavy chef's knives held parallel
- Italian mezzaluna and wooden bowl

* Pastry blender (the kind with blades, not wires) for chopping soft items, such as eggs or avocados

### CHOPSTICK HOLDER/HASHI-OKI (ceramic, metal, or wood triangle; used as part of a place setting to rest chopsticks between eating)
* Wine cork
* Well-washed pebble, seashell, or section of twig
* Bag clip

### CHURRO/CRULLER PRESS (tube-like tool with a wooden plunger; used for pressing out churros)
* Pastry bag fitted with a 3/4-inch, star-shaped decorating tip (or a freezer bag with a 3/4-inch section cut off a bottom corner)

### CITRUS REAMER/LEMON JUICER (wooden or metal grooved cone; used for juicing halved citrus fruits)
* One of the beaters from a handheld electric mixer, heavy fork, or kitchen tongs held in a closed position (place it in the halved fruit and use a twisting motion to extract the juice)
* Nutcracker, or spring-loaded tongs (squeeze the halved fruit to extract the juice)
* Food processor and strainer (pulse whole peeled fruit and then push it through the strainer [for quantity juicing])

### CLAM KNIFE/OPENER (small, round-tipped knife for opening clams)
* Stubby screwdriver with a 1 1/4-inch blade
* Parmesan cheese knife/gouger
* Butter knife (to make the clams easier to open, blanch a few at a time for 15 seconds or pour boiling water on them and then shuck)
* Freezer (freeze the clams for 30 to 60 minutes until they crack open)

### CLAY BOWL (large, rustic, terra-cotta bowl for holding fruit and nuts)
* New unglazed terra-cotta flowerpot saucer scrubbed and dried

**CLAY COOKER/TERRA-COTTA POT/CLAY CHICKEN POT/RÖMERTOPF/
SCHLEMMERTOPF** *(unglazed, lidded clay pot; used for oven cooking
without fat and little if any liquid);* see also *DONABE; CHINESE SAND
POT/SAH BO; TEGAME; TERRINE/PÂTÉ MOLD*

- New, unglazed terra-cotta flowerpot plus matching saucer as a lid or
  base (soak the clean pot and saucer in cool water 30 minutes before
  use and then place in a cold oven set at 450°F; do not clean with soap
  or detergent; scrub the cooled pot with a brush or plastic sponge using
  coarse salt or a solution of baking soda and water—stains and dark
  spots are natural with clay or terra-cotta cookware)
- Deep, heavy, lidded casserole, earthenware covered casserole, daubière,
  or Dutch oven (reduce oven temperature by 100°F and cooking time by
  30 minutes)

**CLEANING SOLUTION, ALL-PURPOSE** *(liquid spray for cleaning most
kitchen surfaces)* **— 8 ounces**

- One teaspoon baking soda and one tablespoon distilled white vinegar
  added to one cup hot water; cooled and then poured into a spray bottle
- One tablespoon liquid dishwashing soap added to one cup water in a
  spray bottle

**CLEANING SOLUTIONS;** *see GOO REMOVER; OVEN CLEANER; SANITIZING
SOLUTION; SCOURING POWDER; SCOURING PASTE/SOFT SCRUBBING
MULTI-PURPOSE PASTE*

**CLEAVER/CHINESE KITCHEN CLEAVER SIZ #1** *(heavy butcher's knife with
a large square blade; used for cutting through bone)*

- Small axe or hatchet
- Flat/blunt side of a heavy-bladed chef's knife

**CLOCHE/LA CLOCHE/BREAD DOME/COVERED BAKER (*heavy stoneware pan with domed lid for baking artisan bread*);** see also COVERED BAKER, LONG
- Inverted cast-iron Dutch oven or large metal bowl that fits closely over a shallow baking dish; remove after 10 to 15 minutes to continue baking
- Four- to five-quart unglazed earthenware baking pot, or large well-seasoned clay flowerpot without drainage hole, soaked in cold water 30 minutes and then placed in a cold oven set at 400°F; remove the cover the last 10 to 15 minutes of baking to brown the crust

**COCKTAIL SHAKER/COBBLER SHAKER (*tall, stainless-steel, three-piece vessel with built-in strainer; used for shaking/mixing cocktails*)**
- Boston mixing glass and shaker tin
- One-quart, wide-mouth canning jar with a screw band and two lids (one plain lid for shaking and one with several holes drilled in for straining)
- Tempered 16-ounce lidded glass jar plus strainer, or Nalgen-type plastic container plus strainer; *see HAWTHORNE STRAINER/COCKTAIL STRAINER*
- Blender bottle plus strainers (or hold the cover slightly askew while pouring)

**COCKTAIL STRAINER;** *see HAWTHORNE STRAINER/COCKTAIL STRAINER*

**COCONUT SCRAPER/GRATER (*metal serrated wheel with sharp teeth; used for scraping coconut from the shell*)**
- **For scraping/prying chunks from the shell:** metal bottle cap with the edge slightly flattened, flat-head screwdriver, or small dull knife
- **For peeling strips from the shell:** Y-shaped vegetable peeler
- **For making it easier to separate the meat from the shell:** freeze the whole coconut 8 to 12 hours, or bake it for 25 minutes at 325°F

**COCOTTE; see** CASSEROLE DISH/COCOTTE

**COFFEE ESPRESSO MAKER; see** ESPRESSO COFFEE MAKER

**COFFEE FILTER, PAPER**
- Piece of plain paper towel folded into quarters and then opened up to form a wedge or basket
- Paper napkin trimmed or folded so it fits in the basket
- Triple piece of cheesecloth (piece of cheesecloth folded three times)
- Piece of clean nylon hose or unbleached cotton muslin

**COFFEE FILTER, REUSABLE (fine mesh nylon or gold-plated basket for holding ground coffee in a drip coffee maker)**
- Piece of unbleached cotton muslin cut to size (use a paper filter as a pattern, adding enough for a hem if desired; it will last for up to four months if rinsed in hot water after each use)

**COFFEE GRINDER (small electric appliance for grinding coffee beans for brewing)**
- High-powered blender using the grinding setting or the highest setting (use small amounts in small spurts)
- NutriBullet using the milling blade (use small amounts in small spurts)
- Mortar and pestle or molcajete using elbow grease
- Rolling pin, mallet, or hammer plus freezer bag (enclose the beans in the bag, place the sealed bag on a cutting board, and then crush the beans into grinds)

**COFFEE MAKER/COFFEE POT (automatic or manual appliance for brewing coffee)**
- Deep pot (heat water to boiling and add coffee grounds; let mixture return to a boil and then remove from heat; sprinkle a few drops cold water on the surface, and then wait a minute until coffee grounds sink to the bottom)

- Jug (pour boiling water over medium-ground coffee in the preheated jug; stir, cover, wait three or four minutes, and then drag a spoon across the surface to settle the grounds)
- Coffee mug and funnel (place filter-lined funnel over the mug, add medium-ground coffee and then boiling water; wait a few minutes for water to drain through, adding more water as required)

## COFFEE ROASTER, HOME (electric machine for roasting raw (green) coffee beans)

- Hot-air popcorn popper with vents on the side of the popping cylinder (such as Whirleypop)
- Perforated pizza baking sheet in a 500°F oven (listen for the first popping sound, 5 to 10 minutes for a light roast)
- Heavy, stainless-steel skillet or cast-iron Dutch oven preheated to 500°F on a stovetop with a powerful exhaust fan or on an outdoor grill (constantly turn and mix the beans only until golden brown, 5 to 10 minutes; if too dark, their taste will be bitter)

## COLANDER (perforated, bowl-shaped utensil; used for rinsing and draining food); see also SIEVE/STRAINER

- Salad spinner insert
- Deep-fat fryer basket
- Pasta pan insert
- Loosely woven bamboo basket
- Clean grill basket, or grill wok with perforations
- Large disposable foil pan (make holes or cuts in the bottom and bend the sides upward if necessary)
- Clean, empty, 4-pound yogurt container; 1/2-gallon ice-cream container; or large, clear, rigid container from prewashed greens (make holes or cuts in and around the bottom)
- **For draining water from the cooking pan:** crescent-shaped pan strainer
- **For draining salad greens, fruit, and vegetables:** over-the-sink dish drainer, or free-standing dish drainer/rack with drain board

- **For draining small amounts of pasta, and blanched fruit or vegetables:** pasta strainer or wire skimmer/spider
- **For draining a very small amount:** collapsible steamer basket, mesh strainer, wire skimmer/spider, or steel mesh coffee filter

## COLANDER, SOAK AND STRAIN (*two-piece vessel for washing and straining berries and other items*)
- Colander set in a deep bowl (hold both together when straining water)

## COLD TRAY; *see* ICE BOWL/CHILL BOWL

## COMAL (*Mexican, round, unglazed earthenware, or cast-iron griddle; used for cooking tortillas*)
- Cast-iron griddle or skillet
- Non-stick, wide aluminum skillet

## COMPOST LINER ANCHOR (*gadget for securing the liner to the bin*)
- Heavy-duty rubber band or wide strip cut from an old rubber glove (to go around the outside)
- Magnets for a metal bin (to position around the outside)
- Paper-coated produce tie or bread-wrapper tab (to gather the excess for a tighter fit)

## CONDIMENT BOWLS/SMALL SAUCE DISHES (*ceramic dishes for holding dipping sauces or individual food portions*)
- Custard cups
- Demitasse or espresso cups or saucers
- Glass or crystal punch cups
- Silicone baking cups
- Clear votive candle holders
- Small 1/2-cup cazuelas/cazuelitas
- 3- to 6-ounce ramekins
- Large, traditional eggcups

- 2-inch ceramic tea-bag holders
- Wide-mouth, 4-ounce canning or storage jars
- Clean, empty, baby-food jars or similar small jars
- Asian soup spoons
- Stainless-steel, glass, or ceramic prep bowls
- 2 1/2-inch scallop shells, or 3- to 6-inch clam shells (cushion them in a bed of raw rice, dried beans, crushed ice, or crumpled foil)
- Hollowed out bell peppers, citrus halves, gourds, small winter squash, or miniature pumpkins (cut a thin slice off the bottom to stabilize them)

**CONFECTIONERS' SUGAR SHAKER; see** *SUGAR DUSTER*

**CONTAINERS, PAPER; see** *PAPER BOWLS/BOXES*

**CONVECTION OVEN CONVERSION (*formula for adapting a conventional recipe to convection cooking*)**
- Lower the convection oven temperature by 25°F; reduce the cooking time by 25 percent; and use low-sided baking pans for best air circulation

**COOKBOOK HOLDER/EASEL (*transparent stand for holding a cookbook in an open position*)**; see also *RECIPE CARD HOLDER*
- Bookstand or plate stand, sheet-music holder, or clear acrylic napkin holder (for propping up a magazine or cookbook)
- Large, shallow salad or mixing bowl (for propping up a cookbook at an angle)
- Two heavy 2-inch magnetic spring clips (for weighting down each side of a magazine or cookbook to keep it open)
- Two heavy rubber bands (for securing each side of a cookbook to keep it open)
- Trouser or skirt hanger (for hanging an opened magazine, or page, on a cabinet knob)
- Magnetic spring clip (for attaching a magazine page to a range hood, refrigerator, hanging pan, or other metal object)

**COOKIE CUTTER, 1 1/2-INCH ROUND** (*implement for cutting out shapes for canapés or cookies*)
- 1 1/2-inch round vitamin bottle cap
- Inverted liqueur glass or sturdy champagne flute
- Alternatively, form dough into a 1 1/2-inch roll, wrap in plastic wrap or waxed paper, and place in an empty paper-towel roll, slit lengthwise; chill until firm (or freeze) and then slice into desired widths

**COOKIE CUTTER, 2-INCH ROUND** (*implement for cutting out dough for biscuits, canapés, cookies, crackers, crostini, petits fours, or scones*)
- Lid from a condiment jar, spice jar, or honey container
- Cap from a large vitamin bottle
- Clean, empty (6-ounce) tomato paste can with both ends removed
- **For cookies and crackers:** Form dough into 2-inch-diameter logs, chill until very firm (or freeze), and then slice into 1/8- or 1/4-inch thick rounds. Or, pack the dough into a 1-cup adjustable measuring cup (such as Adjust-A-Cup or Wonder Cup); chill until firm, and then push the base through to the correct width and slice

**COOKIE CUTTER, 2–INCH SQUARE**
- Pack dough into an empty kitchen wrap box (foil, parchment, plastic, or wax) lined with plastic wrap; chill until firm (or freeze); then slice into desired widths

**COOKIE CUTTER, 2 1/2–INCH ROUND**
- Clean, empty, 8-ounce tomato sauce can (not pop-top) with both ends removed
- 2 1/2-inch, fine-edged, straight-sided drinking glass

**COOKIE CUTTER, 3-INCH ROUND** (*implement for cutting out dough for empanaditas, kreplach, piroshki/pierogi, ravioli, sambusak, schlutzkrapfen, shortcakes, tarts, or tostadas*)
- Upturned drinking glass or measuring cup

* Clean, empty (15-ounce) food or soup can with both ends removed

### COOKIE CUTTER, 3 1/2-INCH ROUND
* Wide-mouth canning jar ring

### COOKIE CUTTER, 4-INCH ROUND (implement for cutting out dough for Asian dumplings, calzones, cannoli, small crostatas, Eccles cakes, empanadas, panzarotti, pierogie, shortcakes, tartlets, turnovers, or vol-au-vents)
* Base of a two-part, hinged, mini pie mold/dumpling maker that cuts, crimps, and seals the dough
* Clean, empty, 29-ounce food can with both ends removed
* 4-inch diameter bowl, inverted

### COOKIE CUTTER, 4-INCH SQUARE; see PASTRY CUTTER, 4-INCH SQUARE

### COOKIE CUTTER, 6-INCH ROUND; see PASTRY CUTTER, 6-INCH ROUND

### COOKIE CUTTER, LEAF-SHAPE
* Small fresh leaf, washed and patted dry (place on the dough and cut around it)

### COOKIE CUTTER, SQUARE, SCALLOP-EDGE
* Use the curved edge of a dry lasagna noodle to cut out the cookie dough

### COOKIE MAT (silicon liner with circular markings; used for baking evenly spaced cookies)
* Parchment paper (draw circles on the paper, using a small upturned glass as a guide; or select your size: 1 teaspoon, 1 tablespoon, or 3 tablespoons, then turn the paper over for baking)

### COOKIE MOLD (small wooden mold; used for shaping cookie dough into disks)
* Small, sturdy paper cup cut down to a 1/2-inch base

**COOKIE SHEET (*rectangular sheet with two to four unrimmed edges; used for baking cookies and pastries*)**
- Shallow, inverted roasting pan, baking pan, or baking sheet (cover with foil or parchment paper if necessary)
- Oven rack covered with heavy-duty foil, with a 2-inch margin on all sides (place the cookies on the foil-lined rack and slide in place; remove the rack using heavy oven mitts)
- Large wire cooling rack or broiler pan top covered with heavy-duty foil
- Two layers of heavy-duty foil (for light or delicate cookies)

**COOKIE SHEET, MARKED/ZONED (*nonstick cookie sheet with marked circles for placement of dough; used for baking cookies the appropriate distance apart*)**
- Parchment paper (draw circles on the paper, using a small upturned glass as a guide; then turn the paper over for baking)

**COOKIE STAMPS (*small, decorative molds for imprinting designs on cookie dough*)**
- Perforated/grid potato masher
- Bottom of a decorative glass, cut crystal container, or patterned spoon
- Coarse-toothed surface of a mallet/meat tenderizer
- Bottom of an empty plastic thread spool
  Bottom of a food processor feed tube
- Carved section of a potato (especially to make a raised initial)
- Engraved rolling pin to make the pattern before cutting with a cookie cutter
- **For creating indentations for thumbprint cookies:** clean rubber wine cork, thimble, or back of a small melon ball scoop

**COOKING FAT/BACON GREASE CONTAINER (*receptacle for disposing of liquid fat in the garbage/trash*)**
- Empty yogurt container; used cardboard take-out cup; frozen juice container; opened cardboard milk or cream carton; or other empty, disposable container (let sit until fat solidifies, refrigerating if necessary, and then discard)

- Small bowl lined with foil (when fat solidifies, fold up the foil and discard)
- Shredded newspaper in an old plastic bag (let newspaper absorb the fat; then seal the bag and discard)

**COOKING OIL DISPENSER; see** *OIL MISTER, COOKING; OLIVE OIL SERVING CAN*

**COOKING PLANKS (hardwood boards; used for holding food during grilling, broiling, or baking)**
- Untreated cedar shingles, or other 1/4-inch untreated "construction-grade" wood (soak clean planks at least one hour before using, weighted to keep them submerged)
- Cedar paper wraps soaked following package directions (place food parallel to the grain of the wood, fold over the edges, and secure with kitchen twine; discard wrap after use; papers can be used only once)

**COOKING PLANK TRAY (7-x-15-inch stainless-steel tray for transporting and/or serving planked food)**
- Heavy jellyroll pan (not nonstick)

**COOKWARE, HEAVY-BOTTOMED/HEAVY-BASED; see** *PAN/POT, HEAVY-BOTTOMED*

**COOKWARE, NON-REACTIVE (pots and pans with a non-porous cooking surface that does not react to acidic ingredients)**
- Enamelware or enamel-lined cookware
- Earthenware or stoneware
- Glass or glass-ceramic cookware
- Nonstick cookware
- Stainless-steel cookware
- Lined copperware

**COOKWARE, NONSTICK; see** NONSTICK COOKWARE

**COOKWARE, REACTIVE (pots and pans with a porous cooking surface that can give a metallic taste to acidic ingredients)**
* Aluminum cookware
* Cast iron and ironware
* Unlined copperware

**COOLING PITCHER (glass or plastic decanter/pitcher with an ice tube insert)**
* Regular decanter or pitcher plus a gel-filled tube, such as Corkcicle or Freezer Stick (freeze tube/stick for two hours ahead of time; then insert into the pitcher)
* Regular decanter or pitcher plus small frozen bottle of water (remove some of the water from the bottle before freezing)

**COOLING RACK (metal or wood grid for holding hot baking pans straight from the oven);** see also TRIVET
* Perforated insert from a pressure cooker
* Stovetop grate
* Oven or toaster oven rack (prop it up with small condiment containers or balls of crumpled foil)
* Two same-size food cans spaced a little apart
* Two inverted empty cardboard egg cartons spaced a little apart
* Inverted metal muffin pan
* Sturdy metal desk organizer
* Heat diffuser or copper defroster plate
* Heavy oven mitt or folded towel
* Several dinner knives laid out in opposite directions
* Flan/tart ring, or collar from a springform pan (for a cookie or sheet pan)

**COOLING RACK/WIRE RACK** *(footed, open-weave metal grate for cooling baked goods removed from the pan)*
- Footed grill rack
- Splatter shield with little legs (or one without legs set over a large skillet)
- Flat rack from a broiler or roasting pan, indoor grill, or toaster oven, set on a flan ring or two cans, one at either end
- Inverted pizza crisper/perforated pizza pan
- **If no substitute**: turn cookies upside down on a tray or countertop; lay muffins on their side in the muffin pan; place breads or other firm items on a clean towel

**COPPER BOWL, UNLINED** *(bowl reserved for beating egg whites)*
- Stainless-steel, round-bottomed bowl plus 1/8 teaspoon cream of tartar per each egg white, added after whites start to foam (to acidify the bowl's surface and remove all traces of grease, rub the inside with a cloth dampened with vinegar or lemon juice)

**COPPER CLEANER** *(natural cleaner for copper cookware)*
- Cream of tartar mixed to a paste with lemon juice (apply and let it sit for five minutes before washing with warm water)
- Salt moistened with lemon juice or white vinegar (or rub pan with a cut lemon dipped in salt)

**COPPER DEFROSTER PLATE** *(flat alloy disc; used for thawing frozen food)*
- Aluminum or stainless-steel (not nonstick) skillet, grill, or flat lid (place frozen, unwrapped food on the unheated metal)
- Zip-lock bag and cold water (seal frozen, unwrapped food in the bag; submerge it in the water; and then change the water every half hour until the food is thawed)

### CORDIAL GLASSES (2 1/2-ounce footed or colored glasses for serving liqueurs and cordials)
- Glass votive candle holders

### CORK REPLACEMENT/BOTTLE STOPPER (device with expandable seal for sealing any opened bottle)
- Plastic wrap and then foil stretched over the opening (secure with a tightly wound rubber band)
- Candle stub wrapped in plastic wrap (microwave the candle stub until softened, 1 or 2 seconds; then form it to fit the opening)

### CORKSCREW (wire spiral device for removing a cork from a wine bottle)
- Slip-joint pliers or small paring knife, for gently prying the cork loose
- Drywall screw inserted into the cork with a screwdriver and then pulled out with pliers
- If all efforts fail: push the cork into the bottle and close the top with a piece of foil, candle stub, or cork saved from another bottle (if the cork has crumbled or disintegrated, pour the wine through a piece of cheesecloth or a coffee filter secured over the mouth of the bottle)

### CORN COB HOLDERS (implements for holding hot corn on the cob)
- Poultry skewers/turkey lacers or cocktail forks, pressed deeply into the husks
- Corn husks (cook with husks intact after removing silks and washing corn; pull down the husks and use as a handle)

### CORN STRIPPER/CORN ZIPPER/CORN SCRAPER (stainless-steel cylinder for removing kernels and liquid from the cob)
- Chef's knife and tube pan (rest the corn in the center so the cut kernels will fall in the pan, or use a large wide bowl with a smaller bowl upended in the center; use the knife's cutting edge for removing kernels and the back/blunt edge (or a hand grater) for removing leftover pulp and juices)

* Mandoline set to 1/4-inch thickness (use the cutting guard and watch your fingers)

**CORZETTO (Italian handcrafted wooden pasta stamp); see** COOKIE STAMPS

**COUCHE, BAKER'S (flax linen cloth; used for supporting baguettes during final proofing)**
* 1/2 yard of 26-inch-wide unbleached baker's linen, linen canvas (like artist's canvas), old linen tablecloth, or a double layer of large linen tea towels pinched lengthwise to form a walled compartment for each loaf (place a tightly rolled kitchen towel at each long edge to provide support)
* Parchment paper bunched lengthwise to form a compartment/half sphere for each loaf (place a tightly rolled kitchen towel at each long edge to provide support)
* Empty paper-towel rolls cut in half lengthwise and lined with cotton dishtowels

**COUPON HOLDER (container for clipped food coupons)**
* Old checkbook cover

**COUSCOUSIÈRE/CUSCUZEIRO (double-decker vessel with a cooking pot on the bottom and an uncovered, perforated steamer on top)**
* Small-holed, stainless-steel colander set atop a large pot, plus a strip of twisted foil or a damp cloth wedged between the rim of the pot and the colander to prevent steam from escaping; alternatively, seal the gap with luting paste (a moist dough made with 1 to 1 1/4 cups flour and 1/3 to 1/2 cup lukewarm water)

**COVERED BAKER, LONG (long, narrow, unglazed stoneware lidded pan; used for baking artisan loaves)**
* Two new, well-seasoned terra-cotta planters (use one for the base and the other for the top)

**CRAB FORK/LOBSTER PICK** *(long, very thin, two-pronged fork for extracting meat from crab or lobster shells)*
- Nutpick, olive fork, teaspoon handle, bamboo skewer, or Japanese chopstick

**CRAB/LOBSTER CRACKER** *(handheld tool for cracking open crab or lobster shells)*
- Seafood scissors
- All-purpose kitchen shears (serrated area between the finger holes and the blades)
- Nutcracker
- Slip-joint pliers
- Rolling pin, small hammer, wooden mallet, or dull side of a chef's knife (cover the shells/claws with a kitchen towel; then whack them in several places)

**CRAB/OYSTER GLOVE** *(steel-reinforced glove; used for protection when opening seafood)*
- Leather gardening glove
- Welder's glove
- Folded towel

**CREPE PAN** *(5- to 12-inch flat-bottomed, low-sided, round metal pan)*
- Omelet pan
- Nonstick skillet
- Smooth-surfaced comal

**CROCK, BRINING** *(ceramic or glazed stoneware vessel; used for fermenting food and vinegar)*
- Wide-mouth glass jar wrapped in brown paper (or heavy-duty foil), plus plate or board for a lid; or for a loose lid, a dishtowel or coffee filter
- One-gallon food-safe plastic bucket (for a vented lid, drill or poke a hole in the lid)

**CROCK, TOOL; see** *TOOL CADDY*

**CROCK WEIGHT, PICKLING/FERMENTATION WEIGHT (heavy tempered glass or stoneware weight; used for submerging food in wide-mouth jars or crocks)**
* One-gallon vinegar or water jug
* Large lidded jar or empty milk jug filled with water
* Quart or gallon freezer bag filled with water (or with salt brine for weighting pickles)
  (Use a saucer or dish that fits inside the container or covers the food; then set the weight on top)

**CRUETS (small glass serving bottles for holding oil and vinegar)**
* Double-spouted soy sauce bottles
* Small empty condiment bottles

**CRUMPET/ENGLISH MUFFIN RINGS (metal rings for holding batter in place as it cooks on a griddle or baking sheet)**
* Small flan rings
* 3 1/2- or 4-inch round, metal pastry cutters
* Non-stick aluminum foil folded into 1/4-inch, triple-thickness strips; then formed into circles 3 1/2 or 4 inches in diameter
* Clean, empty 2-inch-deep food cans (PBA-free and not pop-top) with label and both ends removed (will make smaller crumpets or English muffins)

**CULINARY TORCH; see** *BLOWTORCH, BUTANE KITCHEN/CHEF'S TORCH/ CRÈME BRÛLÉE TORCH*

**CUPCAKE CARRIER (container for transporting cupcakes)**
* Roasting pan, lasagna pan, or 13-x-11-inch baking pan (tent with foil or with plastic wrap coated with cooking spray)
* Upside-down deli container or plastic storage container (place cupcakes on the lid and then snap the container on top).

* Muffin pan tented with foil (for a dozen cupcakes)
* Bamboo steamer (for a few cupcakes)

### CUPCAKE CORER (small plunger tool; used for creating a cavity for extra frosting or a filling)
* Apple corer, melon baller, or small paring knife (core out a section from the top of the cupcake; spoon in the frosting/filling, and then replace the trimmed cap flush with the top)
* Wooden skewer or chopstick (poke a hole in the bottom of the cupcake and twist it around to make room for the filling; pipe the frosting/filling into the center, using a Bismarck tip or section of a fat straw)

### CUPCAKE LINERS/PAPER BAKING CUPS; see also MUFFIN PAN/CUPCAKE PAN, REGULAR
* Nonstick, heavy-duty foil cut into 4 1/2-inch squares, molded on the outside of the muffin pan and then inserted into the cupcake wells (snipping off the corners of the foil makes for a smoother fit)
* Parchment paper cut into 5- or 6-inch squares, crumpled tightly, and then opened up and inserted into the cupcake pan wells (or molded over the base of an inverted bottle or drinking glass and then fitted into the cupcake pan wells)
* Paper nut cups (for miniature liners)

### CUPCAKE LINERS, TULIP
* Trimmed, blanched cornhusks or banana leaf (fresh, thawed frozen, or dehydrated dried) cut into 2-x-6-inch strips and then laid crosswise in each muffin cup, allowing two strips per cup

### CUPCAKE PAN; see MUFFIN PAN/CUPCAKE PAN

## CUPCAKE PAN, HEART-SHAPED
* Regular cupcake/muffin pan plus marbles (place a clean marble between the paper cupcake liner and the cupcake/muffin pan)

## CUP WARMER (small, flat electric device with a circular indentation; used for keeping a cup of hot beverage warm)
* Drip coffee maker base plate
* Lidded cup, such as Japanese *chawan*, or a regular cup with a small saucer or condiment dish placed on top (to keep contents warm longer)

## CURD CUTTING KNIFE (long-bladed knife with a rounded top; used in cheese making)
* 10-inch-long, narrow, offset cake-decorating spatula

## CURING CHAMBER (cool storage area for curing cheese and dry-cured meat)
* Wine refrigerator

## CUSTARD CUPS (Pyrex or glazed porcelain tapered cups; used for individual baked desserts)
* Dariole molds
* Ramekins
* Jumbo espresso cups
* Ovenproof or tempered teacups (temper cups by covering them with cold water in a large pot, bringing the water to a boil, and simmering, covered, 10 minutes; let cool in the water)
* Japanese *chawan* cups (for large custard cups)

## CUTLET BAT; see MEAT POUNDER/CUTLET BAT

**CUT-RESISTANT GLOVE; see** CRAB/OYSTER GLOVE

**CUTTERS; see** ASPIC/JELLY CUTTER; BISCUIT CUTTER; CAKE CUTTER/
DIVIDER; CANNOLI CUTTER; CHEESE CUTTER; DOUGHNUT CUTTER;
EGG TOP CUTTER;MEZZALUNA/CRESCENT CUTTER; PASTRY CUTTER;
PIZZA CUTTER; SEA URCHIN CUTTER; VOL-AU-VENT CUTTER

**CUTTING BOARD, DISPOSABLE (single-use, flexible paperboard sheet;
used for cutting raw poultry or meat)**
* Piece of butcher paper, opened produce plastic bag, or other food-safe
  plastic or paper bag (use kitchen shears for cutting chicken; use herb
  shears or herb mill for chopping herbs)
* Regular cutting board covered with plastic wrap; discard plastic when
  finished
* Dishwasher-safe chopping mat

**CUTTING-BOARD HOLDER (rack for holding cutting boards upright)**
* Desktop file sorter

**CUTTING BOARD, NONSLIP (wooden cutting board with a rubberized,
nonskid bottom)**
* Regular wooden cutting board resting on a damp dishtowel, piece of
  nonskid/rubberized shelf liner, or a rubber sink mat
* Regular cutting board with rubber bands wrapped diagonally across each
  corner

**CUTTING-BOARD OIL (replenishing oil; used for keeping the board
smooth and free of cracks)**
* Food-safe mineral oil

**CUTTING-BOARD SANITIZER *(solution used for sanitizing wood or plastic cutting boards)***

- Distilled white vinegar and hydrogen peroxide (lightly spray with the vinegar followed by a light spray of hydrogen peroxide; let sit 10 minutes, and then rinse and dry
- Undiluted rubbing alcohol/isopropyl alcohol (wipe or spray it on and let sit a few minutes; then rinse and dry)
- Salt (for wood boards: let it sit on the board 8 to 12 hours; then rinse, scrub, and finish with a light coat of mineral oil)
- Dishwasher for hard polyethylene or polypropylene plastic boards

# D

**DAIRY THERMOMETER; *see*** THERMOMETER, CHEESE

**DANISH PANCAKE PAN; *see*** AEBLESKIVER PAN

**DARIOLE/TIMBALE MOLDS (*small bucket-shaped molds; used to bake timbales and various other sweet or savory items*)**
* Custard cups
* Small ramekin dishes
* Porcelain or tempered ceramic teacups or cappuccino cups

**DARK-COLORED GLASS CONTAINER; *see*** BOTTLE, OPAQUE

**DAUBIÈRE (*French, potbellied, earthenware pot with a concave lid; used for stovetop or oven slow-cooked dishes*)**
* Deep earthenware casserole, bean pot, or Chinese sand pot (place a wet piece of crumpled parchment paper, preferably unbleached, directly atop the food before putting on the lid)

**DECANTER; *see*** WINE DECANTER/CARAFE

**DECORATING BAG, DUAL COLOR STRIPING (*two-chambered pastry bag insert for piping two different colors of frosting through one tube*)**
* Homemade parchment decorating bag (lay the chilled frosting in two horizontal strips before folding the paper into a cone shape and snipping off the tip)
* Two small decorating bags plus one larger bag fitted with a piping tip (slightly flatten the filled smaller bags to fit into the larger bag, and squeeze both bags at the same time)

**DECORATING BAG/PIPING BAG/CORNET** *(cone-shaped bag with inter-changeable tips; used for piping frosting into decorative designs);* see also *PASTRY BAG/PIPING BAG*
- Plastic sandwich or freezer bag with a bottom corner snipped off (slip the decorating tip into the opening or use the bag without one, closing the snipped-off section with a clothespin or bag clip when refilling the bag)
- Parchment paper cut on the diagonal to make a triangle and then folded into a cone shape (enlarge the tiny opening, if necessary, by snipping a small curved piece off the bottom)
- Clean, empty, plastic squeeze bottle

**DECORATING/PASTRY BAG SUPPORT** *(7-inch tall, polypropylene cone for holding a decorating bag while being filled)*
- One-quart, wide-mouth canning jar; beaker from an immersion blender; or tall drinking glass (turn the top of the decorating bag over the rim of the support and hold in place with a rubber band, if necessary)

**DECORATING PEN** *(battery-operated device for applying decorative icing)*
- Empty, well-washed mustard, ketchup, or mayonnaise plastic squeeze bottle (hold bottle at a 90° angle for making dots, and at a 45° angle for making lines or writing)
- Plastic bag with a 1/8-inch corner cut off (for piping)
- New hair-dye bottle, or plastic bag with a 1/16-inch corner cut off (for fine-line drawing)

**DECORATING TIP CLEANING BRUSH** *(small brush for cleaning piping tips)*
- Q-tip
- Cotton-wrapped orange stick
- Dental pick brush

**DEEP-FAT FRYER (electric or stovetop appliance with wire basket insert; used for cooking food in hot fat)**
- Deep, heavy pot and a deep-fat frying thermometer, if possible (fill the pot no more than a third of the way; position it on a back burner on the stove, making sure the pot is larger than the burner; and avoid adding too many ingredients at one time or letting the oil get too hot and smoke)

**DEEP-FAT FRYER THERMOMETER; see** THERMOMETER, DEEP-FAT FRYER

**DEHYDRATOR, ELECTRIC (appliance for drying food at low temperatures using fan-circulated air);** see also OVEN DRYING RACK
- Oven (preferably convection) set at 140°F (or the lowest possible setting), with the oven door propped slightly open and a small electric fan positioned by the oven door (if oven heat is coming from the top, place the food on a lower shelf with an empty cookie sheet on the top shelf)
- Oven preheated to 200°F and then turned off—repeat cycle for as long as necessary; alternatively, turn off the heat but leave the oven light on

**DEHYDRATOR SHEETS (nonstick Teflon-coated flexible sheets; used when drying fruit leathers and other soft food)**
- Parchment paper cut to size and oiled if necessary

**DEMITASSE/ESPRESSO SPOON (small stirring spoon served with espresso coffee)**
- Baby-feeding spoon
- Egg spoon

**DESSERT DISHES, INDIVIDUAL (small porcelain or glass dishes for cold or frozen desserts)**
- Small wine glasses, juice glasses, cordial glasses, highball glasses, margarita glasses, or champagne flutes
- Punch cups or small teacups
- Opaque glass cups from a yogurt maker

* 4-ounce, wide-mouth canning jars; quilted jelly jars; storage jars; or small repurposed food jars
* Hollowed-out citrus fruit halves with a small slice removed from the bottom to stabilize
* 1/4-cup vodka or shot glasses, saké cups, demitasse cups, or aperitif glasses (for small, extra rich desserts)

## DESSERT MOLDS, INDIVIDUAL (small molds for chilled or frozen desserts); see also GELATIN MOLDS, INDIVIDUAL

* Foil-coated or unbleached parchment cupcake liners (set in the cupcake pan to freeze; then unmold or tear away the liner before serving)
* 3- to 4-ounce paper drinking cups (unmold or cut away the paper before serving)

## DESSERT SERVING DISH, LARGE (glass or crystal footed serving bowl for trifle and other cold desserts)

* Small cut-glass punch bowl
* Large tempered-glass mixing bowl
* Large, round, glass food storage container
* Round Pyrex casserole dish
* Outer bowl of a small salad spinner

## DEVILED EGG PLATE/STUFFED EGG PLATE (plate with several indentations for holding stuffed eggs)

* Small serving tray or platter (line with a bed of greens, such as arugula, baby spinach, or parsley; or use small sterilized pebbles. For extra stability, cut a small slice off the bottom of each egg half.)
* Clean, empty egg carton; or shallow plastic container plus cupcake liners (for transporting to picnics or potlucks)

## DIP AND CHIP BOWL (shallow bowl with a center cup for holding the dip)

* Ring mold pan (place dip container in the pan's hollow and chips in the pan)

* Inverted cake or decorating stand, or footed compote (use the hollow base for dip and the pedestal top for chips)
* New terra-cotta plant saucer plus mortar or suribachi

## DIP BOWL (small bowl for holding a savory or sweet dipping mixture); see also DESERT DISHES, INDIVIDUAL; SOUP BOWL

* Sugar bowl, gravy boat, large mug, cream pitcher, or mortar or suribachi
* Small stoneware or stainless-steel bowl nestled in a larger bowl containing chopped ice (for a chilled dip)
* Grapefruit with top third removed (hollowed out and small sliver cut off the bottom if necessary to stabilize)
* Zucchini or marrow boat (large zucchini or marrow halved lengthwise, hollowed out leaving a 1/2-inch shell, and then a small sliver cut off the bottom if necessary to stabilize)
* Green or red pepper cup (large pepper with top third removed, insides hollowed out, and then a small sliver cut off the bottom if necessary to stabilize)

## DIPPING FORK/CANDY DIPPING FORK (long, two- or five-prong fork for dipping pastries and candies into melted chocolate or icing)

* Two-pronged mussel or seafood fork
* Plastic fork with center two tines removed
* Toothpick/cocktail pick (for light items)

## DIPPING SAUCE DISHES; see CONDIMENT BOWLS/SMALL SAUCE DISHES

## DISH DRAINER (rack used for air drying dishes next to the sink)

* Clean dish towel or folded bath towel
* Large cooling rack for cups and glasses

## DISH SOAP; see DISHWASHING SOAP/DISH SOAP

### DISHTOWEL (dish drying towel)
- **For drying dishes:** flour sack towel, old linen napkin, or unbleached auto shop towel (soft, lint-free, absorbent, and fast-drying)
- **For rubbing off toasted hazelnut skins:** clean microfiber cloth, or plastic netting from fruit or vegetables

### DISHWASHER RINSE ADDITIVE (anti-spotting agent for hard water)
- Distilled white vinegar (add 1/4 to 1/2 cup to the rinse dispenser)
- Citric acid, Epsom salts, or unsweetened lemonade mix (add a little to the detergent)

### DISHWASHING SOAP/DISH SOAP (liquid cleaning agent for hand-washed dishes)
- Castile soap (citrus or unscented)
- Baby shampoo, or other plain shampoo without conditioners

### DISINFECTING SPRAY; see SANITIZING SPRAY, KITCHEN

### DOCKER/PASTRY PRICKER (thick roller with protruding spikes; used for making uniform holes in unbaked puff pastry, crackers, or flatbread)
- Chocolate chopper
- Dinner fork
- Metal or other sharp-toothed comb

### DONABE (Japanese earthenware lidded pot; used for stovetop or table-top one-pot meals)
- La Chamba, Chinese sand pot, or seasoned clay cooker that can be used on the stovetop with a heat diffuser
- Covered cast-iron pot, Dutch oven, or covered flameware casserole

**DOUBLE BOILER/DOUBLE SAUCEPAN** *(double-decker pan with the lower pan for water and the upper lidded one for food; used for gentle, low-temperature cooking)*
- Stainless-steel or any heatproof bowl, set over a saucepan and resting snugly into the rim (make sure the bottom of the bowl is a few inches above the water)
- Colander set over a saucepan and a heatproof bowl set in the colander (make sure the bottom of the bowl is a few inches above the water)
- Cast-iron skillet set over a low flame (place a saucepan or heavy metal bowl directly in the dry skillet, or add 1/2 inch of water to the skillet, adding more when it runs low)
- Heavy saucepan used with a heat diffuser over a low flame

**DOUBLE BOILER/DOUBLE SAUCEPAN MINDER; see** *PAN/POT MINDER/ WATCHER*

**DOUBLE BOILER INSERT, UNIVERSAL** *(cone-shaped metal insert for elevating heat-sensitive ingredients above water)*
- Metal or Pyrex bowl that sits in the rim of a saucepan, without touching the water below

**DOUFEU** *(heavy French oval pot with an indented lid to hold water or ice; used for slow-cooked dishes)*
- Cast-iron or other heavy metal pot, plus a cast-iron skillet for a lid
- Enameled cast-iron cocotte or Dutch oven (used without water or ice)

**DOUGHNUT COOKER, ELECTRIC** *(nonstick pan for cooking doughnuts)*
- Cast-iron aebleskiver/ebelskiver pan

**DOUGHNUT CUTTER** *(two metal circles joined by a handle; used for cutting out doughnuts)*
- 2 1/2- or 3-inch biscuit cutter (or clean, empty 15-ounce food can with both ends removed) plus 7/8- or 1-inch aspic cutter for the center hole (or use the large end of a decorating tip, deep bottle cap, or apple corer)

**DOUGHNUT PAN** *(nonstick pan for baking 6 or 12 standard doughnuts)*
- 6- or 12-cup muffin pan plus aluminum foil (roll pieces of foil into balls and press one into the center of each muffin cup; grease muffin cups and foil with cooking spray or shortening)

**DOUGH-RISING BUCKET** *(covered container with markings for tracking the rise of the dough)*
- Large, straight-sided, tempered-glass food storage container; or large, clear, straight-sided canister; or small, acrylic, food-safe storage bucket (write measurements in 1-quart increments on the outside; or use a large elastic band for marking the dough's height, placing it around the container after adding the dough)
- 1-quart Pyrex measuring jug (for a small dough bucket)

**DOUGH SCRAPER/PASTRY SCRAPER;** *see BENCH SCRAPER*

**DREDGER;** *see SHAKER/SIFTER/DREDGER*

**DRINKING GLASS COVERS, OUTDOOR** *(beverage covers for protection from dust and flying insects)*
- Paper cupcake liners or thin plastic food container lids (cut a slit in the top for the straw; then invert it over the glass)

**DRINKING GLASS MARKERS (tags or customized glass decals; used for identifying a guest's wine or beverage glass)**

- Different-colored thick rubber bands or regular wide rubber bands (write guest's name with a permanent marker after placing the band around the glass)
- Washi tape strip (for attaching to a drinking straw or wrapping around a glass stem; write guest's name on the strip before attaching it to the straw or glass)
- Different colored ribbon, fabric strips, yarn, or pipe cleaners (for wrapping around the base of stemmed glasses)
- Wine Glass Writer (washable wine marker), wax pencil, or washable window crayon (for writing the guest's name directly on the glass)
- Color-coated paper clip opened into a triangle (for looping around a glass stem)

**DRINKING GLASS SLEEVE/GLASS COZY (silicone cover; used to prevent condensation and provide a better grip)**

- Stretchable exercise wrist band
- Cotton or paper cocktail napkin (wrap around the glass and secure with a colored rubber band or raffia)

**DRINKING STRAW DISPENSER**

- Clean empty Pringles container; or other tall, narrow, cylindrical container

**DRINKING STRAWS; see** STRAWS, PAPER OR PLASTIC, DRINKING

**DROP LID/OTOSHI-BUTA (Japanese wooden disk; used for placing atop simmering food to keep it submerged in liquid)**

- Flat, lightweight, non-domed pan lid or heatproof plate, 1/2 inch smaller than the diameter of the pan (place directly atop the food to be cooked)

• Poaching paper/parchment paper lid/*cartouche* (circle cut from parchment paper with a small ventilation hole made in the center; place directly atop the food to be cooked)
• 12-x-15-inch piece of parchment paper, crumpled and flattened (place directly atop the food to be cooked, letting the edges come up the sides of the pan)

**DRYING RACK; *see*** *CHOCOLATE DRYING RACK; DYED EGG DRYING RACK; HERB DRYING RACK; PASTA STAND/DRYING RACK; OVEN DRYING RACK*

**DUMPLING PRESS/MAKER (4- to 6-inch round plastic or metal hinged gadget; used for making Asian dumplings, ravioli, pierogi, or turnovers)**
• 4-inch round cookie cutter (cut circles out of the thinly rolled dough, and then fill, fold, seal, and crimp the edges with a fork, ones fingers, or a pastry wheel)

**DUMPLING SCOOP; *see*** *SCOOP, MUFFIN AND SCONE*

**DUSTING BRUSH/TELESCOPIC WAND (cleaning tool used for dusting crevices and hard-to-reach areas)**
• Broom with an old flannel pillowcase tied over the end (for high, hard-to-reach areas)
• Yardstick with an old sock tied over the end (for crevices between or under appliances)

**DUTCH OVEN/FRENCH OVEN (large, heavy, cast-iron, or enameled cast-iron pot with two handles and a tight-fitting lid; used for stovetop and oven slow-cooked dishes)**
• Large, cast-iron skillet with tight-fitting lid
• Heavy-duty, flameproof casserole with lid
• 6-quart, heavy, stainless steel soup pot or stockpot with tight-fitting lid

* Stainless steel casserole
* Ceramic insert from a slow cooker (for oven cooking up to 400°F)
* Pressure cooker (for stovetop cooking; replace the lid with a heavy lid from another pan)
* Pressure cooker used as intended (reduce amount of liquid in recipe by 20 to 40 percent, reduce seasoning by 50 percent, and reduce cooking time by two-thirds)
* Slow cooker (reduce amount of liquid in recipe by one-half—usually 1 cup liquid is adequate for most recipes; increase cooking time to 8 to 10 hours for Slow or 3 to 5 hours for High)

## DUTCH OVEN, OUTDOOR; see CAMP DUTCH OVEN/BASTABLE

## DYED EGG DRYING RACK (rack for supporting dyed/decorated eggs)

* Piece of foam (floral or heavy Styrofoam) or other rigid polystyrene plastic, with metal T pins pressed into the top

# E

**EARTHENWARE (high-fired glazed bakeware and cookware)**
- Stoneware
- English ironstone
- Porcelain enamel
- Porcelain
- Pyrex glass

**EGG CODDLERS (small stoneware or porcelain lidded pots for cooking and serving eggs)**
- Custard cups, dariole molds, *petits pots*, small ramekins, or tempered ceramic teacups (cover with small saucers, condiment dishes, or pieces of foil)
- Japanese lidded custard cups/*chawans*
- Pots de crème set

**EGG COOKER (small electric appliance with timer; used for boiling eggs)**
- Electric kettle plus timer (cover eggs with water and set timer when water comes to a boil: 3 or 4 minutes for soft boiled or 12 minutes for hard boiled; pour off water before removing cooked eggs)

**EGG CUPS (small, footed cups; used for holding soft-boiled eggs)**
- Shot glasses
- Demitasse cups
- Wooden or silver napkin holders

**EGG PIERCER/EGG PRICKER (small device used for making a pinprick in the large end of an egg to prevent it from cracking during boiling)**
- Heavy sewing needle/darning needle

* Thumbtack
* Push pin

### EGG POACHER (shallow, covered pan containing an insert with three to six shallow indentations)
* Covered skillet or sauté pan plus egg poaching pods or silicone baking sups (simmer them in a minimum amount of water)
* Nonstick muffin pan (fill muffin wells with 3 tablespoons boiling water, add the eggs, and bake in a preheated 425°F oven until the whites are firm, about seven minutes)

### EGG POACHER, SINGLE (small, shallow, covered pan with an insert for poaching one egg)
* 1- or 2-cup microwave-safe bowl (fill bowl with 1/2 cup water, add the egg, cover with a saucer, and microwave on High until the white is firm, about one minute)

### EGG POACHING PODS (3-inch nonstick silicone cups for poaching eggs)
* Ovenproof and microwave-safe silicone baking cups

### EGG RINGS/POACHING RINGS (metal forms for frying or poaching perfectly shaped eggs)
* Wide-mouth canning jar rings (grease or coat with cooking spray)
* 3- or 3 1/2-inch round metal biscuit cutters (grease or coat with cooking spray)
* Clean, empty, 2-inch-deep food cans (PBA-free and not pop-top) with both ends removed (grease or coat with cooking spray)
* Large bell pepper, cored, seeded, and cut into thick rings

### EGG SEPARATOR (small slotted device for separating yolk from white)
* Small metal funnel (the egg white will slip through the bottom, leaving the yolk in the funnel)
* Fat separator mug (the egg white will slip through the spout)

- Large slotted spoon anchored over a small bowl
- One's cupped hand (let the white slip through separated fingers, leaving the yolk in your palm)

**EGG SPOONS (small, thin, stainless-steel spoons; used for soft-boiled eggs)**
- Demitasse or cappuccino spoons

**EGG TOP CUTTER/EGG TOPPER (small spring-loaded or scissor-style cutter; used for removing the top from soft-cooked eggs)**
- Serrated knife (tap the tapered top third of the eggshell to crack the shell; then use a gentle sawing motion to remove the top)

**ENGLISH MUFFIN RINGS; see** CRUMPET/ENGLISH MUFFIN RINGS

**ENGLISH MUFFIN SPLITTER (wide fork with thick, flat tines or wire prongs; used for halving muffins while preserving their texture)**
- Chocolate chopper
- Serving fork

**ESCARGOTIÈRE; see** SNAIL PLATE/ESCARGOT DISH/ESCARGOTIÈRE

**ESPRESSO COFFEE MAKER (electric steam pressure machine for making strong-brewed coffee espresso style)**
- Manual espresso maker (such as Presso Espresso or AaeroPress)
- Small Italian *moka* pot

# F

**FAT SEPARATOR/DEGREASING PITCHER (heatproof jug with a spout extending from the bottom or with a bottom opening; used for draining fat from liquid)**
- Clean, empty yogurt container or other food container (pour the drippings/pan juices into the container, let fat rise to the top (or freeze to let it start to solidify), and then make a small hole near the bottom for the defatted liquid to pour out; stop before the fat layer reaches the opening; discard fat or plug the hole
- Zip-top freezer bag (rest the opened bag in a bowl or glass measuring jug, and pour in the drippings and seal; then, after the fat rises, snip off a bottom corner and let the defatted liquid drain out, stopping before the fat reaches the opening)
- Bulb baster or large spoon for skimming fat from the top of the liquid (move the pan halfway off the burner so only one half has contact with the heat—the fat will move to the cool side making it easier to remove; alternatively, pour the liquid into a large measuring jug and wait until the fat rises to the top, about five minutes)
- Refrigerator or freezer (chill the liquid until fat rises or congeals; then scoop it off)

**FERMENTATION WEIGHT; see** *CROCK WEIGHT/FERMENTATION WEIGHT*

**FILLETING KNIFE (knife with a thin, narrow, flexible blade and sharp point; used for filleting fish and cutting bones from meat)**
- Flexible or semi-stiff boning knife
- Japanese-style fish filleting/slicing knives (*yanagiba* or *sashimi bocho*), or for large whole fish, the *deba bōcho* or an electric knife

*FILTRATION BAG; see* NUTMILK BAG

**FINANCIER MOLDS (1 7/8-x-2 3/4-inch tin pans for making financiers/**
**almond pastries)**
- Miniature pastry molds/petits fours molds, preferably oval or rectangular shaped
- Mini muffin pan

**FIRE BLANKET, DOMESTIC (fire-resistant wool blanket; used for extin-**
**guishing small stovetop fires)**
- Large pan lid, baking/cookie sheet, or wet towel (for placing over the top to smother small flames)
- Baking soda or salt (for throwing on top to douse small flames or smother spills in the oven)

**FIRE KETTLE/STEAMBOAT POT/MONGOLIAN FIRE POT/HUO-GUŌ/**
**KUO-HOKO-NABE (large, round-bellied metal pot with a central funnel**
**for a heat source; used for holding boiling stock or soup at the table)**
- Chinese electric hot pot
- Large fondue pot
- Deep electric skillet or wok
- Heatproof casserole dish, straight-sided deep skillet, chicken fryer, or deep sauté pan placed over a gas or alcohol burner, electric hot plate, or an induction burner

**FIRE PASTE (odorless and tasteless fire starter paste)**
- Cotton balls rubbed with petroleum jelly, such as Vaseline (store in a sealed container)

**FISH DEBONER/FISH BONE TWEEZERS/HONENUKI (long, tweezer-type**
**tool for removing fish bones);** see also *FISH SCALER/SCRAPER*
- Needle-nose pliers or flat-ended tweezers (for pin bones, bend the fish slightly to expose the bones; then dip the tweezers in water to remove the bones from the tweezers)

* Claw-type ice tongs, or elbow pliers with a small crook at the end (for big bones)

## FISH GRILLING BASKET/FLEXI GRILLING BASKET (*flat, hinged shallow basket for grilling fish*)

* Quesadilla grill basket
* Two wire cooling racks joined together at one side (use two or three metal key rings, large paper clips, or wire from twist ties to join the racks; use grill tongs to move the basket to and from the grill)
* Two thin spatulas with long blades for turning the fish (use one spatula to lift and the other to support the fish as it's turned)
* Cast-iron griddle set on the grates
* Soaked wooden skewers for whole fish (thread two skewers crosswise through the wide area of the body, or lay two or three across the grate and rest the fish on top)
* Dried fennel stalks (place directly on the grill grate with the fish on top)

## FISH POACHER/FISH STEAMER/TURBOTIÈRE (*long, deep, narrow pan with lid and removable rack; used for poaching or steaming whole fish*)

* Covered roasting or baking pan containing a wire cooling rack set atop balls of crumpled foil (position pan over two stovetop burners)
* Two large aluminum foil baking pans nested together and covered with parchment paper and then foil (position over two stovetop burners; make sure the parchment paper is inside the foil and not near any flame)
* Large saucepan or Dutch oven (wrap cleaned fish in cheesecloth and then curl it inside the pan with its backbone facing upward)
* Preheated 250°F oven (cook cleaned fish on a greased, foil-lined baking sheet with a baking pan of boiling water placed on the oven floor or lowest oven rack; or double wrap the fish securely in greased heavy-duty foil and place directly on the oven rack, baking until done, about 1 1/2 to 2 hours for a 3-pound fish)

* Preheated 350°F oven (cook cleaned fish wrapped in 8 to 10 layers of thoroughly soaked newspaper [inner pages] until the paper is completely dry, about 60 minutes for a 3-pound fish)
* Electric dishwasher (double-wrap cleaned fish in foil, sealing it thoroughly, and place on the upper rack and run it through a wash cycle at 150° without prewash or dry; remove and cool in the foil)
* Skillet with tight-fitting lid for salmon fillets or small fish (rest fish on thick lemon slices and use 1 cup poaching liquid only)

## FISH SCALER/SCRAPER (*jagged-edged tool for removing fish scales*)
* Bread knife
* Frozen food knife
* Serrated blade of kitchen shears
* Scalloped cookie cutter
* Crinkled edge of a scallop or clam shell
* Flat/blunt edge of a chef's knife or any blunt kitchen knife
  (Rubbing fish with distilled white vinegar and leaving it on 10 minutes makes scaling easier; and scaling fish under running water or in a large heavy plastic bag keeps scales from flying about.)

## FISH SPATULA (*long, silicone-edged, slotted metal turner; used for turning fish without tearing the skin*)
* Thin spatula with a long blade
* Heatproof silicone spatula
* Small, flexible cutting board
* Two dinner knives for flipping big fish

**FISH TWEEZERS;** *see FISH DEBONER/FISH BONE TWEEZERS/KOTOBUKI*

**FLAME TAMER;** *see HEAT DIFFUSER/FLAME TAMER/SIMMER MAT*

**FLAN CASES (*metal rings for pastry cases baked directly on a baking sheet*)**
- Clean, empty, 2-inch-deep food cans (PBA-free and not pop-top) with both ends removed

**FLAN RING/TART RING (*3/4- to 1-inch-high metal band; used for a free-standing tart or shell baked directly on a baking sheet*)**
- Piece of heavy-duty foil folded lengthwise into a thick, 1-inch strip and formed into a ring; pinch the ends together with the fold outside, or overlap the ends and then staple, pin, or clip them together (set the ring on a parchment-lined baking sheet)

**FLATBREAD PAN (*round earthenware dish for cooking flatbreads on the stovetop*)**
- 12-inch unglazed terra-cotta plant saucer; unglazed, flat-bottomed tagine base; La Chamba skillet; or earthenware comal (used with a heat diffuser)
- 12-inch cast-iron griddle or skillet

**FLATBREAD PRESS; *see* TORTILLA PRESS/TORTILLERA**

**FLAX GRINDER (*small electric appliance for grinding 1 cup of flaxseed at a time*)**
- Clean, blade-type coffee grinder (grind raw rice, torn-up bread, or kosher salt to clean and remove any coffee odor)
- Pepper mill or empty glass peppercorn jar with removable grinding mechanism for individual servings.
- NutriBullet using the milling blade
- High-powered blender using the grinding setting (or the highest setting)
- Whole flaxseed soaked in water 8 to 10 hours (use in place of ground flaxseed)

**FLOUR DUSTER/WAND (*small squeezable device for sprinkling flour in a fine, even layer*)**
- Piece of folded cheesecloth doubled up a few times and then gathered together and tied at the top
- Clean, empty spice bottle
- Cheese shaker with a perforated, screw-on lid (one with small holes, or cover half of the holes with tape)
- New powder puff
- Mesh tea or spice infuser, or extra-fine-mesh sieve (gently tap the infuser or sieve on the side)

**FLOUR SIFTER; *see* SIFTER, FLOUR**

**FONDUE POT/CAQUELON (*wide-based pot set over low heat; used for keeping dipping ingredients warm [usually cheese mixture or chocolate]*)**
- Small, heavy, wide-based saucepan set on a single-burner electric hot-plate or tabletop butane burner (use lowest possible heat setting for fondue/melted cheese mixture, plus a heat diffuser for melted chocolate)
- Small slow cooker (set on low for fondue or warm for chocolate)
- Stoneware bowl or enameled cast-iron pan placed on a warming tray or a heating pad set to high
- Small chafing dish using a candle
- Double boiler with bottom section filled with hot water (refill with hot water as needed)
- Microwavable bowl nestled in a larger microwavable bowl containing hot water (reheat bowls in the microwave as needed)

**FOOD CARRIER, INSULATED COLD (*ice chest for transporting a cold dish*)**
- Picnic hamper or plastic box, plus crumpled newspaper and frozen ice packs

* Prechilled slow cooker or ice-cream-maker freezer bowl, plus flexible ice packs (for a carton of ice cream or a dessert dish)

### FOOD CARRIER, INSULATED HOT (*padded bag for transporting a hot dish*)

* Picnic hamper or cardboard box (cover dish with a double layer of foil and then wrap the dish in a few clean kitchen towels (for more insulation, pack heavy towels or crumpled newspaper below, above, and around the covered dish)

### FOOD CHOPPER; *see* CHOPPER, SPRING ACTION/SPRING LOADED

### FOOD DEHYDRATOR; *see* DEHYDRATOR, ELECTRIC

### FOOD MILL (*hand-cranked strainer for separating pulp and juice from seeds and skins*)

* Ricer (or potato masher) plus sieve (rice or mash the ingredients; then press them through the sieve)
* Food processor or blender plus sieve (puree the ingredients; then press them through the sieve)

### FOOD MOLDS/CHEF'S RING MOLDS/PRESENTATION RINGS (*metal molds for shaping fish cake, grains, vegetables, and composed salads*)

* Clean, empty, small food can (PBA-free and not pop-top) with both ends removed (use the lid to press the ingredients in place)
* Disposable cup cut in half (use the top half as a mold and the base to press the ingredients in place)
* Egg ring or deep, round pastry cutter (with the handle removed if necessary)
* Plastic pint container (for lightly dressed greens)
* Lightly oiled ramekin, custard cup, ice-cream scoop, or adjustable or regular measuring cup (for packed and shaped rice or grains)

**FOOD PRESS; see** *BACON PRESS; BURGER PRESS, ADJUSTABLE; CHURRO/ CRULLER PRESS; CROCK WEIGHT/FERMENTATION WEIGHT; DUMPLING PRESS/MAKER; FOOD PRESS/REHYDRATING WEIGHT; FUNNEL CAKE PRESS; GRILL PRESS; ICE-CREAM PRESS; MEAT PRESS; SANDWICH PRESS/ SANDWICH GRILLING IRON/PANINI PRESS; SPÄETZLE PRESS/SPÄTZLE MACHINE; TOFU PRESS/TSUKURIKI; TORTILLA PRESS/TORTILLERA*

**FOOD PRESS/REHYDRATING WEIGHT (*object used for keeping a small amount of dried food submerged in liquid while it rehydrates*)**
- Potato masher
- Heavy spoon
- Cup, bowl, or jar filled with water
- Plunge-filter coffee maker/French press (place ingredient under the press mechanism)

**FOOD PROCESSOR (*small appliance with attachments for slicing, shredding, grating, chopping, and pureeing*)**
- **For pureeing, blending, mincing, and crushing small amounts:** blender on low speed
- **For slicing, grating, and shredding:** mandoline, box grater, or julienne shredder
- **For chopping and slicing:** chef's knife or food chopper
- **For crushing crumbs:** rolling pin
- **For producing fine shavings:** box grater
- **For cutting fat into flour:** pastry blender or two butter knives; see also *PASTRY BLENDER*

**FOOD PROCESSOR SPATULA (*small implement for scraping the corners of the processor bowl*)**
- Rubber spatula (for scraping down the sides of the bowl)
- Bamboo skewer or chopstick (for reaching the crevices)

**FOOD SCOOP** *(flat stainless-steel shovel for transferring ingredients from cutting board to pan or compost pail or garbage bin)*
- Colander scoop
- New mini- or regular-size dustpan
- Pizza peel
- 8-inch-wide sheet rock taping knife
- Large inverted pot lid, such as a Universal or stockpot lid
- Cleaver's broad blade or bench scraper (for small amounts)
- Cutting mat, or bend and pour cutting board (for chopping and funneling ingredients directly to the pan)

**FOOD UMBRELLA** *(free-standing mesh dome for protecting food from flies and insects)*
- Tented cheesecloth or nylon net
- Inverted wire mesh colander, large sieve, fryer basket, or salad spinner insert
- Splatter screen or bamboo sushi mat (for placing over food bowls)

**FOOD WARMER, INFRARED/CULINARY HEAT LAMP** *(overhead lamp for keeping prepared food warm)*
- Lamp containing a 250-watt infrared bulb
- Oven preheated to 200°F

**FOOD WARMING TRAY/HOT TRAY** *(electrically heated tray; used for keeping prepared food warm)*
- Opened waffle iron set on low and covered with several sheets of heavy-duty foil
- Electric heating pad set on high
- Wire cooling rack set over a heavy casserole dish filled with an inch or so of boiling water
- Wire cooling rack or grate set over a baking pan or deep cake pan containing votive candles

- Broiler pan with hot water in the lower section (set over two stovetop burners if necessary)
- Electric griddle, electric skillet, or opened indoor electric grill set at the lowest temperature setting
- Heavy, stainless-steel grill set over a low flame, or preheated and used at the table with a trivet
- Slow cooker set on low (to hold a single serving dish; or place the food directly in the cooker, set it at warm, and place a linen dishtowel under the lid)
- Stainless steel insulated casserole
- Heat diffuser/flame tamer atop a stovetop burner set on low (for a single serving dish)
- Preheated baking/pizza stone set on a trivet (will keep food warm 30 or more minutes)
- Warming surface of an electric drip coffee maker
- Top of a toaster oven while the oven is in use, or back of the stovetop while the oven is on
- Rimmed tray or platter containing heated rock salt
- Soapstone dish or platter heated beforehand
- Indented lid of a round doufeu pan while the pan is in use

## FOOD WEIGHT/PRESS (heavy object for compressing a food item to expel the liquid)
- Cast-iron skillet
- Two or three heavy food cans
- Stack of plates
- Freezer bag (or bowl) filled with water
- Foil-wrapped brick
  (Set the weight on a plate or small cutting board placed atop the food)

## FREEZER LABELS (white, removable labels for identifying food packages or jars)
- Freezer tape
- Low-tack painter's tape or masking tape

- Peel-off office labels
- White plastic tape
- Sharpie pen (for writing directly on the packaging material or container)
- Whiteboard erasable marker (for writing on the packaging materials or container; will wash off)

**FREEZER TAPE** *(specialty tape for sealing food packaged for the freezer)*
- Low-tack painter's tape or masking tape

**FRENCH FRY SHEET/CRISPER PAN** *(nonstick, metal, perforated pan for baking French fries)*
- Cookie sheet with a perforated insert
- Splatter screen set over a cast-iron skillet (for a small amount)

**FRITTATA PAN** *(double pan with interlocking handles for making a frittata)*
- Rolled omelet pan with central divider
- Two 10-inch omelet pans (invert one over the other to flip the frittata)
- Nonstick skillet plus removable bottom of a tart pan or a large plate (cover the frittata with the base or plate, flip it quickly, and then return the frittata to the pan, uncooked side down)

**FROTHER, BEVERAGE/HOT CHOCOLATE SWIZZLE/MOLINILLO** *(electric, battery-powered, or manual stirrer; used for whisking drinks to create froth)*; see also *CAPPUCCINO FROTHER/ESPRESSO MACHINE STEAMING WAND*
- Immersion/stick blender with beaker (or use a tall container—such as a clean, empty 32-ounce yogurt container—and fill no more than two-thirds full)
- Rotary beater/egg beater
- Electric hand mixer using one beater only
- Thin wire whisk twirled with both hands

**FRUIT AND VEGETABLE CORER; see** APPLE CORER; ZUCCHINI CORER

**FRUIT AND VEGETABLE WASH (commercial spray for removing pesticide residue) — 1 cup**
* 2/3 cup water and 1/3 cup distilled white vinegar (put in a clean, empty spray bottle)
* 1 teaspoon baking soda mixed with 1 cup water (use as a wash solution and then rinse with cold running water; for non-organic lemons used for zest, dip them in boiling water and then scrub under cold running water)

**FRUIT BOWL/BASKET (glass or wooden container for holding fresh fruit)**
* Large cazuela, dinner plate, shallow bowl, pasta dish, or terra-cotta plant saucer
* Round, shallow basket or large repurposed bread basket
* Large colander

**FRUIT FLY TRAP, KITCHEN (solution for trapping fruit flies)**
* Small bowl of apple cider vinegar, plus a few drops liquid dish soap (stir to combine and then leave on the countertop)
* Fresh basil as a deterrent (keep a little in the fruit bowl or keep a basil plant nearby)

**FRUIT SALAD SERVING BOWL (glass, wood, or ceramic round bowl for holding fruit salad)**
* Clean, hollowed-out cantaloupe, pumpkin, or watermelon (brush inside with diluted lemon juice and cut a small slice from the bottom to stabilize, if necessary)
* Pineapple shell (use a pineapple slicer/corer to hollow out the pineapple; or make a pineapple boat by slicing the top quarter off lengthwise, leaving the green top intact, and hollowing it out manually)

* Clean, empty coconut shell halves, especially for tropical fruit salad (sanitize shells in a dishwasher)
* Clean, hollowed-out orange or grapefruit halves (for individual servings)

### FUKIN (Japanese kitchen cloth; used for straining stock and squeezing excess water from tofu)

* Tightly woven, unbleached muslin; or triple-layer of cheesecloth (see also CHEESECLOTH/TAMMY CLOTH/ÈTAMINE)

### FUNNEL CAKE PRESS (device for drizzling funnel cake batter into hot cooking fat)

* Fat separator, preferably depositor-style, bottom opening type
* Bulb baster
* Squeeze bottle
* 1/2-cup capacity funnel (keep a finger over the hole while filling)
* Pastry bag with a 1/8-inch round tip, or freezer bag with one lower corner snipped off

### FUNNEL, CANNING (bowl-like funnel with a wide-mouth; used for filling canning jars)

* Wide plastic funnel (cut off the bottom part)
* Clean plastic yogurt container or other plastic container (cut a hole in the bottom, smaller in diameter than the canning jar)
* Small ladle or wide-mouth, heat-resistant pitcher (to ladle or pour in the ingredients)

### FUNNEL, LARGE (cone-shaped utensil; used for transferring dry or liquid ingredients into a small opening)

* Gallon plastic water bottle or clean plastic juice jug, with the bottom third cut off and turned upside down
* Freezer bag with a bottom corner cut off (cut off the corner after liquid is in the bag)

### FUNNEL, SMALL (cone-shaped utensil; used for pouring small amounts of dry ingredients into a small opening)

* Cone-shaped paper cup with the bottom snipped off
* Cone-shaped coffee filter with the bottom snipped off
* Piece of heavy-duty foil or large Post-it Note, rolled into a cone shape
* Small paper plate, 5-x-7-inch card, or piece of waxed or parchment paper bent in half (the fold will be the chute)
* One corner of an envelope cut off diagonally, with its end point then removed
* Paper cupcake liner with the edges held together (for pouring freshly grated nutmeg or ground pepper into a measuring spoon)

### FUSILLI PIN/FERRETTO (thin, square metal rod; used for shaping spiral-shaped pasta)

* Long knitting needle or thick metal skewer
* Piece of straw (for more delicate fusilli)

# G

**GALICIAN EMPANADA PAN/EMPANADEIRA (shallow metal pan with a 1-inch rim; used for baking large, double-crusted savory pies/empanadas gallegas)**
- Pizza pan
- Paella pan
- Rimmed baking sheet

**GARBAGE DISPOSAL CLEANING TABLETS (cleaning tablets for refreshing the garbage disposal) — 16 tablets**
- Vinegar and lemon cubes (1 cup each distilled white vinegar and water plus chopped lemon peel, frozen in ice-cube trays and then stored in a freezer bag)
- Baking soda cubes (1 cup baking soda mixed with 1 1/2 cups water, frozen in ice-cube trays and then stored in a freezer bag)

**GARGANELLI BOARD (ridged wooden board; used for making garganelli/ridged pasta tubes)**
- Butter paddle
- Sushi mat
- Undyed bamboo placemat (with slats)

**GARGANELLI DOWEL (small wooden tool; used for curling pasta dough to make tubes)**
- Thick pencil
- Piece of dowel
- Wooden spoon handle
- Candle wrapped in waxed paper or foil

### GARLIC PEELER (silicone tube for loosening garlic skins without squashing the cloves)

* Silicone potholder or rubber jar opener/lid grip (roll the garlic cloves in the doubled-over potholder or jar opener while applying downward pressure)
* Heavy dishwashing gloves (wear the gloves and rub the cloves firmly between the hands)
* Mallet/meat tenderizer or flat side of a large chef's knife (pound down once on the cloves; the skins fall away easily)
* Microwave oven (heat the garlic cloves on High 15 seconds; then cool and peel)

### GARLIC POT/GARLIC KEEPER (small ventilated stoneware crock for storing fresh garlic)

* Small terra-cotta flowerpot inverted over its saucer or small plate (use a flowerpot with a hole in the base)

### GARLIC PRESS (small, handheld, hinged tool; used for crushing garlic cloves)

* Mortar and pestle plus a little salt
* Meat pounder/cutlet bat, clean palm-size rock, or the edge of a heavy skillet (cover the peeled cloves beforehand with parchment paper or plastic wrap, if desired)
* Dinner fork pressed face down against a cutting board (rub the peeled garlic back and forth over the edge of the tines closest to the board, and then turn the fork over and mash the garlic to a paste)
* Microplane/rasp-type grater (rub the peeled garlic along the holes to reduce it to a paste)

### GARLIC ROASTER (terra-cotta or cast-iron dish with a bulb-shaped vented lid; used for roasting one garlic bulb)

* Oven-safe porcelain soup bowl (double-handled, chowder, or Asian), small pudding bowl, or large ramekin covered with tented, perforated foil
* Piece of heavy-duty foil gathered into a package

**GELATIN MOLD, LARGE** *(metal container for forming a jellied dessert or salad)*
- Casserole dish or soufflé dish
- Small serving bowl or mixing bowl
- Tempered glass loaf pan
- Glass refrigerator or freezer storage container
- Decorative bread or cake pan, especially Bundt, brioche, savarin, Kugelhopf/Turk's head, or other fluted or tube mold
- Wide-mouth glass canning jar (1-pint size for small gelatin packages; 1-quart size for large)

**GELATIN MOLDS, INDIVIDUAL** *(small metal containers for forming jellied desserts)*
- Custard cups or ramekins
- Small teacups
- Opaque glass cups from a yogurt maker
- 4-ounce wide-mouth canning jars
- Clean empty containers from store-bought gelatin desserts
- 8-ounce Japanese custard cups/*chawans*
- Hot and cold cups/plastic party cups
- Clean, empty, BPA-free food cans
- Jumbo muffin pan cups

**GINGER GRATER/OROSHIGANE/OROSHIKI** *(small dish with a raised, rasp-type ceramic center)*
- Microplane/rasp-type grater (freeze ginger 30 minutes before grating)
- Smallest holes on a box or sheet grater (place plastic wrap over the grater and grate the ginger over the plastic wrap; freezing ginger makes it easier to grate)
- Garlic press (for a small amount)
- Rotary grater (for a large amount)

**GINGER PEELER AND GRATER** *(long, thin grater with one sharpened edge; used for peeling and grating fresh ginger)*
- Oyster knife or teaspoon (for scraping off the peel)
- Microplane/rasp-type grater (for grating the flesh)

**GLASS BOTTLE, DARK-COLORED; see** *BOTTLE, OPAQUE*

**GLASS-LIDDED JAR/CLAMPED JAR/LUMINARC JAR/WECK JAR** *(locking-lid jar used for holding solutions containing salt or vinegar)*
- Metal-lidded jar with a piece of waxed or parchment paper placed between the lid and the jar

**GLOVE, KITCHEN; see** *KITCHEN GLOVE/RUBBER GLOVE; PLASTIC GLOVE, DISPOSABLE*

**GOO REMOVER** *(solution for removing sticker and tape residue from hard surfaces)*
- WD-40
- Rubbing alcohol (isopropyl alcohol)
- Equal parts vegetable oil and baking soda
- Vegetable oil

**GRABBER TOOL** *(long handled, spring-action tool; used for retrieving hard-to-reach items)*
- Long-handled grill tongs

**GRAIN MILL** *(hand-operated or electric machine for grinding or crushing grain into flour or meal)*
- Heavy-duty or high-performance blender (such as Vita Mix or Blendtec)
- Flax grinder or regular coffee grinder (grind in small batches)
- Food processor (for some grains)

**GRANITE CLEANER (non-abrasive cleaning solution for sealed granite) — 1 cup**
* 1 cup purified water, 1 1/2 tablespoons undiluted rubbing alcohol (isopropyl alcohol), plus 1/4 teaspoon liquid dishwashing soap (combine in a spray bottle)

**GRAPEFRUIT KNIFE (small knife with a short, slightly curved serrated blade; used for removing grapefruit segments)**
* Small serrated steak knife, or paring knife

**GRATER, BOX, SHEET, OR ROTARY (handheld tool with perforations or slits; used for grating, slicing, or shredding)**
* **For grating hard cheese, nuts, vegetables, and most other hard foods**: food processor with the metal blade (chill nuts or grind with a little sugar from the recipe)
* **For shredding carrots, potatoes, cabbage, and other hard food, and for grating chocolate**: food processor with the shredding attachment (chill the chocolate in the refrigerator at least 1 hour)
* **For grating nuts and chocolate**: blender (chill the chocolate and break or chop it into smaller pieces)
* **For grating small amounts of nuts, chocolate, bread, and hard cheese:** spice/coffee grinder
* **For slicing cheese or making chocolate shavings:** cheese plane/slicer
* **For zesting citrus peel:** vegetable peeler (remove peel in strips and then mince or process until fine)
* **For slicing cheese:** vegetable peeler (chill soft cheese in the freezer 10 to 30 minutes to make it easier to slice)
* **For shredding or shaving soft or aged cheese:** metal colander or perforated potato masher
* **For grating small amounts of hard cheese:** serrated steak knife, blade of serrated kitchen shears, or fork

**GRATIN DISH/FRENCH TIAN/CASSOLO (*shallow, round or oval, fireproof baking dish; used for recipes topped with buttered crumbs or cheese*)**
- 9-inch pie pan, quiche dish, round layer-cake pan, or any ovenproof, broiler-safe shallow dish
- Inverted top of a metal or flameproof casserole dish or roaster (flat type without a knob)

**GRAVY BOAT; *see* SAUCE BOAT**

**GRAVY WARMER (*small electric appliance; used at the table for keeping gravy and sauces warm*); see also BUTTER WARMER**
- Wide-mouth thermos bottle/jar, or thermal coffee carafe (preheat five minutes with boiling water)
- Small repurposed electric coffee percolator (inside component removed)
- Small double boiler with the base filled with boiling water
- Small jug preheated with boiling water and then set in a bowl filled halfway with boiling water

**GREEK ROLLING PIN (*long, thin wooden pin; used for rolling out phyllo dough*)**
- 1/2-inch wooden dowel cut into a 3-foot length (lightly sand and then rub with food-grade mineral oil; let dry before using)

**GREEK YOGURT MAKER; *see* YOGURT MAKER/YAOURTIÈRE or ELECTRIC PRESSURE COOKER WITH A YOGURT SETTING**

**GRIDDLE (*thick, heavy, cast-iron or cast-aluminum rimless pan; used for searing and cooking foods quickly*)**
- Cast-iron comal
- Large inverted cast-iron skillet

* Opened indoor electric grill
* Metal pizza pan set over two burners

## GRILL, CHARCOAL (heavy metal grate set over charcoal; used for cooking outdoors for barbecue flavor)

* Japanese cast-iron hibachi or earthenware *shichin* (smaller and space-saving)
* Gas grill with metal smoker box (or wood chips wrapped in perforated foil)
* Large terra-cotta/clay pot plus an oven rack or grill rack (half fill pot with rocks or pebbles, cover the rocks/pebbles and top insides of the pot with heavy-duty foil, and then set pot on two bricks for air circulation)
* Old galvanized bucket plus a metal rack (drill a few vents holes close to the bottom; then set on two bricks)
* Old metal wheelbarrow plus a metal grate or oven rack
* Old cast-iron Dutch oven plus a cooling rack (set it on a piece of heavy-duty foil)
* Garden firepit—if lawful with local fire codes—plus grill rack. Place gravel and sand in the bottom of the hole, line with firebricks or landscaping stones, and then place two bricks on either side to hold the rack. Alternatively, lay three large sheets of heavy-duty foil on tarmac or paving, place three bricks in a Y formation, and top with a grill or oven rack.
* Indoor wood-burning fireplace using seasoned hardwood logs. Place two bricks a foot apart over waning, burning embers; then cover with an oven rack, heatproof wire rack, or metal grate. (Use a disposable aluminum drip pan to keep the fireplace clean, and coat the exterior of cooking pans with liquid soap to make cleanup easier.)
* Stovetop burner plus two bricks (for skewered, non-juicy (drippy) items such as tofu or peppers; place a brick at each side of the burner to act as supports, and use thin metal grilling skewers placed parallel)

## GRILL BASKET (perforated metal container; used for holding food while it grills)

* Old fryer basket
* Old perforated pizza pan/pizza crisper

* Disposable aluminum pan (poke holes in the bottom with the tip of a paring knife)
* Large sheet of heavy-duty foil (poke holes in the foil and curl up the sides)

**GRILL BASKET, FLEXI/EXPANDABLE; see** *FISH GRILLING BASKET/FLEXI GRILLING BASKET*

**GRILL BASTING BRUSH/MOP (long-handled brush for basting grilled food as it cooks);** see also *GRILL CLEANING BRUSH (for cleaning the grill)*
* New, untreated, natural-bristle paint brush; long-handled pastry brush; or silicone bristle brush
* New cotton dishwashing mop
* Large stalks of fresh rosemary, sage, thyme, or other woody herbs (tied together or tied to a stick, twig, handle of a wooden spoon, or long-handled carving fork)
* Woody tops of lemongrass stalks (flattened and frayed with a cleaver or knife handle, and then tied together)
* Food-safe plastic spray bottle (for applying a thin basting sauce or a moisturizing mist)
* New, plastic, food-safe squeeze bottle; or well-washed mustard, ketchup, or mayonnaise plastic squeeze bottle (for applying a basting sauce)

**GRILL BELLOWS/BLOWER (hand-crank fire-starter for applying oxygen to the coals)**
* Large, sturdy bamboo fan, such as an Asian *uchiwa*
* Rolled-up newspaper (be careful that it doesn't catch fire)

**GRILL CLEANING BRUSH (long-handled brush with stainless-steel or brass bristles; used for loosening residue from a grill grate)**
* Crumpled wad of aluminum foil (for a hot grill; use a pair of long-handled tongs to grip the foil)
* Steel wool pad (non-soapy kind) followed with paper towels (for a cold grill)

**GRILL DOME** (*metal grill cover; used for concentrating heat, moisture, and smoke*)
- Inverted disposable roasting pan
- Wok lid/cover
- Large metal bowl
- Tented heavy-duty foil

**GRILL DRIP PAN** (*metal pan for catching meat drippings when cooking by indirect heat*)
- Large disposable aluminum pan, such as a roasting or baking pan
- Double layer of heavy-duty foil (mold the foil over an inverted baking pan; pinch corners together and remove the pan)

**GRILL FLARE SPRAY** (*commercial food-safe liquid spray; used to douse flare-ups caused by dripping fat*)
- Grill cover or dome (to cut off oxygen); or if room, move food to another part of the grill while flare-up burns out
- Spray bottle filled with tap water

**GRILL FORK** (*long-handled fork with two tines; used for lifting and moving grilled food*)
- Long-handled grill tongs or spatula

**GRILL GLOVES** (*heavy-duty gloves used to protect the hands while grilling*)
- Leather or welder's gloves, or gloves or mittens made of Kevla or silicone

**GRILL GRIDDLE** (*large stainless-steel griddle; used for frying food on the grill*)
- Piece of thin sheet iron
- Stainless steel or cast-iron griddle
- Stainless-steel baking sheet

**GRILL GRID/GRILL TOPPER (*perforated metal grilling tray; used to prevent small items from falling through the grates*)**
- Extra grill rack (place so its bars are perpendicular to the grates)
- Sturdy metal cooling rack (place upside down with wires perpendicular to the grates)
- Large piece of heavy-duty non-stick foil (fold in half, curl up the edges, and then poke slits or holes in the bottom at 1/2-inch intervals)
- Two foil-wrapped bricks for skewered items (place bricks upright and 4 to 8 inches apart; rest the skewer ends on top of the bricks)

**GRILL HUMIDIFIER (*vented cast-iron box for holding liquid; used for releasing steam during cooking*)**
- Metal grill smoker box/wood-chip box
- Large disposable foil pan plus piece of foil (poke large holes in the foil and crimp it over the top of the pan)

**GRILLING STONE; see *GRILL GRIDDLE***

**GRILL PAN (*heavy stovetop skillet with raised ridges that create grill marks on food*)**
- Grill side of a reversible grill-griddle
- Indoor electric grill
- Large cast-iron skillet (food will not have the grill marks)

**GRILL PAN LID (*grill accessory used to cover grilled food while cooking*)**
- Grill dome
- Wok lid/cover
- Large inverted aluminum bowl or disposable roasting pan
- Heavy-duty foil (tented over the food)

**GRILL PAN, PERFORATED; see *GRILL BASKET***

**GRILL PRESS** *(heavy metal plate for keeping food flat while it cooks)*
- Clean cement cinder block, wrapped in heavy-duty foil
- Two (6-pound) clean bricks, wrapped in heavy-duty foil
- Baking or cookie sheet weighted with a cast-iron skillet or heavy pot lid

**GRILL RIB RACK** *(vertical rack for cooking several rib racks at a time)*
- 18-inch pieces of foil crumpled into 9-inch-long rolls (place one roll between each section of ribs to stand them in place)

**GRILL SCREEN** *(rack for holding small items that could fall through the grates);* see also *GRILL BASKET; GRILL GRIDDLE; FISH GRILLING BASKET/ FLEXI GRILLING BASKET*
- Double thickness of heavy-duty foil (poke holes through both layers)
- Sturdy metal cooling rack (place upside down with wires perpendicular to the grate's)
- Stovetop splatter shield
- Perforated pizza pan/pizza crisper
- Large wire skimmer/spider (for few items)

**GRILL SKEWER SUPPORTS** *(grill accessories that add extra height; used for providing steady, indirect heat and preventing wood skewers from burning)*
- Two long metal bars, or foil-wrapped bricks, or coils of heavy-duty foil placed across the grill, parallel to each other and 6 to 8 inches apart (suspend the skewers between the two supports so the food is over the coals and skewer ends rest on the supports)

**GRILL SKILLET** *(12-inch, two-handled, nonstick skillet for cooking food on the grill)*
- Large, well-seasoned cast-iron skillet

**GRILL SMOKER BOX (vented metal box for holding soaked wood chips; used to impart a smoky flavor to gas-grilled food);** see also WOOD CHIPS
- Commercial one-time smoker tray (contains chips)
- Disposable foil pan (poke 8 to 12 large holes in the bottom)
- Large piece of heavy-duty foil (fashion into a loose pouch, and then make three or four slits in the top)
- Clean, empty tuna can or disposable pie tin (use grill tongs to set the can on the turned-on burner)

**GRILL SPATULA (long-handled metal tool for turning food on the grill)**
- Grill tongs or long sturdy kitchen tongs
- Chinese or Japanese cooking chopsticks or long silicone chopsticks (for turning small or delicate items)

**GRILL TONGS/BARBECUE TONGS (long-handled tongs for picking up food from the grill)**
- 16-inch locking kitchen tongs
- One or two metal spatulas (for turning or picking up food)
- Chinese or Japanese cooking chopsticks, or long silicone chopsticks (for turning or picking up small or delicate items)

**GRILL TOPPER; see** GRILL GRID/GRILL TOPPER

**GRILL WOK (8-inch, bowl-shaped, perforated pan for cooking food on the grill)**
- Vertical poultry grill roaster, with the centerpiece removed

**GRINDING BOWL; see** MORTAR AND PESTLE/MOLCAJETE Y TEJOLOTE/ SURIBACHI & SURIKOGI

**GROCERY BAG HOLDER; see SHOPPING BAG HOLDER/GROCERY BAG HOLDER**

**GSAA (Moroccan, large, shallow earthenware or metal basin for working and drying couscous)**
- Large, new, unglazed flowerpot saucer
- Rimmed baking sheet
- Large pizza pan

# H

**HAMAS (North African shallow clay plate; used for cooking flatbread over an open fire)**
- Large cast-iron griddle or skillet (for cooking over a firepit, charcoal grill, or gas burner)

**HAMBURGER BUN CUPS; see** CRUMPET/ENGLISH MUFFIN RINGS

**HAMBURGER BUN/MUFFIN TOP BAKING SHEET; see** MUFFIN-TOP PAN

**HANDAI/HANGIRI (Japanese wooden tub; used for cooling and mixing sushi/vinegared rice)**
- Wide, shallow wooden or glass salad bowl or large platter (use a wooden or plastic rice paddle or flat wooden spoon for tossing and folding the rice)

**HAWTHORNE STRAINER/COCKTAIL STRAINER (metal coiled ring that sits atop a cocktail shaker; used for filtering ice and herbs from a mixed drink)**
- Julep strainer, mesh tea strainer, wide slotted serving spoon, or small strainer with a handle (place over the glass rim to catch the ice and herbs)
- Mixing glass or beaker (insert the bottom end inside the shaker to hold back the ice and herbs)
- Fat separator (pour out the drink and leave the ice and herbs behind)

**HEAT DIFFUSER/FLAME TAMER/SIMMER MAT (perforated metal disk; used over a stovetop burner to help regulate heat output)**
- Heavy-duty foil (roll up lengthwise, and flatten into a 1-inch thick ring that will fit the burner, with an even thickness so the pot will rest on it evenly)

* Ring trivet from a round-bottomed wok (use it on a back burner, preferably)
* Cast-iron skillet (use it for holding a covered saucepan for dishes requiring low, even heat)
* Double boiler (use it for cooking heat-sensitive food, such as egg dishes)

**HEATING TRAY;** *see FOOD WARMING TRAY/HOT TRAY*

**HERB DRYING RACK (***circular hanging frame with hooks; used for drying herbs***)**
* Multi-armed circular clothesline hanger with attached clips
* Old umbrella plus clothespins or clips (remove fabric from the umbrella frame)
* Metal coat hanger plus clothespins or clips

**HERB DRYING SCREEN (***fine-mesh screen for air-drying fresh leaves or sprigs***)**
* Piece of plastic or stainless-steel window screening stapled to strips of wood or an old picture frame
* Wire cooling rack set in a rimmed baking sheet and covered with cheesecloth

**HERB KEEPER/FRESH HERB CONTAINER (***tall, vented, covered container for holding fresh herbs***)**
* Drinking glass, jar, or cut-down 1-liter plastic bottle plus plastic vented bread or produce bag (place leafy herbs in container with 1 to 2 inches of water and cover loosely with the bag; keep in the refrigerator and change the water every few days (keep basil and other cold-sensitive herbs on the counter, out of direct sunlight, not in the refrigerator)

**HERB STRIPPER (***handheld perforated tool; used for stripping greens and herbs from their stems***)**
* Colander (pull the stems through the holes, leaving the leaves on the inside of the colander)

* Dinner fork (comb the tines through the herbs to pull off the leaves)
* Slotted spoon (thread the stems through the holes and pull the herbs through)

**HOCHMESSER; see** *MEZZALUNA/CRESCENT CUTTER*

**HONEY DIPPER/SERVER (small wooden sphere; used for lifting a small amount of honey from a honey pot)**
* Narrow spoon handle
* Popsicle stick

**HOT DOG BASKET (mesh container used for cooking hot dogs on the grill and turning them all at one time)**
* Long metal skewer (thread the skewer crosswise through a row of hot dogs, lining them up on the same skewer)

**HOT TRAY; see** *FOOD WARMING TRAY/HOT TRAY*

# I

### ICE BATH (water and ice for force-chilling hot food)
* Large aluminum bowl or stainless-steel pan set in a larger container holding ice and coarse salt (metal dissipates heat faster and salt lowers water temperature faster)
* Frozen jell packs, or stainless-steel or plastic water bottles containing frozen water (for using in place of ice)
* Set covered food outdoors when temperature is between 32°F and 40°F (for natural chilling)

### ICE BOWL/CHILL BOWL (serving container for chilled foods)
* **For holding chilled food, such as shellfish, over ice:** freezer-proof serving bowl halfway filled with water and frozen
* **For holding chilled food in ice:** large metal bowl filled with crushed ice, plus a smaller metal bowl filled with weights (press the small bowl into the center of the crushed ice, cover the crushed ice with water, freeze several hours, and then remove the smaller bowl)

### ICE COOLER, LARGE (insulated container for holding canned drinks and ice)
* Galvanized bucket or garbage pail
* Planter box or garden trough plugged with a trimmed-to-fit cork (if necessary) and lined with plastic
* Rigid plastic storage container lined with double-thick bubble wrap
* Washing machine lined with a large towel

### ICE CREAM BOWLS (small footed bowls for holding individual servings of ice cream); see also DESSERT DISHES, INDIVIDUAL; DESSERT MOLDS, INDIVIDUAL
* Wide-mouth wine glasses

### ICE-CREAM CONE CUPCAKE BAKING RACK/CUPCKE CONE BAKING RACK (*sectioned wire pan for baking cupcakes inside ice-cream cones*)

* Inverted foil baking pan with holes cut in the bottom and set on a baking sheet

### ICE-CREAM CONE RACK (*small serving tray for keeping cones standing upright*)

* Cupcake cone baking rack
* Upended wire basket with open weave
* Tray containing drinking glasses

### ICE-CREAM MAKER, HAND CRANK (*appliance for churning ice cream mixtures*)

* Yonanas Frozen Dessert Maker (use it with frozen ice-cream ingredients)
* 1-gallon freezer bag (place 2 cups prechilled mix in the bag; place it inside a tightly sealed container holding 2 to 3 pounds crushed ice and 1/2 cup rock salt; and shake the container until the mixture thickens, 10 or more minutes)
* Prechilled stainless-steel bowl (place 2 cups prechilled mix in the bowl; place it inside a larger bowl holding three parts crushed ice and one part rock salt; and stir constantly until the mixture thickens, 20 to 30 minutes)
* Shallow, metal baking pan (place 2 cups prechilled mix in the pan, cover with foil and freeze for 45 minutes, and then stir with a fork or immersion blender; return it to the freezer and repeat every 20 minutes for the next two hours, and then let freeze solid)
* Food processor (place 2 cups chilled mix in the pre-chilled processor bowl and freeze for one hour; then scrape the mix from the sides of the bowl and run the machine for a few seconds; return it to the freezer and repeat every 30 minutes for the next two to three hours, and then let freeze solid)

**ICE-CREAM PRESS (*handheld tool for dispensing uniform-size disks of ice cream*)**
- Nonstick adjustable measuring cup set to desired depth (push the measuring cup into the ice cream, twist and pull, and then reattach the plunger and push the ice cream out)

**ICE-CREAM SANDWICH PAN (*baking pan with wide, shallow indentations*)**
- Muffin-top pan
- Whoopie pie pan
- Tart pan with shallow, 2 1/2-inch-wide indentations (for smaller size)

**ICE CRUSHER, MANUAL (*hand-crank device with metal teeth; used for crushing ice cubes*);** see also *LEWIS BAG*
- Lewis bag, or heavy-duty freezer bag with a small opening at the top for air to escape, plus a wooden mallet or rolling pin for pounding the ice (rest the bag on a cutting board, stack of newspapers, or folded towel to protect the countertop); alternatively, freeze water in plastic freezer bags, laying them flat on a baking sheet and then pounding them when frozen.
- Empty, well-washed cardboard milk or juice carton (freeze water in the carton, and then pound the frozen carton with a hammer to break up the ice)
- Heavy-duty/high-performance blender (for crushing small ice cubes)

**ICE CUBE TRAY (*plastic or aluminum sectioned rectangular tray for making ice cubes*)**
- Bottom half of a Styrofoam egg carton
- **For small-size ice cubes:** teacake or muffin pan
- **For large ice cubes to use in pitchers with a pinched pouring lip or filter:** paper or Styrofoam cups; clean, empty yogurt containers; popover pans; or jumbo muffin pans

- **For ice rings to use in punch bowls:** tube cake pans; ring molds; metal mixing bowls; or round, shallow food containers (include lemon or lime slices and fruit pieces that complement the punch)
- **For ice to use in ice chests/coolers:** empty, well-washed cardboard milk or juice cartons, or heavy plastic juice bottles (leave head space when filling the containers)

### ICED TEA SPOON (long-handled spoon served with iced tea)
- Bar spoon

### ICE PACKS, FLEXIBLE (reusable ice packs for keeping food chilled)
- 4 cups water and 2/3 cup rubbing alcohol (isopropyl alcohol) poured into freezer bags and sealed; freeze 8 to 12 hours, and then secure each bag inside a second freezer bag

### ICE PACKS, LARGE (reusable ice packs used for keeping food chilled)
- Rinsed out empty wine bags or gallon freezer bags (seal securely and lay flat to store)
- Rinsed out empty waxed cardboard or plastic milk or juice containers (leave head space at the top)

### ICE PICK (handheld tool for chipping ice)
- Long, flat-head screwdriver
- Metal chisel
- Leather punch

### ICE POP MOLDS/POPSICLE MOLDS (plastic molds for making ice pops)
- 3-ounce paper Dixie cups (or small plastic juice glasses) plus wooden craft sticks or sturdy plastic spoons (cover top of each cup tightly with foil or with plastic wrap held in place with a rubber band; then insert stick or spoon into center by making a small slit in the foil or plastic)

### ICE POP STICKS/POPSICLE STICKS (wooden sticks for holding ice pops)
* Plastic spoons (press the handle end into the mold)
* Large wooden skewers cut to size

### ICE SHAVING MACHINE (electric device for shaving small amounts of ice for cocktails)
* Mandoline
* Blender using the crush function
* Heavy knife or dinner fork

### ICE TRAY (tray with ice in the bottom compartment; used for keeping serving food cold)
* Large platter, preferably stainless steel, nestled inside a large plastic-lined tray holding crushed ice
* Shallow broiler pan with ice in the bottom section
* Glass bowl set in a larger bowl filled with ice and a little water
* Egg poacher with ice in the bottom section (for keeping condiments cold)

### IMMERSION BLENDER/STICK BLENDER; see BLENDER, IMMERSION/STICK BLENDER

### IMMERSION CIRCULATOR; see SOUS VIDE MACHINE/WATER OVEN WITH THERMAL IMMERSION CIRCULATOR

### IMPULSE SEALER (electric tool used for sealing Mylar bags)
* Vacuum sealer with a heat strip
* Clothing iron set to medium plus a wooden or aluminum yardstick to serve as an ironing board
* Hair straightener, preferably with thin, wide plates

**INSTANT POT (6-quart stainless steel programmable appliance; used for multi-purpose applications); see** PRESSURE COOKER; RICE COOKER; SLOW COOKER; SAUTÉ PAN, DEEP; STEAMER; YOGURT MAKER

# J

**JAM/JELLY MAKER/KETTLE (*stovetop or electric pot used in making jams, jelly, and preserves*)**
- Large, heavy nonstick skillet (a wide surface and small batches reduce cooking time, which helps keep fruit flavor at its peak)

**JAPANESE BENRINER; see** *ADJUSTABLE BLADE SLICER/BENRINER CUTTER/ MINI MANDOLINE*

**JAPANESE FLOATING WOODEN LID; see** *DROP LID, WOODEN/OTOSHI BUTA*

**JAPANESE OMELET PAN/TAMAGOYAKI-NABE/MAKI YAKI-NABE/ TAMAGOYAKI-KI (*heavy square or rectangular skillet for making rolled omelets*)**
- Rolled omelet pan (such as Nordic Ware)
- 10-inch nonstick skillet
- Small flat griddle (trim the edges after cooking, if desired)

**JAR, GLASS-LIDDED (*jar for holding acidic ingredients; used to prevent corrosion from a metal lid*)**
- Metal-lidded jar with lid lined with plastic wrap or waxed paper

**JAR WRENCH (*adjustable metal device for opening various size jars*)**
- Damp cloth, rubber glove, silicone potholder, old computer mouse pad, or heavy rubber band from broccoli or other produce (place around the jar lid to obtain a firmer grip)

- Bottle opener or the tab/screwdriver feature on all-purpose kitchen shears (gently apply under the lid, avoiding the lid's notches, to release the vacuum seal)
- Small dish of hot water (submerge the jar, lid down, for a few seconds to release the vacuum seal; make sure the glass is at room temperature—otherwise, it might crack)
- Regular nutcracker, slip-joint pliers, or the jar opener feature on all-purpose kitchen shears (for small jars and bottle screw caps)

### JELLY BAG AND STAND (3-legged rack for holding a washable nylon or cotton-poly bag; used for straining crushed fruit to make jelly)

- Chinois/ultra-fine-mesh sieve (or colander lined with triple thickness of cheesecloth held in place with clips) set over a bowl or measuring jug

### JELLY BAG/JELLY-STRAINING BAG (finely woven cotton or nylon-mesh bag, often cone-shaped; used for straining crushed fruit to make jelly)

- Nutmilk bag or cloth sprouting bag
- Chinois/ultra-fine mesh sieve
- Nylon strainer lined with a double layer of cheesecloth
- Colander lined with several layers of cheesecloth
- Several thicknesses of cheesecloth gathered together at the top with kitchen twine
- Piece of unbleached muslin doubled over and sewn at the sides, and then tied at the top with kitchen twine

### JELLY BAG STAND (plastic or metal support; used for suspending a jelly bag over a container)

- Faucet handle, wire coat hanger suspended from a hook, struts of an upturned stool, or broom or mop handle set between two chairs (attach the jelly bag and then position a bowl underneath)
- Deep bowl or pot (for supporting a strainer with handles)

**JUICER/JUICE EXTRACTOR (small electric appliance; used for extracting juice from fruits and vegetables by centrifugal force)**
- Heavy-duty/high-performance blender plus ice
- Regular blender plus fine-mesh sieve (blend soft fruits and vegetables with a little water; then press through the sieve, discarding solids)

**JULEP STRAINER (small, round, stainless steel strainer that fits over a mixing glass; used to trap ice and solid ingredients);** see also HAWTHORNE STRAINER/COCKTAIL STRAINER
- Large slotted serving spoon

**JULIENNE PEELER/SLICER (handheld tool for creating matchstick-like strips)**
- Food processor using the julienne blade or shredding disk
- Mandoline or handheld slicer using the julienne feature
- Box grater using the large holes
- Chef's knife (slice the vegetable into thin slices; then stack and slice them into sticks)

# K

**KABOB SKEWER (double or four-pronged skewer with wide-spaced tines; used for cooking two to four kebabs at once)**
- Two to four long, flat skewers—preferably Japanese yakitori skewers/ *Teppo Gushi* with a flat tab on one end—plus two coils of rolled-up foil (place the foil rolls parallel to each other; then balance the ends of the skewers on top)

**KADHAI/KADAI/KARHAI/KARAHI/BALTI PAN, LARGE (Indian two-handled, circular, deep cooking pot; used for preparing one-pot meals)**
- Wok
- Cast-iron skillet
- Deep-sided, heavy-bottomed, stainless-steel skillet
- Heavy sauté pan

**KALE AND HERB STRIPPER; see** HERB STRIPPER

**KATSUO-BUSHI SHAVER (Japanese implement; used for shaving dried fish into flakes)**
- Clean carpenter's plane or strong cheese plane

**KAVVAM/MADHANI (Indian churning stick; used for mixing chhaachh or lassi)**
- Beverage frother/hot chocolate swizzle/*molinillo*
- Small whisk
- Immersion/stick blender with beaker (or use a tall container—such as a clean, empty 32-ounce yogurt container—and fill no more than two-thirds full)

* Rotary beater/egg beater
* Electric hand mixer using one beater only
* Standing blender

**KETTLE, ELECTRIC (vessel for heating water); see** STOVETOP (gas or electric heating elements used for cooking)

**KETTLE, VARIABLE TEMPERATURE (electric kettle with temperature settings for green tea and coffee)**
* Regular electric kettle (let water come to a rolling boil; then let sit a few minutes to drop down to 170°F to 180°F for green tea or 195°F to 205°F for coffee.

**KITCHEN CHEF'S MAT/WELLNESS MAT (nonslip, cushioned mat for providing comfort while standing)**
* Repurposed yoga mat

**KITCHEN GLOVE/RUBBER GLOVE (protective glove for handling chiles and other skin-irritating substances);** see also PLASTIC GLOVE, DISPOSABLE
* Oil hands generously beforehand, or handle and seed chiles by holding them by the stem

**KITCHEN SANITIZING SPRAY; see** SANITIZING SPRAY, KITCHEN

**KITCHEN SHEARS; see** SHEARS, KITCHEN/KITCHEN SCISSORS, ALL-PURPOSE

**KITCHEN STRING; see** TWINE, KITCHEN/WHITE KITCHEN STRING

**KITCHEN WRAP HOLDER (sectioned container for holding boxes of kitchen wrap upright)**
* Empty, cardboard six-pack beverage container

**KNIFE BLADE GUARD; see** *KNIFE HOLDER/GUARD/PICNIC KNIFE HOLDER*

**KNIFE BLOCK CLEANER/BRUSH (implement for cleaning slots in a knife block)**
- Micro bottle brush cleaner
- 12-inch pipe cleaner/chenille stem
- Compressed air using the slender extension tube

**KNIFE, CHEESECAKE; see** *CHEESECAKE KNIFE*

**KNIFE, CHEF'S; see** *CHEF'S KNIFE /COOK'S KNIFE/FRENCH KNIFE*

**KNIFE, HARD CHEESE; see** *CHEESE KNIFE, HARD/PARMESAN KNIFE/GOUGER*

**KNIFE HOLDER/GUARD/PICNIC KNIFE HOLDER (hard plastic sheath for covering a knife blade; mostly used for picnics and camping)**
- Pot handle sheath
- Flattened cardboard insert from foil or waxed paper (cut to size and then cover the top opening with masking tape, if necessary)
- Plastic binding spine from a vinyl report cover (cut to size and then secure with a rubber band, if necessary)
- Roll of paper towels (insert the knife blade into the slightly flattened roll)
- Bubble wrap or several thicknesses of newspaper folded over a few times and secured with a rubber band
- Plastic travel toothbrush holder for small 7-inch paring knife (such as 3-inch bird's beak)

**KNIFE, FILLETING; see** *FILLETING KNIFE*

**KNIFE, ITALIAN CHOPPING; see** *MEZZALUNA/CRESCENT CUTTER*

**KNIFE, NONSTICK; see** *NONSTICK KNIFE*

**KNIFE, OYSTER;** *see* OYSTER KNIFE/SHUCKING KNIFE

**KNIFE, PARING;** *see* PARING KNIFE

**KNIFE, PASTA;** *see* PASTA KNIFE

**KNIFE, PICNIC;** *see* KNIFE HOLDER/GUARD/PICNIC KNIFE HOLDER

**KNIFE, SANDWICH;** *see* SANDWICH SPREADER/BISTRO SPREADER

**KNIFE SHARPENER STONE/CARBORUNDUM STONE/WHETSTONE**
  ⁕ Unglazed base of a ceramic slow-cooker insert, ceramic pot/mug/vase, or terra-cotta flowerpot saucer, soaked in water five minutes

**KNIFE, TOMATO;** *see* TOMATO KNIFE

**KUGELHOPF/GUGELHUPF MOLD/TURK'S HEAD MOLD (*metal cake pan with a spiraled, fluted design and narrow center post; used for making fruited sweet bread*)**
  ⁕ Bundt pan, angel-food pan, or tube pan (using the same amount of batter); *see* BAKING PAN EQUIVALENTS

# L

**LABEL REMOVER (solution for removing labels from jars)**
- Fill the jar with hot water, put on the lid, and immerse in hot water for 30 minutes; or cover the label with a wet paper towel or dishtowel and keep it wet until the label can be peeled off (remove any sticky residue by rubbing it with vegetable oil, equal parts vegetable oil and baking soda, WD-40, adhesive remover, or rubbing alcohol/isopropyl alcohol)

**LADLE (long-handled, metal half cup for serving liquids)**
- **For ladling soup or punch:** coffee mug; teacup; or long-handled, stainless-steel measuring cup
- **For transferring stock:** small saucepan
- **For ladling small amounts of soup or sauces:** jumbo cookie or ice-cream scoop
- **For pouring soup or punch:** large jug

**LAME; see** BREAD LAME/FRENCH LAME

**LARDING NEEDLE/LARDOIR (long, hollow-bodied needle; used for inserting fat strips into meat)**
- Skewer or long, thin boning knife (pierce the meat and force the fat strips through the holes)
- Bulb baster with injecting needle or large syringe without needle (for inserting melted fat or oil instead of fat strips)

**LASAGNA PAN (rectangular pan for baking lasagna)**
- Roasting pan or broiler pan base (for large party-size lasagna)
- Large covered skillet (cut or break the lasagna noodles into 3- or 4-inch pieces)

- Standard nonstick loaf or bread pan (for a small two-person lasagna)
- Ramekins (for individual servings; cut the softened lasagna noodles into rounds with a cookie cutter)

## LAUNDRY FABRIC SOFTENER (liquid solution for reducing static cling)
- Distilled white vinegar (add 1/4 to 1/2 cup to the final rinse cycle)

## LAUNDRY STARCH (sprayable solution for imparting a crisp finish to ironed linens and garments)
- 1 tablespoon cornstarch mixed with 1 cup cold water (place in a clean spray bottle and shake before using; for a lighter finish, use less cornstarch; for a heavier finish, use more.)

## LEMON REAMER; see CITRUS REAMER/LEMON JUICER

## LEMON SPOUT/JUICE EXTRACTOR/CITRUS TRUMPET (small hollow cone; used for inserting into a lemon to extract a small amount of juice)
- Skewer, food pick, or small knife (make a hole or slit in the scrubbed lemon, squeeze out the juice, wrap with plastic wrap (optional), and refrigerate; to extract more juice, roll the lemon on the countertop and then heat in the microwave for 20 seconds)

## LETTUCE KNIFE (wide-bladed, plastic knife for cutting greens)
- Sturdy, serrated plastic knife
- One's own hands (the torn lettuce will last longer)

## LEWIS BAG (heavy-duty, drawstring canvas bag; used to hold ice for crushing)
- Linen kitchen towel
- Piece of canvas or duck, such as pastry cloth
- Piece of denim, such as a pant leg from a pair of old jeans

*LID; see* PAN/POT LID, DOMED; PAN/POT LID, FLAT; PAN/POT LID, TIGHT-FITTING; ROASTING PAN LID/ROASTER PAN LID; SKILLET LID/FRYING PAN LID

*LID WAND; see* CANNING LID WAND/LID LIFTER

*LOAF PAN (ceramic, metal, nonstick, or glass deep rectangular baking pan; used for baking breads, pound cakes, fruit cakes, and meatloaves);* see also *BREAD PAN; MEATLOAF PAN*
- **For meatloaf, sweet bread, or cake**: shallow casserole dish or large, clean, empty coffee can
- **For meatloaf, sweet bread, or cake:** ring mold (use the center space for a small bowl of sauce, cream cheese, butter, or other suitable accompaniment)
- **For meatloaf, sweet bread, or cake:** 12-x-4-x-2-inch tea loaf pan, brownie pan, or cake pan (reduces baking time by 25 percent)
- **For individual portions of meatloaf or sweet/quick breads:** muffin pan (reduces baking time by about half)
- **For less-fat meatloaf:** broiler pan (line the base with foil for easy cleanup)
- **For quicker-cooking meatloaf:** rimmed baking sheet (form meat into a long, narrow loaf to reduce the cooking time, and cook atop stale bread slices to soak up grease)

*LOAF PAN, DISPOSABLE ALUMINUM*
- Double layer of heavy-duty foil (shape over an inverted loaf pan or brick, crimp the edges, and then remove foil; bake on a baking sheet)

*LOAF PAN, DOUBLE (two-in-one pan for baking yeast loaves)*
- 8- or 9-inch square baking pan (place two loaves into the pan, greasing their adjoining sides; increase the baking time)

**LOAF PAN, GLUTEN-FREE** *(tall, narrow 9-x 9-x-4-inch pan; used for baking gluten-free bread requiring more support)*
  * Small lidded Pullman pan/pan de mie (use without the lid)

**LOAF PAN, SMALL PULLMAN/PAN DE MIE** *(9-x-4-x-4-inch straight-sided, lidded pan; used for baking soft-crusted white sandwich bread with a flat top)*
  * One (9-x-4-x-4-inch) gluten-free loaf pan, such as King Arthur; or (9-x-5-x-3-inch) loaf pan, preferably straight sided (generously grease top of the loaf before its final rise inside the pan, and then let rise until 1/2-inch short of the top; cover pan with a baking sheet weighted with a brick or cast-iron-skillet; remove the cover and weight after 20 minutes baking time and then continue baking until done, 20 to 25 minutes)

**LOAF PAN, THREE-PIECE/TRIO/THREE-IN-ONE/LINKED** *(three-channel pan for baking three yeast loaves)*
  * One (9 1/2-x-13-x-2 1/2-inch) baking pan containing two (9-x-5-x-3-inch or 8 1/2-x-4 1/2-x-2-inch) loaf pans (place one pan at each end, leaving the empty middle area for the third loaf; then increase the baking time)

**LOBSTER CRACKER;** *see* CRAB/LOBSTER CRACKER

**LOBSTER PICK;** *see* CRAB FORK/LOBSTER PICK

# M

**MACARON/MACAROON MAT (*silicone mat with circles; used for piping perfectly uniform pastries*)**
- Parchment paper cut to fit the baking pan, and then 16 (1 1/2-inch) circles, 1 1/2 inches apart drawn on the paper (use a small upturned glass as a stencil and turn the paper over for baking)

**MALLET; *see* MEAT POUNDER/CUTLET BAT/MEAT TENDERIZER/MANUAL NEEDLER**

**MANDOLINE/MANDOLINE SLICER; *see* ADJUSTABLE BLADE SLICER/BENRINER CUTTER/MINI MANDOLINE**

**MARBLE SLAB (*large marble board; used for keeping pastry dough cold when rolling it out*)**
- Large wooden cutting board
- Plastic or silicone mat chilled in the refrigerator 30 or more minutes
- Smooth countertop chilled with ice packs or with freezer bags filled with water and frozen flat (make sure chilled surfaces are dry before rolling out pastry)

**MATCHES, LONG (*matches for lighting outdoor grills and wood-burning fires [for pilot lights, request the gas company to re-light them if possible—it might be mandatory after a natural disaster]*)**
- Paper drinking straw
- Strand of raw spaghetti
- Wooden stirrer or bamboo skewer
- Tongs to hold a regular match or a piece of cardboard or tightly rolled paper

### MEASURING CUP — 1/8 cup
- Plastic or metal coffee scoop
- No. 30 baking scoop
- 1-ounce shot glass, or jigger with 1-ounce increments
- Small plastic cup from the top of a cough medicine bottle
- 1-tablespoon measuring spoon, used twice

### MEASURING CUP — 1/4 cup
- 2-ounce portion-control sauce spoon
- Number 16 scoop or 2-inch dumpling scoop
- 2-ounce jigger or measured shot glass, or 1-ounce jigger used twice
- Clean, empty take-out condiment container

### MEASURING CUP — 3/4 cup
- Rice cooker measuring cup

### MEASURING CUP — 1 cup
- 1-cup marker on a fat separator
- Clean, empty, 6-ounce yogurt container
- Number four baking scoop
- 8-ounce ladle

### MEASURING CUP — 2 cups
- 2-cup pub-style beer pint glass (American, not British)

### MEASURING SPOON — 1 teaspoon
- Number 140 baking scoop
- Long-handled bar spoon
- Large (1-inch-wide) end of a melon baller

*MEASURING SPOON — 1 tablespoon*
 * Number 50 baking scoop
 * Measured shot glass/jigger with markings for every half-ounce
 * Small plastic cup from the top of a medicine bottle, which has markings in tablespoons
 * Twist-top cap from the cooking oil bottle (for oil)

*MEASURING STICKS; see ROLLING PIN*

*MEATBALL BAKER (baking pan with rack, which drains fat from the meat as it cooks)*
 * Broiler pan
 * Fine-mesh cooling rack set in a baking sheet
 * Mini or regular-size muffin pan (excess fat drips down into the well)

*MEAT GRINDER (free-standing electric appliance, or grinder attachment to a stand mixer)*
 * Manual grinder with a 3/8 plate (cut meat into 1/2-inch cubes and freeze completely; then grind one piece at a time through a prechilled grinder into a prechilled bowl)
 * Food processor (cut meat into 1/2- to 1-inch cubes and partly freeze; then pulse 1 cup at a time in a thoroughly prechilled processor, pulsing no more than 8 to 10 times per batch)
 * Sharp knife (working in small batches, chop half-frozen meat into 1/16-inch dice)

*MEATLOAF PAN (loaf pan containing a perforated tray for draining fat from the meat as it cooks)*
 * Ridged-bottomed loaf pan
 * Cast-iron or other ovenproof grill pan

* Broiler pan
* Heavy-duty foil cut into a 10-x-6-inch rectangle with holes then poked in the bottom every 1/2 inch (set on a cooling rack placed on a rimmed baking sheet)

## MEAT POUNDER/CUTLET BAT (metal disk or hammer-like mallet for pounding meat or chicken breasts)

* Rolling pin
* Rubber coated hammer/plumber's mallet, or regular hammer
* Heavy food can
* Three-pound barbell
* Flat/blunt side of a cleaver or heavy chef's knife
* One's own fist (for flattening boneless chicken breast between two sheets of plastic wrap)

## MEAT PRESS (cast-iron weight for grilling meat on both sides at once)

* Cast-iron skillet, griddle, comal, or foil-wrapped brick, heated until hot and then placed on meat as it grills (will not produce grill marks)

## MEAT TENDERIZER/MANUAL NEEDLER (small spiked tool; used for breaking down connective tissue in meat); see also MEAT POUNDER/CUTLET BAT

* Blunt side of a heavy chef's knife or cleaver, or edge of a saucer or small plate (place meat between plastic wrap and pound in a crisscross pattern)
* Pizza cutter (place meat between plastic wrap and roll the cutter back and forth in a crisscross pattern

## MELON BALLER (small device with hollow half-spheres on either end; used for scooping out fruit into uniform balls)

* 1/2-teaspoon-size metal measuring spoon (for a small 1/2-inch-diameter bowl)
* Number 140 size scoop or teaspoon-size metal measuring spoon (for a 1-inch-diameter bowl)
* 1 tablespoons (for a large 1 1/2-inch-diameter bowl)

**MELON KNIFE** (*long-bladed knife with calibrated serrations; used for cutting thick rind*)
- Bread knife

**MEZZALUNA/CRESCENT CUTTER** (*double-handled, crescent-shaped blade; used for chopping and mincing herbs and vegetables*)
- Chef's knife
- Japanese-style *nakiri* knife
- Sharp all-purpose knife

**MICROPLANE GRATER/RASP-TYPE GRATER** (*stainless-steel grater with tiny, sharp teeth; used for finely grating citrus, nutmeg, and other hard food items*)
- Smallest holes on a box grater
- Citrus zester
- Channel knife (for zest: remove in thin strips; then mince until fine)
- Serrated steak knife or serrated blade of kitchen shears (for grating small amounts of hard cheese)

**MICROWAVE COOKING LID/FOOD COVER** (*10- or 11-inch vented plastic dome; used for covering food being cooked or warmed in the microwave*)
- Round Pyrex casserole cover (to cover a bowl)
- Inverted microwave-safe shallow bowl, pasta dish, or plate, large enough to cover cooking food
- Piece of waxed paper, parchment paper, or microwave-safe white paper towel

**MILK FROTHER; see** *FROTHER, BEVERAGE/HOT CHOCOLATE SWIZZLE/ MOLINILLO*

**MINT JULUP CUPS/GOBLETS** (*traditional sterling silver drinking glasses; used for preventing condensation*)
- Borosilicate glass, double-walled drinking glasses
- Insulated tumblers

**MISE EN PLACE CONTAINERS;** *see* PREP BOWLS/MISE EN PLACE
CONTAINERS

**MIXER, ELECTRIC HANDHELD, SPLATTER SHIELD/SPLATTER GUARD**
*(cover for handheld/portable mixer; used for preventing food splatters)*
- Disposable aluminum pie pan or plastic gallon-size ice-cream lid (cut a hole in the center, invert it over the bowl, and insert the beater stems through the hole)
- High, narrow mixing bowl; or, if possible, place the mixing bowl in the sink to make cleanup easier

**MIXER, ELECTRIC/STAND MIXER (machine for aerating, blending, creaming, mixing, beating, and whipping)**
- Inversion blender, rotary beater, rotary whisk, pastry blender, large serving fork, wooden spoon, or large slotted/perforated spoon
- Food processor (for creaming butter and sugar for pound cakes; eggs and sugar first and then soft butter)
- Large bowl and balloon whisk (for whipping cream; chill bowl and whisk beforehand)
- Jar with tight-fitting lid (for whipping cream; fill chilled jar 1/4 full and shake vigorously until cream is thick or doubled in volume, two to four minutes)
- Strong wooden spoon or one's own hands (for kneading dough with a dough hook)

**MIXER, ELECTRIC/STAND, SPLATTER SHIELD/SPLATTER GUARD (cover for stationary mixer; used for preventing food splatters while in use)**
- Plastic produce bag, plastic bowl cover, or new shower cap to drape over the bowl (make two holes in the plastic for the beater stems to fit through, and then insert the stems through the holes into the beater base)
- Paper plate or large piece of waxed paper to cover the bowl (make two holes for the stems, and then insert them through the holes into the beater base; alternatively, cut one hole in the middle and put both stems through)

* Damp dishtowel to drape over the front of the mixer and the bowl
* Paper bag with the bottom cut out to cover the mixer and the bowl

**MIXING BOWL, LARGE (flat-bottomed stoneware or stainless-steel bowl);** see also *BATTER BOWL*
* Stainless-steel bowl from a stand mixer
* Plain glass, inexpensive punch bowl
* Stainless-steel saucepan or small stockpot
* Gallon-size plastic milk or water container with the top half cut off
* Small plastic pail
* Round-bottomed dishpan
* Glazed ceramic plant pot (without drainage hole)

**MIXING BOWL, NONSLIP (mixing bowl with a rubberized, nonskid bottom)**
* Regular mixing bowl placed on a silicone hot pad/pot holder or dampened facecloth
* Regular mixing bowl with a dampened dishtowel twisted into a circle and placed around the base; for more stability, place the bowl in a heavy pot lined with a dampened cloth

**MOLD/MOLDS; see** *BABA MOLDS/BABAS AU RHUM MOLDS; CHEESE MOLD/FORM/FAISELLE; CANNELÉ/CANELÉ MOLDS; DARIOLE/TIMBALE MOLDS; DESSERT MOLDS, INDIVIDUAL; FOOD MOLDS/CHEF'S RING MOLDS/PRESENTATION RINGS; GELATIN MOLD, LARGE; GELATIN MOLDS, INDIVIDUAL; PANETTONE MOLD; PASKHA/PASHKA MOLD; RING MOLD/ SAVARIN MOLD; STEAMED PUDDING MOLD/PUDDING BASIN; SUSHI MOLD/PUSH FRAME/OSHIWAKU/OSHIZUSHI; TERRINE/PÂTÉ MOLD; TUILES MOLD/MOULE À TUILES*

**MOLINILLO (Mexican wooden whisk for whipping chocolate); see** *FROTHER, BEVERAGE/HOT CHOCOLATE SWIZZLE/MOLINILLO*

**MONGOLIAN BARBECUE PAN/TAN GUO (12-inch convex cast-iron pot; used at the table with a heat source)**
* Cast-iron griddle or wide skillet, plus a small portable butane stove

**MONGOLIAN HOT POT; see** *FIRE KETTLE/STEAMBOAT POT/MONGOLIAN FIRE POT/HUO-GUŌ/KUO-HOKO-NABE*

**MORTAR AND PESTLE/MOLCAJETE Y TEJOLOTE/SURIBACHI & SURIKOGI (marble, stone, or wooden bowl plus club-shaped rod; used for grinding and pulverizing spices, herbs, and other ingredients)**
* Spice/coffee grinder, blender using high speed, or NutriBullet using the milling blade
* Wooden or heavy earthenware bowl, plus a sterilized palm-size rock (or the underside of a wooden spoon, a heavy mug, or the thick handle of an ice-cream scoop)
* Small freezer bag plus rolling pin, smooth side of a mallet, or bottom edge of a heavy skillet (for crushing peppercorns and hard spices)
* Two sterilized rocks, preferably one flat and one round (for crushing and grinding peppercorns and hard spices)
* One large spoon or ladle and a smaller spoon as a pestle (for crushing seeds)

**MUDDLER (wooden or glass narrow pestle for crushing fruit or herbs in mixed drinks)**
* Bar spoon
* Wooden honey dipper/swizzle
* Handle tip of a wooden spoon
* End of an Asian rolling pin
* Dinner fork

**MUFFIN PAN/CUPCAKE PAN, REGULAR (rectangular pan with 6 or 12, 1 3/8-inch-deep cups)**
* Foil-coated cupcake liners or Pyrex custard cups set on a baking sheet (reduce oven temperature by 25°F)

- Clean, empty 1 1/2- to 2-inch-deep food cans (PBA-free and not pop-top) set on a baking sheet
- Doubled-up paper cupcake liners set very close together in a cake pan or skillet with ovenproof handles
- Mason jar canning bands plus cupcake liners
- Ice-cream wafer cones set in a baking pan that has heavy-duty foil stretched over the top and holes poked in it to insert the cones; alternatively, use flat-bottomed cones and set them close together on a baking sheet

### MUFFIN PAN, JUMBO (rectangular pan with six, 2-inch-deep cups)
- Regular size muffin pan (fill nine cups and reduce baking time by three to five minutes)
- Silicone baking cups or 6- or 8-ounce ceramic coffee cups set on a baking sheet (check whether coffee cups are microwave safe, which will make them safe for the oven)

### MUFFIN PAPERS/LINERS; see CUPCAKE LINERS/PAPER BAKING CUPS

### MUFFIN RINGS, ENGLISH; see CRUMPET/ENGLISH MUFFIN RINGS

### MUFFIN SCOOP; see SCOOP, MUFFIN AND SCONE

### MUFFIN-TOP PAN (baking sheet with wide, 1/2-inch-deep cups; used for making thin, flat muffins)
- Whoopie pie pan
- Ice-cream sandwich pan
- Tart pan with shallow, 2 1/2-inch-wide cups (for a smaller size)
- Parchment-lined baking sheet (drop the batter in 2-tablespoonful mounds, about 2 inches apart)

### MUSHROOM BRUSH (small brush with soft, 1-inch bristles for cleaning dirt off mushrooms)
- Short-bristled pastry brush

* Small, soft paint brush
* New, soft-bristled toothbrush
* Barely damp cloth or paper towel

**MUSHROOM SLICER *(device for cutting fresh, firm mushrooms into neat, even slices)***
* Egg slicer

**MUSLIN; *see* CHEESECLOTH/MUSLIN**

# N

**NONSTICK ALUMINUM FOIL; see** *ALUMINUM FOIL, NON-STICK HEAVY DUTY*

**NONSTICK COOKING MAT (baking pan liner; used for oven heating previously fried food)**
* Crumpled Heavy duty or Heavy Duty Non-Stick aluminum foil

**NONSTICK COOKWARE (cookware with interior nonstick finishes)**
* Well-seasoned cast-iron cookware
* Silicone-coated cookware designed for use over high heat
* Ceramic-coated cookware with a slick finish that also browns meat
* Hard porcelain enamel-coated cookware
* Hard-anodized coated cookware

**NONSTICK KNIFE (coated knife for chopping dried fruit and other sticky ingredients)**
* Chopping knife lightly greased with vegetable oil or nonstick cooking spray

**NONSTICK-SAFE UTENSILS (utensils that do not scratch or damage nonstick surfaces)**
* Bamboo, polypropylene, silicone, or wooden utensils
* Plastic takeout utensils (for stirring small amounts such as scrambled eggs, or for loosening cakes or muffins from baking pans)

**NUT CHOPPER; see** *CHOPPER, SPRING ACTION/SPRING LOADED*

**NUTCRACKER (small hinged tool for cracking the hard outer shell of nuts)**

- All-purpose kitchen shears (serrated area between the finger holes and the blades)
- Slip-joint pliers
- Crab cracker
- Meat pounder, mallet, or hammer (place nuts between towels and pound gently to crack the shells. To make them easier to crack, either freeze them 8 hours, soak them in salted water 8 to 10 hours, or bake them 15 minutes at 400°F and then let cool before shelling.)

**NUTMEG GRINDER (small spring-loaded mill with a horizontal hand crank; used for grating nutmeg)**

- Rasp-type Microplane grater
- Smallest holes on a box grater
- Mini food processor (using the grinding feature, pulse about five times; then process continuously to desired consistency)

**NUTMILK BAG (reusable fine-mesh bag; used for straining nut milk from nut pulp)**

- Large piece of white or unbleached cotton muslin, or white nylon or polyester ultra-fine curtain fabric (place in a strainer; then gather ends together and squeeze to expel remaining liquid; alternatively, hang it from a wooden spoon suspended over a bowl in the refrigerator)

# O

**ODOR REMOVER BAR; see** *STAINLESS-STEEL SOAP/ODOR REMOVER BAR*

**OFFSET SPATULA; see** *BAKING SPATULA/OFFSET SPATULA*

**OIL MISTER, COOKING (aerated dispenser for applying oil sparingly)**
- Pump-style spray bottle (such as Misto)
- Oil spreader (small plastic container fitted with a short, round brush)
- Small food-grade squirt or spritz bottle
- Clean, empty ketchup bottle with a flip-top lid
- Double-spouted soy sauce bottle (use a pastry brush or small piece of paper towel to spread the oil)

**OIL STRAINER POT (stainless-steel container with perforated insert; used for straining and storing cooled cooking oil)**
- Old coffee percolator
- Large, empty coffee can or Mason jar, plus strainer lined with two layers of cheesecloth or coffee filters

**OLIVE OIL SERVING CAN (small, long-spouted metal can for dispensing oil at the table or stove)**
- Tiny stainless-steel watering can

**OLIVE PITTER/STONER (handheld, punch-type tool for pitting olives)**
- Cherry pitter
- Small funnel (push the funnel through the center to force the pit out)
- Flat side of a chef's knife, or heel of the hand (crush the long side of the olive, pushing pit through the flesh and then removing it with the other hand)

 Rolling pin or mallet (sandwich the olives between paper towels or waxed paper, about an inch apart, and then roll the pin over them several times (or gently pound with the mallet) to lightly squash them before picking out the pits from the split fruit)

### OLLA (Mexican earthenware lidded pot used for cooking beans)
 Covered bean pot
 Covered cast-iron (or enameled cast-iron) cooking pot/Dutch oven

### OMELET PAN/FRENCH OMELETTE PAN (6- to 10-inch pan with 2-inch sloping sides and a long handle)
 Nonstick skillet

### OMELET PAN, ROLLED (10 1/2-x-6 1/2-inch rectangular pan for making omelets and frittatas)
 Japanese rectangular omelet pan/*tamagoyaki-nabe* (lacks central divider)
 Medium-size nonstick skillet (lacks central divider)

### ONION GOGGLES (glasses for blocking out eye-irritating fumes while chopping onions)
 Plastic safety goggles, ski goggles, swimming goggles, or painter's mask
 Lighted candle placed near the cutting board (helps reduce fumes, as does having the onions very cold)

### OVEN (gas or electric insulated appliance for baking, cooking, and roasting); see also BRICK OVEN/HEARTH OVEN/BREAD OVEN/PIZZA OVEN; CONVECTION OVEN CONVERSION; STEAM-INJECTED OVEN/BREAD OVEN/ COMBI OVEN
 Solar oven (for clear, sunny days; for up to a 400°F cooking environment using dark-colored, lidded cookware)
 Countertop convection oven, or microwave oven with a convection oven feature
 Electric roaster

- Electric toaster oven
- Stovetop baking oven, such as Omni
- Bread maker/machine with a cake setting
- Rice cooker with a bread/cake setting
- Pressure cooker for cake (preheat the pan 3 to 4 minutes on high, without the pressure valve or gasket, and then "bake" the cake 30 to 35 minutes)
- Stovetop gas burner for baked potatoes (poke holes in one or two potatoes and then wrap in foil; lay them evenly on the burner turned to the lowest possible setting, and then turn the potatoes over halfway through and do the other side.
- Slow cooker for baked potatoes (wrap them in foil and cook on Low 8 to 10 hours without water)
- Slow cooker for braised dishes (brown meat first; reduce total added liquid by half; place vegetables on the bottom; fill cooker one-half to two-thirds full; and double or triple the cooking time, depending upon setting)
- Slow cooker for cake, especially cheesecake (set pan directly in cooker; place a folded, clean dishtowel under the lid; and cook on High 2 1/2 to 3 hours)
- Stovetop for lasagna (using no-boil noodles, cook in a large covered skillet over medium-low heat until done, 20 to 25 minutes)
- Stovetop for flatbreads and scones (cook in a greased cast-iron skillet over medium heat until brown on the bottom; flip, cover, and cook until lightly browned on the other side)
- Stovetop for pizza (cook 1/8-inch-thick pizza dough in a well-greased, heated, 12-inch cast-iron skillet until golden, about five minutes; flip, add toppings, cover with a lid or foil, and cook until done, five to eight minutes)
- Gas grill for baking (use the top shelf)
- Coleman camp oven plus liquid fuel for use outdoors only
- Camp Dutch oven plus charcoal for use outdoors only: (For a 350°F cooking environment, have the pot sitting on a circle of 8 hot coals with 16 hot coals, evenly spaced, sitting on the lid; adjust the temperature by adding or removing coals, and replace coals as required, usually after 50 minutes. Each briquette will produce about 40 degrees of heat.)

- Gas or charcoal grill for pizza (grill 1/8-inch-thick dough on medium-low heat until the bottom is spotty and brown, three to four minutes; flip, add topping, close grill [or tent with foil], and cook until brown and crisp underneath, three to four minutes [use a cookie sheet and tongs to move the pizza to and from the grill, or make small, easily managed pizzas])
- Wood fireplace with glowing embers (wrap food in heavy-duty foil and rotate it periodically using tongs)
- Dishwasher on the dry cycle for warming plates, rolls, or bread

### OVEN BAGS (heat-resistant plastic or nylon resin bags; used for oven roasting food items)

- Heavy-duty foil or parchment paper for tenting or wrapping the item(s); oil or spray the foil or paper and increase the cooking time slightly
- Heavy, covered baking dish, Dutch oven, clay cooker, or tagine (for a clay cooker or ceramic tagine, place the cold dish in a cold oven, set the temperature to no more than 350°F, and then increase the cooking time)

### OVEN CLEANER (nontoxic solution for cleaning oven surfaces)

- Baking soda (mix to a paste with water and then apply a thick layer to stained parts; leave it overnight, and then remove with a spatula and rinse)

### OVEN DRYING RACK (rack used for oven-drying herbs at low temperature)

- Wire cooling rack set in a foil-lined baking sheet (for small items, tightly cover cooling rack with cheesecloth)

### OYSTER GLOVE (stainless-steel mesh glove for protecting the oyster-holding hand)

- Crab glove
- Leather glove
- Welder's glove
- Thick oven mitt

**OYSTER KNIFE/SHUCKING KNIFE** (*small, short-bladed knife with slightly curved tip; used for prying open oyster shells*)

* Sturdy butter knife
* Sandwich spreader
* Parmesan knife/gouger
* Stubby flat-head screwdriver
* Bottle cap opener
  (To make oysters easier to open, soak them in club soda 5 to 10 minutes or freeze them three hours, which expands the shell; or microwave them, uncovered, 20 to 30 seconds on High, placed on the rim of a plate hinged side out.)

**OYSTER PAN** (*cast-iron pan with 12 indentations; used for grilling fresh oysters on or off the half-shell*)

* Swedish cast-iron plätt plan/*plättlagg* (fewer indentations)
* Cast-iron Blini pan (shallower; fewer indentations)

**OYSTER PLATE** (*porcelain plate with six or eight shallow indentations; used for serving oysters on the half-shell*)

* Cast-iron oyster pan with 12 indentations
* Wide, shallow platter lined with a stabilizing base: seaweed, crushed ice, rock or kosher salt, dried beans, well-washed small pebbles, or crushed foil

# P

**PAELLA PAN** *(wide, shallow steel pan with slightly sloping sides, two handles, and a thin base; used for cooking and serving paella)*
- 12-inch nonstick grill skillet
- One or two large skillets (enameled or stainless steel; not cast iron) with short, shallow sides (for larger quantity, divide recipe and cook it in two pans at once)
- Large shallow roasting pan that will fit over two burners

**PALETTE KNIFE; see** *BAKING SPATULA/OFFSET SPATULA*

**PANCAKE BATTER DISPENSER; see** *BATTER DISPENSER/PANCAKE PEN*

**PANCAKE TURNER; see** *SPATULA, METAL/PANCAKE TURNER*

**PANETTONE CUPS, MINI** *(small, wax-lined, sturdy paper cups; used for baking individual pannetones)*
- Foil-coated or unbleached parchment cupcake liners

**PANETTONE MOLD** *(metal or paper, high, round mold; used for baking Italian sweet bread)*
- Large, clean, empty coffee can (or PBA-free food can) plus a greased collar of folded foil tied around the can and extending 2 or 3 inches above the rim (line the bottom of the can with parchment paper)
- Untreated brown paper lunch bag with the top turned down 2 1/2 to 3 inches (grease inside of the bag generously, set it on a cake or pie pan to bake, and then peel away the paper to serve)

**PANINI PAN; see** SANDWICH PRESS/SANDWICH GRILLING IRON/PANINI PRESS

**PAN/POT HANDLE SHEATH (silicone tube for a metal pot handle; used to protect the hands from heat)**
* Silicone garlic peeler (slip it over the handle)

**PAN/POT, HEAVY-BOTTOMED (cooking pot with a reinforced base to prevent scorching)**
* Regular pan or pot plus a heat diffuser/flame tamer

**PAN/POT LID, DOMED**
* Inverted skillet or sauté pan
* Stockpot lid or any large lid, turned upside-down so condensed liquid will fall into the pot instead of down the sides

**PAN/POT LID, FLAT**
* Pyrex pie pan (for a see-through lid)
* Metal cake or pie pan
* Large heatproof plate
* Skillet, crepe pan, or sauté pan
* Two layers of foil wrapped around or covering a splatter shield
* Piece of heavy-duty foil
* Baking sheet or non-perforated aluminum pizza pan (for a roasting pan or other large pan)

**PAN/POT LID, FLOATING WOODEN; see** DROP LID/OTOSHI-BUTA

**PAN/POT LID KNOB, REPLACEMENT (stainless-steel or black phenolic knob)**
* Wine cork or metal drawer knob (attach with a short screw on the underside)

**PAN/POT LID, PAPER; see** *PAPER LID/CARTOUCHE*

**PAN/POT LID, TIGHT-FITTING**
- Piece of parchment paper cut to fit inside rim of pan, or dampened and crumpled and placed directly over the food, before putting on the lid
- Luting paste (a mixture of flour and water), or bread or pizza dough, applied to the pan's rim to seal the lid for long-cooking dishes (not for clay/terra-cotta cookers)

**PAN/POT LID, UNIVERSAL (WITHOUT STEAM VENT)**
- Two pieces of foil molded over the pan and crimped to make a tight seal, tented if necessary to prevent food from touching the foil

**PAN/POT MINDER/WATCHER (stainless-steel or glass disk; used for indicating when water in a steamer or double boiler needs replenishing)**
- Two or three coins or glass marbles, or a small spoon (the rattle will alert)

**PAN/POT SCRAPER/SCRUBBER (abrasive tool for removing baked-on food from sturdy [not nonstick] cookware)**
- Old credit or library card; square plastic tag from a bread bag; or other hard piece of plastic (for scraping)
- Crumpled-up plastic mesh netting from fruit or vegetables, or wadded-up piece of aluminum foil (for scrubbing)

**PAPER BAKING CUPS; see** *CUPCAKE LINERS/PAPER BAKING CUPS*

**PAPER BOWLS/BOXES (disposable containers for holding party nibbles)**
- 6-inch paper plates (cut 2-inch slits at the North and South Poles and at the equator points, fold the four sides up, and then join overlapping flaps with a staple or tape; or wrap the box in place with kitchen twine or a rubber band)
- Basket-type paper coffee filters

- 16-ounce hot/cold cardboard cups or plastic party cups
- Chinese take-out boxes or pint take-out pails
- Mini bread pans

**PAPER LID/CARTOUCHE** *(disposable lid with a hole in the center; used for covering food as it steams or poaches)*
- 8-, 9-, or 10-inch parchment cake pan liner (make a small ventilation hole in the center)
- Square of parchment paper cut to make a circle larger than the diameter of the pan with a small ventilation hole made in the center (place directly atop the food, letting the edges come up the sides of the pan)
- Japanese drop lid/*otoshi-buta*

**PAPER LUNCH BAG** *(small brown or white paper bag)*
- **For dredging/flouring meat or chicken:** plastic produce bag
- **For holding packed lunches to go:** neoprene or cotton lunch bags, or reusable plastic totes
- **For ripening fruit:** wrap it in newspaper or a dishtowel (for faster ripening include a ripe apple or banana)
- **For ripening an avocado:** wrap it in newspaper; put it in an oven mitt or heavy sock; or for several, place them in an empty cardboard beverage holder
- **For storing loose refrigerated mushrooms:** wrap them in a dry paper towel and then place in a perforated plastic bag or clamshell container, or place them in a paper-towel-lined bowl and cover with perforated plastic wrap
- **For steaming the skins off roasted green peppers:** place them in a tightly covered saucepan, a plastic storage container with a tight-fitting lid, or a bowl covered with plastic wrap or a kitchen towel

**PAPER NAPKINS**
- Fabric napkins on a perforated roll (such as MyDrap; can be washed and reused up to six times)

* Package of inexpensive, non-terry cotton dishtowels from Ikea or a dollar store (reuse until ready to wash; use personalized napkin rings, a different-colored napkin for each person, or a white napkin embroidered with the person's name or with the name written in fabric marker or washable fabric paint)
* Unbleached muslin, cotton seersucker, or gently worn clothing cut into 12- or 18-inch squares with pinking shears, or pull several threads out from all sides to create a 1/4-inch fringed border
* New handkerchiefs for cocktail napkins
* New bandanas for picnics

### PAPER PLATES, DISPOSABLE
* Clean Styrofoam trays from prepackaged fresh produce
* Large, sturdy plastic lids from food containers (reusable)
* Banana leaves (cut into pieces; wash and refrigerate until the next use)

### PAPER PLATES HOLDER (container for storing paper plates)
* Round cake carrier

### PAPER-TOWEL HOLDER, STANDING (small free-standing pole for a paper-towel roll)
* Upended heavy meat pounder with a tall handle

### PAPER TOWELS (disposable towels used for various functions)
* **For blotting dry fruits and vegetables:** clean cotton dishtowel
* **For draining fried food:** wire cooling rack set inside a rimmed baking sheet; several thicknesses of newspaper (interior pages, topped with an opened-up paper napkin if desired); cut up or opened up clean brown paper bags; or basket-type paper coffee filters
* **For drying hands:** kitchen towel
* **For cooling non-greasy cooked food:** clean cotton dishtowel
* **For oiling the grill:** standard paper coffee filter or piece of clean rag; alternatively, oil the food to be cooked

- **For washing windows:** old crumpled black-and-white newspaper (at least a week old)
- **For wiping up floor spots:** lightly used paper napkins (saved for the purpose and then discarded)
- **For wiping up spills:** reusable wipes; bar mop towels; old washcloths or dishcloths; cut-up terry towels or dishtowels; or cut up old cotton T-shirts, sweatshirts, or pajamas (stored in a jar, plastic container, or used tissue box; then washed and reused again and again)
- **For wrapping refrigerated greens and herbs:** light/thin dishtowel

## PARCHMENT COOKING BAGS/PAPILLOTES (nonstick, silicone-coated bags; used for cooking foods in their own juices)

- Parboiled leaves: banana; bamboo; large grape; large fig; large green romaine; or large cabbage, preferably savoy (fashioned into an envelope and secured with kitchen twine, skewers, or plain wooden uncolored toothpicks)
- Non-stick foil or heavy-duty foil coated with cooking spray (cut to size, fashioned into a pouch, and crimped to seal)

## PARCHMENT PAPER (nonstick, silicone-coated paper; used for lining cake and baking pans, plus other culinary procedures)

**For lining baking sheets:**
- Reusable silicone baking mat, such as Silpat
- Non-stick foil or plain foil lightly coated with oil or cooking spray
- Multipurpose printer paper lightly coated with oil or cooking spray
- Rice/wafer paper (for macaroons and meringues)

**For lining cake pans:**
- Waxed paper
- Unsalted butter or margarine wrappers
- White or brown wrapping paper greased and floured or coated with cooking or baking spray
- Disposable slow-cooker liners or basket-type paper coffee filters, buttered and floured or coated with cooking or baking spray

**For lining flan cases before weighting them down with pastry weights:**
- Double layer of foil
- Basket-type coffee filter
- Copier paper

**For making pastry or piping cones, or cones for funneling ingredients:**
- Heavy-duty foil (double layer if necessary)

**For making soufflé dish collars or extending the height of baking pans:**
- Double layer of white wrapping paper, copier paper, or foil

**PARCHMENT PAPER LID/CARTOUCHE; see** *PAPER LID/CARTOUCHE*

**PARING KNIFE (small, short-bladed knife for peeling and trimming fruits and vegetables)**
- Japanese-style Petty knife/*wa-petty*; or any small, thin, sharp knife
- Clean penknife
- Clean utility knife/box cutter
- Unflavored dental floss, wire, or kitchen twine held taut (for soft foods, such as goat cheese, polenta, cheesecake, or other food tending to stick to the knife)

**PARMESAN KNIFE; see** *CHEESE KNIFE, HARD/PARMESAN KNIFE*

**PASKHA/PASHKA MOLD (earthenware mold for making a Russian cheese dessert)**
- New, 6-inch (1-quart) terra-cotta flowerpot lined with a double layer of cheesecloth

**PASSAPOMODORO; see** *TOMATO STRAINER*

**PASTA FORK/PASTA LADLE/SPAGHETTI RAKE (long-handled, slotted utensil for serving or removing pasta from the cooking water)**
- Scoop colander
- Wire skimmer/spider

* Steel-locking tongs
* Large perforated spoon

## PASTA KNIFE (sharp, wide-bladed, 9- to 11-inch-long knife for cutting homemade pasta)
* Long chef's knife
* Japanese-style noodle cutting knife/*soba-bocho* or *menkiri-bocho*
* Chinese vegetable cleaver, size 2
* Pastry/pizza wheel

## PASTA MACHINE (hand-cranked tool; used for rolling and cutting homemade pasta dough)
* Pasta rolling pin and pasta knife; *see* PASTA KNIFE; PASTA ROLLING PIN/ MATTARELLO

## PASTA POT (6- to 8-quart pot with a perforated insert for lifting pasta from the cooking water)
* Deep pot plus fryer basket (alternatively, cook the pasta in a smaller pot with less water, using 4 cups per 1/4-pound pasta; boil the pasta for three minutes; then leave it, covered with a kitchen towel and lid, until al dente, five to eight minutes; then drain)
* Microwave pasta cooker, such as Fasta Pasta (reduces cooking time and conserves water)

## PASTA POT, OVAL (large oval pot for boiling filled pasta or long lasagna noodles)
* Oven roaster, set over two burners if necessary

## PASTA ROLLING PIN/MATTARELLO (long, thin 1 1/2-x-24- to 1 1/2-x-32-inch pin for rolling out pasta)
* Straight French rolling pin
* Long piece of dowel, 1- to 2-inches in diameter (lightly sand and then rub with food-grade mineral oil; let dry before using)

- New detached broom handle
- Poster mailing tube
- Sturdy tube from a used 18-inch roll of paper (heavy-duty foil, parchment, or gift-wrapping)

**PASTA STAND/DRYING RACK (*wooden rack for air-drying freshly-made pasta*)**
- **For sheets of pasta before cutting:** dish drying rack, sweater drying rack, or clean cloth
- **For strips of pasta after cutting:** covered with a clean dishtowel: swing-arm dishtowel rack, indoor accordion clothes dryer, standing towel valet, open cabinet door, sturdy coat hanger, chair back, makeshift clothesline, or broom handle balanced between two chairs

**PASTRY BAG/PIPING BAG (*cone-shaped plastic, nylon, or cloth bag with two open ends; used for piping out doughs, batters, and fillings*);** see also *DECORATING BAG/PIPING BAG/CORNET*
- Plastic freezer bag with an opening made in a bottom corner (fill bag half full, close securely, and then cut off the corner; close the opening with a clip or twist tie when refilling the bag)
- Parchment paper rolled into a cone
- Clean, empty, plastic squeeze bottle

**PASTRY BLENDER (*U-shaped tool with five curved wires or blades attached to a handle; used for cutting fat into dry ingredients, usually flour*)**
- Food processor using the metal blade (pulse briefly with chilled butter, or frozen shortening or margarine, cut into pieces)
- Electric mixer with the paddle attachment used on the lowest speed (cut chilled fat into 1/4-inch cubes and toss with the flour before mixing; as an extra precaution, refrigerate fat, flour, and bowl at least 30 minutes before mixing)
- Largest holes on a box grater (grate frozen fat into flour and toss to combine)

* Potato masher (press cold, cut-up fat into flour with up and down motions)
* Blending/Granny fork or large fork (blend cold, cut-up fat into flour with firm, quick motions)
* Two butter knives or dinner knives (cut cold, cut-up fat into flour in a crisscross pattern)
* Wooden spoon (cut cold, cut-up fat into flour with a stabbing motion)
* Cool fingertips (pinch cold, cut-up fat into flour lightly and briskly, using tips of fingers and thumbs)

**PASTRY BOARD *(large piece of wood or marble; used for rolling out pastry and bread dough)*;** see also *MARBLE SLAB*
* Pastry cloth or piece of canvas or cotton duck (place on a piece of non-skid/rubberized shelf liner)*; **see** PASTRY CLOTH*
* Large, nonstick silicone sheet or baking mat
* 18-x-12-inch flexible plastic cutting mat
* Two sheets of lightly floured plastic wrap or waxed paper (roll dough between the two sheets, wetting the counter first to keep the paper anchored)
* Large freezer bag (cut bag lengthwise on both sides before or after rolling the dough)
* 14-inch square pizza peel (for a small amount)
* Clean, smooth countertop, preferably granite or marble
* Cookie sheet (for galette/crostata and other free-form pastry, roll dough directly on the sheet)

**PASTRY BRUSH *(small flat brush; used for applying egg, liquid, or glaze onto dough or pastries)***
* 1 1/2-inch new, untreated, natural-bristle paint brush with a plastic handle (for brushing excess flour off cookie and pie dough; applying egg wash, melted butter, or glaze; or washing sugar down the sides of a pan)
* 1/2-inch-wide brush or No. 9 artist's brush (for delicate brushing and glazing)
* Piece of parchment paper folded into a small rectangle, and then the bottom part cut into a fringe with scissors

* Salt-free butter wrappers or greased waxed paper (for greasing baking sheets and pans)

### PASTRY CLOTH (large canvas cloth; used when rolling out pastry or kneading bread dough)
* Piece of unbleached natural canvas (or duck cloth folded in half) purchased from a fabric store and cut to size, if necessary
* Large silicone baking mat
* Piece of tightly woven linen cloth
* Plain old tablecloth, preferably linen (for making strudel pastry or other large projects)
* Clean, floured countertop

### PASTRY CLOTH WITH MEASURING GUIDES (cloth with marked circles to indicate crust sizes when rolling out pie dough)
* Regular pastry cloth with circles made by a sewing machine or hand stitching
* Parchment paper or plastic-coated freezer paper with circles drawn on the reserve side of the paper

### PASTRY CUTTER, 4-INCH SQUARE (implement for cutting out dough for cannelloni, cannoli, knishes, pansotti, samosas, or other square or triangular applications)
* Roll dough into an 8-inch square and then cut into four quarters (for a fluted square cutter, use a dry, scalloped-edge lasagna noodle to section the quarters)

### PASTRY CUTTER, 6-INCH ROUND (implement for cutting out dough for Cornish pasties, pocket pies, or large turnovers)
* 6-inch-size Asian dumpling press (it will seal as well as cut)
* 6-inch-wide saucer, bowl, or plate (inverted and used as a template)

### PASTRY CUTTER TOOL (tool for cutting fat into dry ingredients); see
PASTRY BLENDER

**PASTRY DOUGH ROLLER** *(small roller with handle; used for areas too small for a regular rolling pin or for rolling dough right in the pan)*
- Small plain juice glass
- Round, glass pill/vitamin bottle
- Spice/herb bottle or small condiment jar
- Baby food jar

**PASTRY SCRAPER;** *see* BENCH SCRAPER/DOUGH SCRAPER/PASTRY SCRAPER

**PASTRY TEMPLATE, LARGE** *(stencil used as guide for cutting dough into a desired shape);* see also **TART/GALETTE/CROSTATA TEMPLATE**
- Small inverted plate, saucer, or bowl
- Lid from a cookie or cake tin, a chocolate or candy box, or a large jar or canister
- Clean lid from a large yogurt or deli container
- Removable base of a tart or springform pan
- Small pan lid
  (Lay the template on the dough and cut around it with a plain pastry wheel or the tip of a knife.)

**PASTRY WHEEL, STRAIGHT-EDGED** *(bevel-bladed tool for cutting rolled-out dough);* **see** PIZZA CUTTER/PIZZA WHEEL

**PÂTÉ MOLD;** *see* TERRINE/PÂTÉ MOLD

**PEDESTAL STAND, INDOOR** *(large, round dish with a wide pedestal foot; used for holding cake, fruit, or pastries)*
- Small inverted bowl plus serving dish (set the serving dish on the bowl, attaching it with a roll of poster putty or with a hot-glue gun on low temperature setting)

**PEDESTAL STAND, OUTDOOR** *(large, round dish with a wide pedestal foot; used for holding condiment bowls or chips and dip)*
  * Small inverted terra-cotta plant pot plus large terra-cotta saucer (set the saucer on the pot, gluing it if necessary)

**PEEL, OVEN; see** *BAKER'S PEEL/PIZZA PEEL/PADDLE*

**PEPPER AND TORTILLA ROASTER, STOVETOP/ASADOR** *(circular mesh rack that fits over an electric stovetop burner; used for charring chiles and toasting tortillas)*
  * Small grill screen
  * Cake cooling rack
  * Wire coat hanger (bend down each end and lay it on the coils)
  * Dry skillet (for toasting nori sheets)

**PEPPER MILL** *(handheld or motorized pepper grinder)*
  * Clean electric coffee grinder (grind raw rice, bread, or kosher salt to clean and remove any coffee odor)
  * Mini food processor (using the grind feature, pulse 10 seconds at a time to desired consistency)
  * Mortar and pestle
  * Two clean rocks, scrubbed and sterilized
  * Freezer bag plus mallet, hammer, or rolling pin (enclose peppercorns in bag and tap, roll, or pound them to desired consistency)

**PESTLE** *(short, club-shaped stick for crushing spices and other food items)*
  * Back of a wooden spoon
  * Palm-size rock (scrubbed and sterilized)
  * Butt end of a cleaver
  * End of a rolling pin
  * Bottom of a heavy mug

**PETITS FOURS PASTRY MOLDS (*miniature tin molds of various shapes; used for making pastry shells*)**
- Inverted mini-muffin pan (fit the pastry over the cups)
- Heavy-duty foil, fashioned into barquettes, ovals, rounds, triangles, and squares (place on a baking sheet to bake)

**PICKLE/FERMENTATION WEIGHT(S) (*ceramic, stoneware, or tempered glass disk; or non-iridized soda glass pebbles; used for keeping pickle ingredients submerged in the brine*); see also** *CROCK WEIGHT/ FERMENTATION WEIGHT*
- Glass lid from a canning jar, such as Weck
- Piece of cabbage core or peeled daikon, cut to size
- Small jar or container filled with water
- Unglazed ceramic pie weights enclosed in a sterilized mesh produce bag

**PICNIC KNIFE (*small knife with blade guard*); see** *KNIFE HOLDER/ GUARD/ PICNIC KNIFE HOLDER*

**PIE BIRD/PIE VENT (*hollow ceramic figurine; used for supporting a pie's top crust and venting steam from the filling*)**
- Small metal funnel
- Piece of rigatoni, paccheri, or other large tubular pasta
- Pastry tubes (for individual pies or tarts)
- Inverted eggcup or ramekin (for supporting the pastry on a large pot pie)

**PIE CARRIER/PIE KEEPER (*lidded pie plate for holding or transporting a baked pie*)**
- Empty pie plate (invert on top of the pie; then wrap foil around the plates to hold them together)
- Plastic wrap for pie topped with whipped cream or meringue (suspend the wrap over the pie with pieces of uncooked spaghetti or toothpicks/ cocktail sticks)

- Foil for meringue-topped pie (tent the foil over the pie, leaving a small opening to prevent moisture buildup)
- Bamboo steamer for more than one pie (secure the steamer lid with kitchen twine or ribbon)

**PIE CHAIN; see** *PIE WEIGHTS*

**PIE CRUST BAG (11- or 14-inch, heavy, food-safe plastic pouch; used for holding pastry while you roll it out)**
- 1-gallon plastic freezer bag (cut bag lengthwise on both sides before or after rolling the dough)
- Two large pieces of parchment paper (roll pastry between the parchments)
- Two large pieces of waxed paper (roll pastry between the waxed paper)

**PIE CRUST SHIELD/PROTECTOR (metal or silicone ring; used for preventing pie edges from over-browning)**
- Inverted and flattened 8- or 9-inch disposable aluminum foil pie pan with the bottom and sides cut out, leaving a 1- or 2-inch rim remaining (for an 8-inch pie)
- Inverted ring/collar from a 10-inch two-piece tart pan (for a 9-inch pie)
- 12-inch square of foil with a 7- or 8-inch circle cut out of the center (loosely mold or crimp it over the edge of the pie; alternatively, use a 2- to 3-inch-wide strip of foil)

**PIE PAN (8- or 9-inch round dish with 1- to 1 1/2-inch sloping sides, usually dark metal, ceramic, or glass)**
- Disposable aluminum pie pan (set it on two nestled baking sheets and increase baking time by up to 10 minutes)
- Inverted flat-top lid from a 2-quart ovenproof casserole dish (set it on a dark metal baking sheet)
- Large plain lid from a round cookie tin
- 8- or 9-inch layer cake pan (keep the crust 1 inch deep)

♦ Baking sheet (make a free-form fruit pie/*galette* by mounding the fruit in the center of rolled-out pastry, leaving a 2- or 3-inch border to fold toward the center)

### PIE PAN, DEEP (9- or 10-inch round dish with 1 1/2- to 2-inch sloping sides)
♦ 1 1/2- or 2-inch deep cake pan or casserole dish
♦ 9- or 10-inch seasoned cast-iron skillet (place on the bottom rack)

### PIE PAN, MINI (4 1/2- to 6 1/2-inch round dish with 1- to 1 1/2-inch sloping sides)
♦ Ovenproof cereal dish, or 8- or 10-ounce ramekin (for a small pan)
♦ Wide soup plate; wide, shallow pasta bowl; or 6-inch cake pan (for a large pan)
♦ Disposable aluminum foil pans (or clean pans saved from oven-baked frozen pot pies)

### PIE PAN, SPLIT/TWO-IN-ONE (pan with a removable divider and base; used for baking two half-pies requiring similar baking time)
♦ 9-inch two-piece tart pan (or 9-inch pie pan) plus heavy-duty foil (line the pan with foil, folding it into a 1 1/2-inch-high peak/pleat in the center)

### PIE SAVER (plastic domed cover for placing over a cooked pie)
♦ Large round storage container (use the lid as the base and the inverted container as the cover)
♦ Large inverted mixing bowl or outer bowl of a salad spinner
♦ Clean domed cover saved from a store-bought cake or pie
♦ Microwave cooking lid (vented plastic dome)
♦ Food umbrella

### PIE SERVER/PIE KNIFE (wedge-shaped, offset spatula with sharp or serrated edges; used for removing slices of pie from the pie pan)
♦ Offset spatula
♦ New mortar trowel

**PIE SHIELD; see** *PIE CRUST SHIELD/PROTECTOR*

**PIE WEIGHTS (small ceramic or metal pellets; used to prevent an empty crust from warping as the dough cooks)**
- Copper coins sterilized in boiling water and then dried
- Stainless-steel teaspoons
- 24 to 30 inches of light metal chain
- Dried beans
- Another same-sized pan placed atop the parchment paper (or coffee filter) and baked upside-down with pastry in the middle (or, bake crust upside-down halfway and right side up, without the other pan, the remainder of the time)
- Small dried beans, well-washed small pebbles, or rice (for tartlets using a paper cupcake liner atop the dough; save the weights for repeated use)

**PIPING BAG; see** *DECORATING BAG/PIPING BAG/CORNET*

**PIZZA CUTTER COVER (protective guard for housing the sharp pizza blade)**
- New sponge with an opening made in the side

**PIZZA CUTTER/PIZZA WHEEL (handheld tool with a sharp-edged cutting wheel; used for slicing individual portions of pizza)**
- Plain pastry wheel
- Heavy-duty kitchen shears or long-bladed scissors
- Single-blade mezzaluna
- Stainless-steel bench scraper
- Clean casing knife

**PIZZA OVEN; see** *BRICK OVEN/HEARTH OVEN/BREAD OVEN/PIZZA OVEN*

**PIZZA PAN** *(round or square aluminum or stoneware pan with a 1/2-inch rim, or 1 1/2 to 2 inches for deep-dish)*
- **For American or Roman style:** baking stone (bake pizza in a preheated 500°F oven, directly on the baking stone)*; see BAKING STONE/PIZZA STONE*
- **For cracker style, pizette, or super-thin style:** double thickness of heavy-duty foil with 1/4-inch holes made in the top (bake the punctured crust five minutes before putting on the topping)
- **For St. Louis style:** heavy-duty cookie sheet
- **For Neapolitan/Naples, New York, or thin-crust style:** cast-iron comal, griddle, or inverted skillet preheated in a 500°F oven 30 to 45 minutes (transfer to a cooling rack after baking to prevent crust becoming soggy, and cut with kitchen shears)
- **For long, foldable New York slices:** heavy-duty cookie sheet (shape dough into a large oval, and slice the pizza crosswise)
- **For Chicago or deep-dish style:** cast-iron skillet; cast-iron crepe pan; 9-x-2-inch dark-colored cake pan; or 8-x-2-inch springform pan
- **For Sicilian or extra-thick style:** heavy-gauge aluminum baking sheet (bake pan on a preheated baking stone five to eight minutes before putting on the topping)

**PIZZA PEEL;** *see BAKER'S PEEL/PIZZA PEEL/PADDLE*

**PIZZA SERVER;** *see PIE SERVER/PIE KNIFE*

**PIZZA SERVING TRAY** *(large round dish for holding baked pizza)*
- Removable carousel from a microwave oven (precut the pizza or cut with scissors)
- Upside-down baking/pizza stone

**PIZZA STONE;** *see BAKING STONE/PIZZA STONE*

**PLACE CARD HOLDERS** *(signage containers; used for indicating seating arrangements)*
  * Small freestanding picture frames (insert snapshots of guests)
  * Wine corks or spools (make slits in the top, and then slide a photo or place card into each slit)
  * Whole walnuts (open shells slightly and insert a place card into each slit)
  * Small pinecones (wedge place cards in the center or hot glue them on)
  * Small bundles of twigs (tie a Kraft place tag to each bundle)
  * Small apples, miniature pumpkins, large radishes, or large chestnuts (make shallow slits on the top and insert place cards)
  * Pomegranates and other hard fruits (write on the fruits using a permanent marker or gold or silver liquid ink)
  * Stemmed fruit, such as pears, clementines, or figs (attach metal plant tags, postal labels with punched holes, or gift tags to the stems)
  * Chocolate bonbon or truffle with the name or initial in melted white chocolate
  * Stand up rectangular cookies (use piping-consistency royal icing to write the names, and use as glue to affix an easel-back to the dried, decorated cookies)
  * Large fall/autumn leaves (write on the back using a gold pen, fine colored marker, or gold or silver liquid ink)
  * Fork as part of the place setting (slip a place card into the fork tines)
  * Napkin (folded in a way as to work as a place card holder)
  * Napkin as signage (use iron-transfer paper to print and iron on name, then peel off the transfer-paper backing)

**PLACE MATS** *(small table mats for holding place settings)*
  * 12-inch square sheets of scrapbooking paper
  * Small heavy tea towels/dishtowels (from a dollar store)
  * Table runners (in place of place mats)

**PLANCHA** *(cast-iron grilling plate; used for grilling quick-cooking foods)*
  * 16-inch untreated slate tile (if necessary, knock off the corners to make it to fit)
  * Cast-iron griddle or skillet

***PLANKS; see** COOKING PLANKS; COOKING PLANK TRAY*

***PLANTAIN PRESS/TOSTONERA; see** TORTILLA PRESS/TORTILLERA*

***PLASTIC AND SILICONE CLEANER (stain-removing formula for discolored cooking utensils) — 1 cup***
- 1 cup 3 percent hydrogen peroxide (soak items 12 to 24 hours and then rinse)
- 1 cup bleach solution: 1 tablespoon plain chlorine bleach mixed with 1 cup cool water (soak items 12 to 24 hours and then rinse)

***PLASTIC BAG AND BOTTLE DRYER/RACK (free-standing, multi-armed wooden rack; used for holding food storage bags or bottles while drying)***
- Baby bottle drying rack
- Jewelry tree
- Free-standing paper towel holder (from a dollar store)
- Clean 2- or 3-liter soda or water bottle
- Toothbrush holder, vase, jar, or jug, containing chopsticks, slotted serving spoons or spatulas, sturdy plastic straws, or dowels (weight the item if necessary; set it on a folded kitchen towel (optional) and drape the bag or bags over it)

***PLASTIC GLOVE, DISPOSABLE (protective mitt for handling messy items)***
- Plastic sandwich bag, produce bag, bread bag, or daily newspaper delivery sleeve (attach to the wrist with a rubber band if necessary)

***PLASTIC PRODUCE BAGS; see** PRODUCE BAGS*

***PLASTIC WRAP (thin, food-safe plastic);** see also MICROWAVE COOKING LID; WAXED PAPER*
- **For covering food being microwaved:** heatproof casserole cover, or inverted microwave-safe ceramic bowl or plate (for a tight seal); for a light covering,

use a basket-type paper coffee filter, inverted paper plate, or microwave-safe paper towel (dampen the edges with water to anchor it in place)

* **For covering proofing dough:** large glass pot lid; large glass inverted bowl or casserole; inverted bowl of a salad spinner; inverted clear-view Sterlite box; cake dome; top from a plastic/silicone cake or cupcake carrier; tented plastic produce bag; new plastic shower cap; or clean, damp dishtowel
* **For covering refrigerated, lidless bowls or containers:** washable and reusable wrap such as beeswax wraps, plates or saucers, clean plastic lids from food containers, washable hemp-cotton squares that cling to the rim of the bowl, stretchable silicone covers, flexible flat silicone covers that rest on the rim of the bowl and create a suction seal, or plastic cut-up produce bags
* **For covering large refrigerated containers:** inverted pan lid, bottom of a tart pan, pizza or baking pan (for a stackable surface), or reusable produce bag (place container in the bag, stretch the bag tight, and then fasten at the side with a twist tie)
* **For crushing ingredients or pounding meat:** inner wrappers from cereal boxes, or plastic or paper produce bags
* **For placing directly on still-warm pudding or pastry cream to prevent a skin from forming:** greased parchment paper or a light film of melted butter

*PLATE WARMER; see WARMING DRAWER*

*PLATTER, SERVING; see SERVING PLATTER/BUFFET TRAY*

*PLETT PAN/PLÄTT PAN/PLÄTTLAGG (cast-iron pan with 3-inch-wide shallow indentations; used for making Swedish pancakes*
* Silver dollar pan
* Large skillet or griddle (use 2 tablespoon batter for each pancake)

*POACHING KETTLE; see FISH POACHER/FISH STEAMER/TURBOTIÈRE*

**POACHING PAPER;** *see PAPER LID/CARTOUCHE*

**POMMES ANNA PAN (6-cup heavy, tin-lined, copper mold with straight sides; used for making pommes Anna)**
- Nonstick, ovenproof skillet
- 8-x-2-inch round cake pan

**POPCORN POPPER, MICROWAVE (glass or plastic lidded container; used for popping corn kernels)**
- Plain untreated (not recycled) brown paper lunch bag (enclose 2 tablespoons kernels in the bag, fold it tightly two or three times, lay it on its side, and microwave on High two to three minutes until pops slow to five seconds apart)
- Large microwave-safe bowl covered with a microwave-safe dinner plate (add 2 tablespoons popcorn kernels to the bowl; microwave on High two to three minutes until pops slow to five seconds apart)

**POPOVER PAN (rectangular metal tray with six 2-inch-deep cups for baking popovers)**
- Dariole molds
- 6-cup jumbo/giant muffin pan
- 6 custard cups, preferably heavy pottery; 2-inch-deep ramekins; or small ovenproof tea or coffee cups (place on a baking sheet, widely separated)
- 12-cup regular muffin pan (pour batter into every other heated muffin cup, filling 2/3 full, and reduce secondary baking time to 25 minutes after temperature has been lowered)

**POTATO MASHER (implement with a flat, round, perforated disk or thick coils; used for mashing potatoes and other soft food)**
- Mallet/meat tenderizer
- Avocado masher or bean masher/*aplastadora*
- Large cooking or serving fork with sturdy prongs

* Wooden spoon
* Single beater from a handheld mixer, removed and used manually (mash the ingredients against the side of the bowl)
* Electric mixer on low speed

## POTS DE CRÈME SET (ovenproof, lidded pots; used for cooking custards in a water bath)

* Custard cups, dariole molds, small ramekins, or tempered ceramic teacups, covered with small saucers, condiment dishes, or pieces of foil or parchment
* Japanese lidded custard cups/*chawans* (filled halfway)

## POULTRY LIFTERS; see TURKEY LIFTERS

## POULTRY NEEDLE (sturdy needle with a large eye; used for sewing up the poultry cavity)

* Darning or upholstery needle

## POULTRY RACK; see ROASTING RACK/TRIVET

## POULTRY ROASTER, VERTICAL; see CHICKEN ROASTER, VERTICAL

## POULTRY SHEARS; see SHEARS, KITCHEN/KITCHEN SCISSORS, ALL-PURPOSE

## POULTRY SKEWERS/TURKEY LACERS AND LACING (thin steel skewers and twine for closing poultry cavities and trussing the bird for roasting)

* Reusable silicone tie (resistant to 480°F; dishwasher safe)
* Plain, uncolored wooden toothpicks
* Long produce ties with the paper stripped off
* Large straightened-out paper clips
* Large new safety pins
* Kitchen or poultry twine plus a poultry needle (for sewing up the poultry vent or securing stuffed meats)

- Clean, thin, stainless-steel nails
- Chicken skin (make a little hole in the fatty skin on each side of the cavity; then stick the legs through, crossing them)
- Heel or chunk of bread or piece of raw potato (in place of trussing poultry; place in the cavity opening to seal it)
- Onion or lemon (in place of trussing poultry; insert in the cavity to prevent the breast drying out)

**POULTRY TWINE; see** *TWINE, KITCHEN/WHITE KITCHEN STRING*

**PREP BOARD (*food preparation board with a lipped edge to keep juices from spilling*)**
- Cutting board set in a rimmed baking sheet

**PREP BOWLS/MISE EN PLACE CONTAINERS (*glass, porcelain, or stainless-steel mini bowls; used for staging ingredients prior to cooking*)**
- Egg cups; cupcake papers/liners; egg poacher inserts; silicone egg poacher pods; small custard cups or ramekins, porcelain tea bag holders, or clean, empty, take-out condiment containers
- Basket-type paper coffee filters (for flour, sugar, and other dry ingredients)
- Single bowl (separate items by sheets of waxed paper or plastic wrap; place them in order of need—first in last out)

**PRESENTATION RINGS; see** *FOOD MOLDS/CHEF'S RING MOLDS/ PRESENTATION RINGS*

**PRESERVING PAN (*large, heavy-bottomed, wide pan with outwardly sloping sides; used for making jams and preserves*)**
- 6- to 8-quart, wide enamel or stainless-steel pot
- Large, heavy, stainless-steel or nonstick skillet or sauté pan (for a small amount; the wide surface reduces cooking time and helps retain the fruit's flavor)

**PRESS, FOOD; see** *FOOD WEIGHT/PRESS*

**PRESSURE COOKER (*heavy, sealable pot for cooking food rapidly under pressure at a very high temperature*)**
- Large heavy saucepan with tight-fitting lid (increase liquid in recipe by 20 to 40 percent, keep ingredients at simmer, and triple the cooking time called for at high pressure)

**PRESSURE COOKER RACK/TRIVET (*pressure cooker accessory; used for keeping food from touching the bottom of the cooker*)**
- 7-inch wire cake rack
- Metal lid of a large jar
- Collapsible steam basket

**PRESSURE COOKER STEAMER BASKET (*pressure cooker accessory; used for steaming long-cooking items*)**
- Adjustable steamer basket
- Two 7-inch colanders (one inverted in the bottom of the pressure cooker, and the other containing the food placed on top)

**PRODUCE BAG HOLDER/DISPENSER (*storage receptacle for reusable produce bags*)**
- Empty tissue box
- Empty box from pre-cut foil sheets
- Empty paper-towel cylinder

**PRODUCE BAGS (*plastic bags for holding bulk fruits and vegetables*)**
- Machine-washable, drawstring, vented muslin or cotton sacks

**PROOF BOX; *see* BREAD PROOFING BOX**

**PUDDING BASIN (*deep pottery or china bowl for steaming suet pudding*); *see* STEAMED PUDDING MOLD/PUDDING BASIN**

**PULLMAN PAN/PAN DE MIE; see** LOAF PAN, SMALL PULLMAN/PAN DE MIE

**PUMPKIN-SHAPED CAKE PAN; see** CAKE PAN, PUMPKIN-SHAPED

**PUNCH BOWL (large decorative or plain glass bowl for holding punch or premixed cocktail)**
- Large glass or crockery mixing bowl
- Large trifle bowl
- Outer bowl of a salad spinner placed on a rimmed dinner or soup plate
- Large Dutch oven or small stock pot
- Large hollowed-out watermelon (cut off the top third and slightly trim the bottom to make a flat surface)
- Large, glass or plastic food storage container

# Q

**QUESADILLA GRILL BASKET; see** *FISH GRILLING BASKET/FLEXI GRILLING BASKET*

**QUICHE PAN (shallow, round dish with fluted, straight sides; used for baking a quiche)**
- Tart pan
- Round layer cake pan
- Metal, glass, or earthenware pie pan

# R

**RAMEKINS (small, shallow, earthenware or ceramic dishes with fluted sides; used for baking and serving individual desserts or soufflés)**
- Custard cups
- Ovenproof ceramic teacups
- Jumbo espresso cups (which hold 1/2 cup)
- Ceramic egg coddlers (minus the tops)
- Jumbo (3-x-1 1/4-inch size) muffin pan wells
- Straight-sided baking dish (for soufflé; bake an additional 15 to 20 minutes longer)

**RASP-TYPE GRATER; see** MICROPLANE GRATER/RASP-TYPE GRATER

**RECIPE CARD HOLDER (gadget for holding a printed recipe while in use)**
- Fork or long plastic spear from a floral arrangement (put the card in the tines of the fork and stand the fork in a glass or mug)
- Clear, 5-x-7-inch freestanding picture frame (slip the card into the frame)
- Open CD or DVD case bent back at an angle (prop the card against the case or attach with a spring clip)
- Standing clipboard
- Magnetic spring clip (attach the clip to a range hood, refrigerator, hanging pan, or other metal object or appliance)
- Cookie sheet (prop the sheet against the wall and attach the recipe with a binder clip or magnet)

**RECIPE FILE (storage receptacle for holding printed recipes)**
- Loose-leaf scrapbook or photo album with peel-up plastic coating on each page (for magazine pages)
- Photo albums with 3-x-5- or 4-x-6-inch slots (for recipe cards)

- Three-hole binders with clear plastic inserts (use a different-colored album for each food category, or different-colored divider tabs for a single album; for computer-generated recipes, use different-colored paper for each category)
- Rolodex file with labeled index cards (to indicate cookbook and page number, or Internet site)
- Computer folder, free at evernote.com and other sites (snap photos of recipes and upload to the folder)

## REFRIGERATOR DEODORIZER (cardboard box of baking soda with porous paper sides)
- New or expired box of cheap baking soda with the top removed
- Activated charcoal (not charcoal briquettes) spread out in a shallow container

## RICE COOKER (large electric pot for cooking plain rice and keeping it warm until serving time)
- Slow cooker (use 1 cup converted rice to 2 cups water and 1 teaspoon oil and cook on Low, 6 to 8 hours; will stay perfect if left on past 8 hours; alternatively, keep warm in a heavy Dutch oven set on a heat diffuser over a stovetop burner turned to low)
- Electric pressure cooker, such as Instant Pot, using the "Rice" feature

## RICE COOKER CUP (measuring cup that accompanies a rice cooker)
- 3/4-cup standard measuring cup

## RICER (tool with small-holed basket for pressing cooked vegetables into even strands)
- Food mill, using the fine disk
- Perforated potato masher
- Pastry blender
- Medium sieve or sturdy, metal, small-holed colander (press food through sieve or colander with a wooden spoon or stiff rubber or silicone spatula)

### RICE SERVER/SHAMOJI (Japanese flat wooden or bamboo paddle for serving rice)

- Hard plastic/polyethylene, silicone, or bamboo spatula
- Ice-cream paddle
- Salad serving spoon or Asian soup spoon

### RICOTTA MOLD (perforated woven container made of food-grade plastic; used for separating curds from whey)

- Repurposed insert from store-bought ricotta containers, such as Angelo & Franco brand
- Small salad-spinner basket

### RING MOLD/SAVARIN MOLD (ring-shaped pan with a large center hole; used for baking cakes or making gelatin molds)

- 2-inch deep cake pan plus greased custard cup or ramekin filled with pastry weights placed in the center, open end up; alternatively, press the ovenproof cup into the center of the batter, open end down, before placing in the oven

### RISOTTO PAN (large, heavy, flat-bottomed pan with straight sides and a clip-on handle that arches over the pan)

- 4-quart sauté pan
- Chicken fryer
- Large shallow saucepan

### ROASTING FORKS, CAMPFIRE (long forks used for toasting marshmallows and roasting hot dogs)

- Extra-long flat metal skewers (from a Middle Eastern market)
- Clean, smooth twigs; sturdy rosemary branches; or slender grapevine branches (bottom three-fourths of the leaves stripped off, sanded if necessary, and then soaked in water 30 minutes)

## ROASTING PAN/ROASTER PAN (large, ovenproof pan with 2-inch sides)

* Broiler pan base
* Cast-iron or other ovenproof skillet
* Flat-bottomed wok or sauté pan with ovenproof handles
* Chicken roaster with insert removed
* Lasagna pan
* 13-x-9-x-2-inch baking pan
* Sturdy rimmed baking sheet
  (Place a roasting rack inside for roasting meat or poultry) **see** ROASTING RACK/TRIVET

## ROASTING PAN LID/ROASTER PAN LID

* Baking sheet or non-perforated aluminum pizza pan

## ROASTING RACK/TRIVET (raised or V-shaped metal rack that fits into a roasting pan and holds the meat or poultry during cooking)

* Small, rectangular cooling rack
* Perforated trivet from a pressure cooker
* Large piece of heavy-duty foil rolled into a long 1 1/2- to 2-inch-wide cylinder and then formed into an "S" shape
* Stovetop grate covered in foil with holes poked in it (use two small covered grates, angled inward, for a large roast or turkey)
* Long skewer (run the skewer through the roast and rest the ends on the sides of the roasting pan to support them
* Crisscrossed carrots, celery, or fennel sticks
* Halved onions, flat side down (or 1/2-inch-thick slices)

## ROLLING MAT (nonstick mat with handy measuring guides to shape pie dough)

* Parchment paper or plastic-coated freezer paper (draw circles to the desired size; then turn the paper over before rolling out the pastry)

**ROLLING PIN (solid cylindrical tool for rolling out dough);** see also *ASIAN ROLLING PIN; PASTA ROLLING PIN/MATARELLO; GREEK ROLLING PIN*
- 16- to 19-inch piece of thick wooden dowel (lightly sand and then rub with food-grade mineral oil; let dry before using)
- Length of clean, thick pipe
- Poster mailing tube or sturdy tube from a used 18-inch roll of heavy-duty foil or parchment paper (roll pastry between two pieces of plastic wrap)
- 2-liter plastic water bottle almost filled with water and frozen (if possible, cover with a clean tube sock to avoid condensation)
- Tall, heavy wine bottle
- Thermos bottle filled with water
- Tall, unopened beverage or food can, or smooth-sided mug or jar (in a pinch)
- One's own hand for pie dough (follow a pat-in-the pan pastry recipe for single pie crust, tart shell, or tartlet shells)
- Pasta machine (for super-thin sheets of dough for flatbread or crackers)

**ROLLING PIN COVER/SLEEVE (fabric stockinet cover for absorbing flour and preventing dough from sticking to the rolling pin)**
- Clean white tube or knee-high sock with the foot section cut off (for tapered or dowel pin, use a stretch sock)

**ROLLING PIN RINGS/SPACERS (disks for helping roll dough to a specific thickness)**
- Thick rubber bands placed on the ends of the rolling pin (stack the bands, one on top of the other, until they match the thickness the dough should be)
- Two rulers or other items of the same thickness (1/8 or 1/4 inch) placed at each side of the dough (set the rolling pin atop the rulers and then roll across the dough)

***RONDEAU;* see** *BRAISING PAN/BRAISER/BRAZIER/RONDEAU*

**ROTISSERIE DRIP PAN (*metal pan for catching the drippings from cooking meat or poultry*)**
* Double thickness of heavy-duty foil fashioned into a tray shape to fit the unit

**RUBBER BANDS, HEAVY-DUTY (*stretchable bands for holding non-food items together*)**
* Wide strips cut from an old rubber glove (lots of give and take)
* Canning jar bands (for a large bundle; not very stretchable)
* Magnets for metal containers (for anchoring a kitchen trash bag or compost liner in place)

**RULER, KITCHEN (*long metal or plastic measuring tool used for various kitchen applications*)**
* 18-inch stainless-steel office or draftsman's ruler (for gauging reduction of liquids, amount of rise in yeast dough, and accurate measurement of rolled dough and bar cookies)
* Metal bench knife/dough scraper (for measuring up to 6 inches)
* 6-inch metal sewing and knitting gauge with a movable slide (for monitoring small amounts of liquid reductions or measuring the thickness of dough)
* Chopstick with markings made at 1/2-inch intervals (for monitoring small amounts of liquid reductions)
* Dollar bill (for measuring up to 6 inches; the bill is a fraction over 6 inches: 6 1/8 inches)

**RUST REMOVER (*nontoxic solution for removing rust from tinware, chrome, and other metal fixtures*)**
* Baking soda plus piece of raw potato (sprinkle on the soda and then rub the item with the potato until clean)

* Distilled white vinegar (apply a vinegar-soaked rag to the area, let sit 15 minutes, and then rub it clean)
* Superfine No. 000 steel wool or a fine steel-wool pad (dip it in a few drops of mineral or vegetable oil and rub it on the area until clean)
* Cola beverage: soak the item overnight; then scrub with an abrasive cloth until clean)

# S

**SAKÉ CUPS (small porcelain cups for serving saké)**
- Glass votive candle holders
- Demitasse or espresso cups

**SALAD BOWLS (small wooden bowls for holding individual servings of salad ingredients)**
- Wide, shallow soup bowls
- Pasta dishes
- Deep saucers
- Small cazuelas
- Red or green outer cabbage leaves or large outer leaves of iceberg lettuce (for savory salads)
- Personal-sized watermelon halves: fruit removed and a slice cut off the bottom (for fruit salad)
- Tortilla baskets: 8-inch flour tortilla pressed into greased jumbo muffin cups and baked at 450°F until golden and crisp, about eight minutes (for taco salad or other savory salad)

**SALAD SERVING BOWL (large wooden container for holding a tossed salad)**
- Outer bowl of a salad spinner
- Large mixing bowl
- Stainless-steel bowl of an electric mixer
- Large Dutch or French oven
- Roasting pan
- Small stockpot
- Insert from a slow cooker, preferably oval

**SALAD SERVING BOWL, SHALLOW (large earthenware or ceramic container for holding an arranged salad)**
- Tray or large platter with a slightly raised edge
- Large pasta bowl

**SALAD SPINNER (centrifugal-forced spinner for drying freshly washed greens)**
- Colander, large strainer, pasta insert, collapsible wire basket, perforated double boiler insert, deep fat fryer insert, perforated plastic clamshell container, or over-the-sink drainer (for draining greens dry)
- Large non-terry dishtowel (for spinning greens dry: gather the towel at the corners and spin it around several times)
- Plastic mesh fruit or onion bag, or lingerie laundry bag (for draining greens dry: suspend bag on the faucet handle, or take it outside and spin it around)
- Clean zipped pillow cover or large net mesh bag (for drying large amounts of greens: shake them until dry, spin them in an empty washing machine one or two minutes, or tumble them in the dryer on the no-heat cycle)

**SALAMANDER (long cast-iron rod with a wooden handle and small fire-heated plate; used for browning tops of gratins or caramelizing sugar-coated desserts)**
- Butane kitchen torch; **see** BLOWTORCH, BUTANE KITCHEN/CHEF'S TORCH/CRÈME BRÛLÉE TORCH
- Self-contained broiler unit used to finish or brown dishes
- Gas oven broiler or toaster oven broiler, preheated to highest setting (place the items 2 inches from the heat; for egg-based dishes such as crème brûlée, set the containers in a roasting pan filled with ice)

**SALOMETER/BRINE TESTER (weighted glass tube with markings for measuring the degree of salt concentration)**
- Food scale with a tare button (weigh the salt and water to obtain the salinity; for example, a 10 percent heavy brine, the strongest used in food

processing and enough to float an egg, is 1 ounce of salt for every 10 ounces water, or 100 grams salt for every 1,000 grams water. To obtain other saline concentrations, divide the salt grams/ounces by the amount of water)

## SALT CELLARS/HOLDERS (small receptacles used on the table for holding finishing salt)

- Small tea light holders
- Oyster, mussel, or other seashells (scrub fresh shells and then soak them in a mild bleach solution for four or five minutes; drain and air dry)
- Inverted porcelain egg cups
- Small stainless-steel egg cups
- 2 1/2-ounce stainless-steel condiment cups

## SALT MILL (small handheld device for grinding coarse granules of sea or kosher salt)

- Pepper mill with plastic, nylon, or stainless-steel grinding mechanism

## SALT PIG/SALT KEEPER (small foghorn-shaped pottery container with an unglazed interior; used for holding cooking salt)

- Tiny terra-cotta flowerpot (without a hole at the bottom)
- Small sugar bowl or parmesan cheese server with a slot in the side for a spoon
- Empty stoneware mustard jar or glass mustard jar with a spoon
- Ceramic ramekin

## SALT SHAKER, KOSHER (small container with a perforated lid; used for sprinkling kosher salt on food

- Clean spice jar with a shaker top

## SALT SPOON (small serving spoon used to accompany a salt cellar/holder)

- 1/8-teaspoon-size metal measuring spoon
- Child's stainless-steel baby spoon (not silver)
- Tiny plastic tasting spoon

**SANDWICH BAGS, PLASTIC** *(small disposable zip-top or foldable bags for holding various food items)*
- Small cellophane bags
- Press'n Seal wrap, cut and pressed into pouches

**SANDWICH BAGS, REUSABLE** *(washable, flap-type or zippered fabric bags; used to replace plastic sandwich bags)*
- Cotton napkins or pieces of clean cloth

**SANDWICH PLATTER; see** *SERVING PLATTER/BUFFET TRAY*

**SANDWICH PRESS/SANDWICH GRILLING IRON/PANINI PRESS** *(heavy, hinged, electric or stovetop cooking griddle; used for grilling Italian-type sandwiches)*
- Square or rectangular waffle iron (not a Belgian waffle iron)
- Round stovetop sandwich grill for single serving (trim overhanging bread to avoid burning)
- Cast-iron skillet topped with another cast-iron skillet heated on the bottom
- Wide-mouth toaster plus toaster bag (set toaster on low setting)
- Ridged grill pan topped with a grill press/*mattone*, bacon press, heavy skillet, foil-wrapped brick, or half-filled tea kettle (cover sandwich with a piece of foil or parchment and flip halfway through cooking)
- Oven or toaster oven set at 375°F (bake panini on a baking sheet until toasted, 7 to 10 minutes; then press down tops for 1 minute with a weight or metal spatula)

**SANDWICH SPREADER/BISTRO SPREADER** *(small, wide-bladed knife; used for spreading sandwich filling)*
- Butter knife
- Fish knife
- Small, narrow offset or pastry spatula
- New spackling knife, palette knife, or putty knife

### SANITIZING SOLUTION (acidic formula for sanitizing beer- and wine-making equipment) — 1 tablespoon

* 1 tablespoon plain chlorine bleach (add to 1 gallon cold water; let equipment soak for 20 minutes, and then rinse with plain water)

### SANITIZING SPRAY, KITCHEN (aerosol spray for sanitizing counters, sinks, and hard, non-porous surfaces) — 1 cup; see also CUTTING-BOARD SANITIZER

* Ten drops grapefruit seed extract (GSE) mixed with 1 cup water (shake well before using)
* 1/4 to 1/2 teaspoon plain chlorine bleach (6 percent sodium hypochlorite) mixed with 1 cup water (allow surfaces to air dry, about two minutes; if desired, rinse or wipe off with a clean wet cloth)
* 1/3 cup distilled white vinegar mixed with 2/3 cup water (not for marble, granite, natural stone, or wood surfaces)
* Undiluted rubbing alcohol (isopropyl alcohol), hydrogen peroxide (3 percent), or undiluted distilled white vinegar (for cutting boards and utensils)

### SARASH (Japanese cotton cooking cloth); see CHEESECLOTH/TAMMY CLOTH/ÈTAMINE

### SAUCE BOAT (shallow, wide-mouth oval jug attached to an oval plate; used to serve sauces)

* Cream jug, small milk jug, or other pouring jug
* Small bowl and ladle
* Wide-mouth thermos bottle/jar or thermal coffee carafe (for keeping sauce warm at the table)

### SAUCEPAN, 1-CUP (small stovetop pan for melting butter or gelatin)

* 1-cup heavy-duty, stainless-steel measuring cup
* Base of an individual egg poacher

**SAUCEPAN, 2-QUART** (*medium-size pan for stovetop cooking*)
* Electric kettle (for cooking asparagus spears, eggs in the shell, or oatmeal; or for heating soups, instant noodles, or hot chocolate; or for blanching peaches and tomatoes for peeling)
* Electric rice cooker (for cooking grains, steaming vegetables, or poaching fruit)

**SAUSAGE KNIFE** (*tool with a blade on one end and tines on the other; used to cut twine and prick filled casings*)
* Small paring knife (to cut casing and twine)
* Casing pricker, or pin or needle sterilized over a flame (to prick casings)

**SAUSAGE PRICKER;** *see* CASING PRICKER

**SAUSAGE STUFFER** (*free-standing metal appliance; used to force meat through a nozzle into a casing*)
* Sausage-stuffer attachment to a manual or electric grinder
* Sausage-stuffer funnel or regular funnel
* Canvas, plastic, or nylon pastry bag with the largest plain tip; *see* PASTRY BAG/PIPING BAG

**SAUTÉ PAN, DEEP** (*wide, enameled cast-iron pan; used for sautéing and slow cooking*)
* Deep covered skillet
* 4-quart Dutch oven, or shallow French oven

**SAUTÉ PAN/SAUTEUSE/SAUTOIR** (*wide, shallow pan with straight or sloping sides; used for quick shallow frying*)
* Chef's pan/multi-function pan/*fait-tout* pan
* Skillet
* Flat-bottomed wok
* Heavy, shallow saucepan

- Braising pan
- Chicken fryer
- Heavy-duty 9- or 10-x-2-inch cake pan
- Base of a nonstick egg-poaching pan
- Shallow roasting pan set over two stovetop burners (for large gatherings)

**SAVARIN MOLD; see** *RING MOLD/SAVARIN MOLD*

**SCALE, LARGE KITCHEN/SPRING SCALE (mechanical or electronic tool for weighing various foods)**
- Bathroom scale and container (for large amounts or fruit and vegetables: weigh the empty container first; then weigh the ingredients in the container and deduct the weight of the container)

**SCISSORS SHARPENER (single-bladed tool for sharpening kitchen scissors and tin snips)**
- Several layers of foil (cut through the foil a dozen or so times; if still dull, cut through a sheet of very fine sandpaper several times; turn the scissors over and repeat to sharpen the bottom blade)

**SCOOP, MUFFIN AND SCONE (half-sphere utensil for ladling out uniform portions; the scoop number indicates the number of scoops per quart)**
- Spring-loaded #16 (2-inch/2 fluid ounces) ice-cream or baking scoop
- 1/4-cup size dry measuring cup with a rounded bottom (spray with oil between scoops)

**SCOURING PASTE/SOFT SCRUBBING MULTI-PURPOSE PASTE (stain-removal paste for enamel and porcelain finishes)**
- Baking soda with enough water to form a paste plus a few drops liquid dishwashing soap
- One part Borax mixed with four parts baking soda (for porcelain stains; sprinkle on wet surface and let sit for a few hours)

**SCOURING POWDER** *(stain-removal powder for enamel and porcelain finishes)*
* Baking soda (keep in an empty shaker container; adding a few marbles will keep the soda from caking)

**SCRAPER, BOWL; see** BOWL SCRAPER, PLASTIC

**SCRUBBER PAD; see** PAN/POT SCRAPER/SCRUBBER

**SCRUBBING GLOVES** *(textured kitchen gloves for loosening grit and dirt from vegetables)*
* New bath/exfoliating mitt (from a dollar store)
* Plastic netting from fruit or vegetables
* Large vegetable brush
* Scrub pad or rough sponge

**SEAFOOD PLATTER/COLD TRAY** *(large serving receptacle for keeping seafood and other food chilled)*
* Shallow broiler pan base filled with ice, and the broiler rack lined with greens, such as lettuce, grape leaves, or regular parsley
* Rimmed tray or large terra-cotta flowerpot saucer lined with plastic wrap and filled with crushed ice
* Stainless steel griddle or grill, pre-chilled in the freezer

**SEAFOOD SCISSORS; see** CRAB/LOBSTER CRACKER

**SEA URCHIN CUTTER** *(9-inch scissor-type tool; used for cutting through sea urchin shells)*
* Nail/manicure scissors
* Paring knife

**SEATING MARKERS; see** PLACE CARD HOLDERS

**SEED GRINDER (*small electric device for grinding seeds, usually flax, 1/2 cup at a time*)**
- Spice grinder or blade-type coffee grinder

**SEED SPROUTING JAR (*container for germinating seeds and grains*);** see also *SPROUT BAG*
- Canning jar with a piece of wire mesh, mosquito netting, or vinyl window screening stretched over the top and held in place by the screw-on band
- Wide-mouth quart jar with piece of cheesecloth (or fine nylon netting, mesh, or hose) stretched over the top and held tightly in place with a thick rubber band

**SERVING BOWL, FRUIT SALAD; *see* FRUIT SALAD SERVING BOWL(S)**

**SERVING CONTAINERS, PARTY (*tableware for holding finger-food items*);** see also *CONDIMENT BOWLS/SMALL SAUCE DISHES; DESSERT SERVING DISH, LARGE; ICE BOWL/CHILL BOWL; SEAFOOD PLATTER/COLD TRAY; SERVING PLATTER/BUFFET TRAY*

**For breadsticks/grissini, cheese straws, celery sticks, skewered tidbits, or extra-long biscotti:**
- Tall containers: wide-mouth canning jars, handle-less mugs, ceramic jars, or clear vases

**For chips, crackers, and pretzels:**
- Cake pans: brioche, Bundt, savarin, fluted tube, or ring mold
- New shallow terra-cotta flowerpots or saucers
- Large inverted container lids

**For popcorn:**
- Plain paper lunch bags turned down a few inches
- 1-quart cardboard pails

**For individual servings of popcorn:**
* Small gift bags
* Squares of parchment or bamboo leaves rolled into cones and fastened at the seam
* Paper baskets fashioned from 6- or 9-inch paper plates (cut 2-inch slits at the pole and equator points; fold the four flaps up, one inside the other, and then staple or tape closed)

**For nuts and nibbles:**
* Large kitchen scoop
* Empty coconut shell halves, sanitized in a dishwasher and set in shallow bowls

*SERVING PLATTER/BUFFET TRAY (large oval or rectangular tray for holding hors d'oeuvres, sandwiches, and baked goods)*
* Cutting board or upended carving board
* Wire-mesh cooling rack, wrapped in heavy-duty foil
* Large terra-cotta flowerpot saucer
* Flat grill pan
* Pizza pan
* Comal
* Base from a large cake carrier
* Large cardboard cake round, or piece of heavy cardboard wrapped in foil
* Cookie or baking sheet
* Toaster oven tray
   (Cover receptacle with paper doilies, linen napkin, or paper place mat)

*SERVING PLATTER/BUFFET TRAY, SILVER OR GOLD (large metal tray for holding hors d'oeuvres, sandwiches, and baked goods)*
* Cutting board, upended carving board, baker's/pizza peel, or cookie sheet covered with silver or gold wrapping paper and secured with double-sided tape

**SERVING TRAY/TEA TRAY/WAITER'S TRAY** *(wooden or silver tray for transporting food and drinks)*
- Sturdy rimmed baking sheet (line with a tray cloth, linen dinner napkin, or large paper napkins)

**SHABU-SHABU POT/PEKING POT** *(Japanese stainless-steel pot with a center chimney for holding charcoal or solid fuel; used for making shabu-shabu)*
- Electric skillet

**SHAKER/SIFTER/DREDGER** *(canister with perforated or mesh screw-on top; used for sprinkling a light dusting of flour, sugar, or cocoa)*
- Tea or spice infuser
- Chinois or small sieve (tap the side to disperse the contents)
- Wide Microplane rasp grater (gently tap the edge to disperse the contents)
- Empty saltshaker, or empty spice container with a perforated, removable top (cover half the holes with adhesive tape, if necessary)
- Canning jar with a piece of cheesecloth stretched over the top and held in place by the screw-on band
- Glass jar or mug with a piece of cheesecloth stretched over the top and held in place with a rubber band (or use plastic wrap instead of cheesecloth: secure with a rubber band and then make holes with a toothpick/cocktail stick or skewer)
- Muslin or cheesecloth bag (unbleached muslin or two or three thicknesses of cheesecloth with ends gathered together and tied with kitchen twine)

**SHEARS, KITCHEN/KITCHEN SCISSORS, ALL-PURPOSE** *(sturdy, short-bladed stainless-steel scissors usually with one serrated blade; used for cutting food and twine plus other functions)*
- Clean, heavy, all-purpose scissors
- Clean, spring-loaded snips (for cutting through chicken backbones and fish fins)

**SHOPPING BAG HOLDER/GROCERY BAG HOLDER** *(stainless steel or plastic receptacle for holding shopping bags)*
- Compartmental wine bottle tote (for sturdy shopping bags)
- Large empty tissue box or wipe container, or liter water bottle with the bottom removed (for thin plastic shopping bags)

**SHORTBREAD PAN/SHORTBREAD MOLD** *(shallow, patterned pan for baking shortbread)*; see also *COOKIE STAMPS*
- Fluted tart or flan pan plus springerle mold or cookie stamp (press mold or stamp into the dough before baking; the decorative pattern will appear on the top rather than the bottom)
- 9- or 9 1/2-inch inverted expandable tart ring set on a parchment-lined baking sheet (press the dough into the ring, prick the surface, and score into 12 wedges before baking)

**SHREDDER/SHAVER;** *see SPIRAL SLICER, VEGETABLE/SPIRALING MACHINE*

**SHRIMPER/SHRIMP DEVEINER** *(small tool for removing a shrimp's intestinal vein)*
- Handheld letter opener/envelope slitter
- Small steel crochet hook
- Blunt end of a toothpick/cocktail stick
- Tine of a dinner fork
- Tip of a paring knife

**SIEVE/STRAINER** *(wire-mesh basket with handle; used for separating lumps from dry materials or liquids from solids)*; see also *CHEESE BAG; CHINOIS/CHINA CAP/BOUILLON STRAINER; COLANDER; FOOD MILL; HAWTHORNE STRAINER/COCKTAIL STRAINER; JELLY BAG/JELLY-STRAINING BAG; NUTMILK BAG; SIFTER; TOMATO STRAINER*

- Pyrex jug or bowl loosely covered with muslin or thin cotton (non-terry) dishtowel and kept securely in place with a rubber band, clothespins, or clips
- Footed metal colander lined with plain white paper towels or basket-type paper coffee filters
- Potato ricer
- Basket of a drip coffee maker lined with cheesecloth or a coffee filter
- Large plunge-filter coffee maker/French press (pour off the liquid, leaving the solids at the bottom)
- Plastic berry basket lined with ultra-fine cheesecloth or muslin and suspended over a bowl or rack (for draining tofu, cheese, and other liquidy solids)
- **For small amounts:** Hawthorne or julep strainer, tea filter basket, large slotted serving spoon, or reverse side of a Microplane or beveled flat grater

### SIFTER, FLOUR (fine-mesh screen with a trigger handle or hand crank; used to aerate flour and combine dry ingredients)

- Fine-mesh sieve or strainer (stir the flour or other ingredient to press it through the sieve)
- Food processor
- Electric mixer on low speed
- Wire whisk
- Pastry blender
- Fork
- One's own hands

### SILICA GEL/SODIUM SILICATE (nontoxic granular desiccant; used for absorbing moisture in stored food items such as cookies) — 1 (5-gram) packet

- 1 to 2 tablespoons dried milk powder from a freshly opened package (wrap in a piece of muslin, thin cotton, or unscented facial tissues)
- Several silica gel packets saved from pill bottles
- 3 tablespoons raw uncooked rice

**SILICONE CLEANER; see** *PLASTIC AND SILICONE CLEANER*

**SILICONE COVER (self-sealing, stretchable cover; used for covering a storage bowl while providing a flat, stackable surface)**
- Clean plastic container lid for covering a bowl of refrigerated ingredients (rest on top of the bowl; save various sizes for different-size bowls)

**SILVER CLEANING PLATE (electrolytic plate for removing tarnish from silver)**
- Piece of heavy-duty foil plus 1/2 cup baking soda (line a shallow basin with foil, add silverware, sprinkle on soda, and then add enough boiling water to cover silverware; remove when tarnish disappears, 5 to 10 minutes; rinse and buff with a soft cloth

**SILVER POLISH (nonabrasive paste or liquid for removing tarnish from sterling or silverware)**
- Equal parts baking soda and club soda (or water) mixed to make a soft paste; use immediately
- White (non-gel) toothpaste plus a little water to make a paste

**SINK MAT/PROTECTOR (perforated rubber or plastic pad; used to protect delicate dishware and stemware)**
- Piece of bubble wrap
- Clean, folded towel

**SIZZLE PLATE (cast-iron griddle used for high-temperate cooking and serving)**
- Indian cast-iron tawa or tava, Mexican metal comal, or small cast-iron griddle or pizza pan, set on a prepurposed wooden board for serving

**SKELETON KNIFE (stainless-steel knife with three large holes in the micro-serrated blade; used for cutting soft or sticky food)**
- Cheesecake knife

* Thin-bladed knife (brush it with a little oil or heat it in a glass of hot water; then wipe dry)
* Unflavored dental floss

**SKEWERS, APPETIZER/FOOD PICKS (wood or plastic sticks for holding bite-size pieces of food);** see also TOOTHPICKS/COCKTAIL STICKS
* 9- or 12-inch bamboo skewers cut in half (use snips for a clean cut)
* 5-inch (child-size) Japanese chopsticks
* Wooden or plastic coffee stirrers
* Sturdy lemongrass stalks, cut in half lengthwise, and then into 4- to 6-inch-long sticks
* Thick, straight, woody sprigs of dried oregano, rosemary, or sage, leaves stripped off and then sharpened at one end; or use a metal skewer to puncture a hole in the food item and then thread it onto the sprigs through the same hole
* Fresh sugarcane stalks, peeled, cut lengthwise into 4- to 6-inch-long sticks, and then sharpened at one end (for canned sugarcane, cut each piece lengthwise into six to eight pieces)
* Pieces of stiff stainless-steel wire or straightened out paper clips (for grilled food)

**SKEWERS, GRILL/BARBECUE SKEWERS (long, thin pointed rods for holding food together during cooking);** see also POULTRY SKEWERS/TURKEY LACERS AND LACING
* Aluminum, stainless-steel, or bamboo knitting needles (soak bamboo needles in water 30 minutes before using)
* Light bamboo or wooden takeout chopsticks (sharpen tapered ends if necessary, and soak in water 30 minutes before using)
* Clean smooth twigs, sturdy rosemary branches, thick lavender branches, or slender grapevine branches, leaves stripped off, sharpened at one end, and sanded if necessary (soak in water 30 minutes before using; use a metal skewer to puncture a hole in the food item and then thread it onto the stalks through the same hole)

- Sugarcane or sorghum cane, peeled and split lengthwise (soak in water 30 minutes before using)
- 15-inch paper-coated metal produce ties with the paper stripped off (use two spaced a little apart for fish, shellfish, and delicate food items)
- Lengths of stainless-steel wire doubled over (for double skewers to balance light items)
- 19 1/2-inch-long single grill basket instead of skewers; *see GRILL BASKET*

### SKEWERS, GRILL/BARBECUE SKEWERS, FLAT (1/2-inch-wide metal skewers for preventing food from spinning around when turned)
- Extra-long flat metal skewers (from a Middle Eastern market)
- Flat yakitori skewers with a tab on one end (from a Japanese market)
- Round skewers plus skewer supports; *see GRILL SKEWER SUPPORTS*

### SKILLET/FRYING PAN (long-handled pan with low, sloping sides; used for frying with a small amount of fat)
- Sauté pan
- Shallow saucepan
- Flat-bottomed wok
- Griddle
- Base of an egg poacher
- 9- or 10-x-2-inch heavy metal cake pan
- Inverted top of a metal or flameproof casserole dish or roaster (flat type without a knob)
- Inverted top of a camp Dutch oven (for cooking directly on the ashes or coals of a fire or grill)
- Large, 1/2-inch-thick rock or stone with one side completely flat (for cooking directly on the ashes or coals of a fire or grill)

### SKILLET/FRYING PAN, NON-STICK (long-handled coated pan with low, sloping sides; used for frying without fat)
- Carbon steel skillet or well-seasoned cast-iron skillet

### SKILLET LID/FRYING PAN LID (large lid for trapping moisture during cooking)

- Inverted skillet having the same (or larger) dimensions
- Stockpot lid
- Aluminum pizza pan
- Baking sheet

### SKIMMER/SPIDER (shallow, wire mesh basket with a long handle; used for lifting food items out of hot oil or water)

- Large perforated spoon
- Long metal tongs
- Cooking chopsticks

### SLOW COOKER/CROCK POT (small insulated electric pot for cooking food with low, moist heat)

- Electric pressure cooker, such as Instant Pot, using the "Slow Cook" feature
- Oven set at 200°F for Low or 300°F for High (place ingredients in a covered Dutch oven or a casserole with tight-fitting lid; add up to 1/2 cup extra liquid if necessary, and cook for the same amount of time specified in the slow-cooker recipe, usually eight hours for Low and three to four hours for High)
- Heavy rice cooker using the "Slow Cook" feature
- Electric roaster set at low
- Covered Dutch oven placed on a heat diffuser set over a stovetop burner on low
- Thermal cooking pot/vacuum insulated pot (have contents brought to a full boil before placing in the outer pot)
- Insulated cooler plus heavy blankets, hay, straw or crumpled newspaper (have the food brought to a rolling boil or long simmer before nestling the pot into the insulated material; weight the pot lid with something heavy such as a cast-iron skillet; and keep the cooler closed until ready to remove the food)

⁕ Wide-mouth thermos bottle/jar covered with a tea cozy or folded towel for making cooked cereal (add boiling water to the cereal and let sit overnight)

**SLOW-COOKER LINER (13-x-21-inch nylon resin bag; used to reduce cleanup time)**
⁕ Nonstick cooking spray (coat the cooker insert before adding ingredients)
⁕ Oven-roasting bag (fold top edges of the bag over the insert rim before putting on the lid)

**SMOKER BOX, GRILL; see** GRILL SMOKER BOX

**SMOKER, STOVETOP/SMOKER COOKER (appliance for smoking food over a heat source)**
⁕ 13-x-9-inch disposable aluminum baking pan plus rack (wrap rack in foil and then poke holes in the foil; if a drip pan if required, use a disposable pie plate and set it over the wood shavings; cover the baking pan with heavy-duty foil, crimping to create a tight seal; if no rack is available, place shavings on one side of the pan and the food on the other)
⁕ Wok plus rack (line the inside of the wok and the lid with heavy-duty foil, allowing a 1-inch overhang in both; then crimp the overhangs together when the shavings begin to smoke)
⁕ Heavy-bottomed pot and collapsible metal steamer (line the pot and lid with heavy-duty foil)

**SNACK BAGS; see** SANDWICH BAGS, PLASTIC; SANDWICH BAGS, REUSABLE

**SNAIL PLATE/ESCARGOT DISH/ESCARGOTIÈRE (small plate with six indentations; used for holding cooked snails)**
⁕ Cast-iron drop biscuit pan, such as Lodge brand
⁕ Danish pancake pan/*aebleskive* pan
⁕ Wide, shallow pasta bowl or soup dish

**SOUFFLÉ DISH** (*white porcelain, flat-bottomed dish with straight sides; used to bake a soufflé*)
- Straight-sided baking dish or charlotte mold (fill dish or mold up to an inch from the top; extend the height if necessary with a strip of double- or triple-folded foil or parchment wrapped around the outside rim)
- Straight-sided ovenproof saucepan with ovenproof handles, or non-metal handles covered with several thicknesses of foil (fill pan up to an inch from the top)
- Custard cups or ramekins for individual soufflés (can be frozen; bake frozen soufflés on a baking sheet in a 350°F oven until golden, about 40 minutes)

**SOUP BOWL** (*shallow, wide bowl for holding an individual portion of soup*)
- Large breakfast cup
- 10-ounce custard cup
- 8-ounce Japanese lidded custard cup/*chawans*
- Small casserole dish or mixing bowl
- Wide-mouth 1/2-pint canning jar

**SOUP LADLE; see** LADLE

**SOUP TUREEN; see** TUREEN

**SOURDOUGH STARTER CROCK** (*stoneware container for storing refrigerated sourdough starter*)
- 1-quart wide-mouth canning jar, measuring jug, or large heavy beer mug, covered with folded cheesecloth secured with a rubber band

**SOUS VIDE MACHINE/WATER OVEN WITH THERMAL IMMERSION CIRCULATOR** (*appliance for cooking food in a low-temperature, precision-controlled, hot water bath*); see also VACUUM SEALER

* Large heavy stockpot plus vacuum-seal (Cryovac) bag or sealable freezer bag (seal food completely airtight and poach in very hot water [140°F for meat or 185°F for vegetables], using a clip-on immersion circulator or a heat diffuser). Make sure the bag is completely submerged by weighting it with a plate or pan; or attach a large binder clip to the bottom of the bag and insert a heavy rod or spoon through the mouth of the clip. Use recipes that take less than one hour, and serve immediately.
* Steamer (steam the bag and contents for about twice the amount of time)

**SPÄETZLE PRESS/SPÄTZLE MACHINE (tool for pressing späetzle dough into boiling water)**
* Potato ricer using the large disk
* Colander with large holes
* Flat cheese grater with large holes
* Cookie press using the smallest holes
* Disposable aluminum pan with 1/4-inch holes poked in the bottom (Hold the substitute press 6 or more inches above the water, and slice dough from the bottom when strands are about 1/2 inch in length.)

**SPATULA, BLENDER; see** BLENDER SPATULA

**SPATULA, FOOD PROCESSOR; see** FOOD PROCESSOR SPATULA

**SPATULA, GIANT/UNIVERSAL (8-inch square metal spatula; used for transferring cake layers and pastry dough)**
* Aluminum baker's peel
* Lightweight, rimless cookie sheet
* Rolling pin for transferring pastry dough (drape the dough loosely over the rolling pin; then unroll it into the pie pan)

**SPATULA, ICING; see** BAKING SPATULA/OFFSET SPATULA

**SPATULA, LARGE (*wide metal spatula; used for turning and lifting large food items*)**
- Dinner plate (slide the food onto the plate; invert skillet over the plate, and flip to return food to the pan)
- Two dinner plates (slide food onto one plate, top with another plate, and then, holding the two plates together, turn them over and slide the food back into the pan

**SPATULA, METAL/PANCAKE TURNER (*tool with a broad, flat blunt blade; used for turning and lifting food items*)**
- One-slot cheese plane
- Wide-blade putty knife
- Wooden cooking chopsticks
- 2-inch wide palette knife (for small or delicate items or for small spaces)
- Heatproof silicone/nylon or wooden spatula or rice paddle (for nonstick pans)

**SPATULA, OFFSET; *see* **BAKING SPATULA/OFFSET SPATULA

**SPATULA, PLASTIC/BOWL SCRAPER; *see* **BOWL SCRAPER, PLASTIC

**SPATULA, RUBBER (*flexible-bladed tool for blending and folding delicate batters*)**
- Wooden spoon or spatula
- Rice server
- Large serving spoon
- One's own clean hands

**SPICE JARS (*glass jars for holding small amounts of spices or dried herbs*)**
- Clean, empty prescription bottles

**SPICE MILL** *(small electric machine for grinding small batches of spices from whole pods and seeds)*
- Blade-type coffee grinder (remove any coffee odor by grinding 2 or 3 tablespoons raw rice, torn-up bread, kosher salt, or coarse sugar, and then wiping clean with a paper towel)
- Mortar and pestle
- Pepper mill or glass peppercorn jar with removable grinding mechanism
- Flat side of a mallet (crush spices between two sheets of waxed paper or in a small freezer bag)

**SPIDER STRAINER; see** *SKIMMER/SPIDER*

**SPIRAL SLICER, VEGETABLE/SPIRALING MACHINE** *(free-standing machine with various settings; used for cutting vegetables into long, spiral-like strands)*
- Mandoline using the julienne blade
- Food processor using the julienne blade
- Julienne peeler or swivel vegetable peeler with serrated blade
- Y-shaped vegetable peeler and knife (shave the vegetable into long, wide strips with the peeler; then slice into thin strands with the knife)
- Box grater using the slicing slot (slice the vegetable into long thin strips; then slice the strips into strands)

**SPIT** *(metal or wooden rod; used to suspend meat being cooked over an open fire or grill)*
- Wooden dowel
- New wooden handle of a broom, mop, or rake, cut to size
- Green branch from a non-toxic species hardwood tree

**SPLASH GUARD; see** *MIXER, ELECTRIC STAND, SPLATTER SHIELD/ SPLATTER GUARD; MIXER, ELECTRIC HAND-HELD, SPLATTER SHIELD/ SPLATTER GUARD*

**SPLATTER SCREEN/SHIELD/GUARD** *(metal mesh cover for preventing grease splatters while allowing steam to escape)*
- Inverted metal colander or large mesh sieve
- Wire skimmer/spider (for a small pan)

**SPLIT-TOP BUN PAN** *(steel pan with 10 indentations; used for baking split-top buns)*
- Hot dog bun pan, covered with an inverted baking sheet weighted with a grill press or cast-iron skillet

**SPOON, SLOTTED** *(large perforated metal spoon for transferring cooked food without the liquid)*
- Wire skimmer/spider
- Perforated disk-type potato masher
- Small sieve

**SPORTS BOTTLE CLEANER** *(antibacterial tablets for cleaning hard-to-reach spots in water bottles)*
- Denture-cleaning tablets (drop in one or two, add water, and let sit an hour; then rinse well)
- Bleach and baking soda (use 1 teaspoon of each, add water, and let sit eight to ten hours; rinse well and air-dry completely)

**SPRINGFORM PAN, WATERTIGHT** *(round metal baking pan with removable sides; used mostly for baking cheesecake in a water bath)*
- Round metal pan slightly larger than the springform pan (set the springform pan inside the larger pan before placing them both in the water bath)
- Regular springform pan wrapped with two pieces of foil

**SPROUT BAG** *(mesh fabric drawstring bag; used for sprouting seeds)*
Cotton cheese bag
- Fine-mesh sieve or nylon strainer lined with cheesecloth or ultra-fine nylon or polyester curtain fabric

* Several pieces of cheesecloth gathered together at the top with kitchen twine

**SPROUTING JAR; see** *SEED SPROUTING JAR*

**SQUEEZO STRAINER (all-metal tool that separates seeds and skins from juice)**
* Food mill
* Ricer or potato masher  plus sieve (rice or mash the ingredients, and then press them through the sieve)
* Food processor or blender plus sieve (puree the ingredients, and then press them through the sieve)

**STAINLESS-STEEL BOWL, LARGE (deep, wide metal bowl)**
* Stainless-steel saucepan or pot

**STAINLESS-STEEL POLISH (nonabrasive solution for cleaning and polishing stainless steel)**
* Baking soda (apply with a wet cloth; for stubborn stains, apply a paste made with water and leave on until completely dry, about 15 minutes)
* Distilled white vinegar (apply with a microfiber cloth; for stained cookware, apply with a stainless-steel pad)
* Almond oil for brushed or polished stainless steel (apply sparingly with a cloth; then buff off excess with another cloth)

**STAINLESS-STEEL SOAP/ODOR REMOVER BAR (metal bar for removing garlic and onion odor from hands)**
* Stainless-steel spoon (rub hands over the spoon while holding them under cool running water; alternatively, rub hands over a stainless-steel faucet and then under running water)
* Toothpaste or diluted lemon juice (rub into the hands and then rinse under running water)

**STEAK KNIFE (sharp straight-edge knife for cutting steak)**
- Super-sharp paring knife

**STEAMED PUDDING MOLD/PUDDING BASIN (deep metal or earthenware bowl used for steaming puddings)**
- Clean, empty 11- to 13-ounce coffee can
- 28- to 32-ounce (PBA-free) food can
- 1-quart earthenware mixing bowl or other heavy, deep bowl
  (Fill the substitute mold two-thirds full, cover with parchment paper, and then seal with heavy-duty foil tied to the bowl with kitchen twine.)

**STEAMER (pot with a perforated insert; used for cooking food suspended over simmering water);** see also *BAMBOO STEAMER; COUSCOUSIÈRE; STEAMER, TALL; STEAMER, STACKABLE; TAMALE/TAMAL STEAMER/TAMALERA/VAPORERAS PARA TAMALES*
- Instant Pot using the steamer function
- Deep, lidded saucepan or electric skillet containing a steamer insert (*see STEAMER INSERT/RACK*) elevated at least 1 inch above the water (set food directly on the insert or in a shallow, heatproof bowl or deep plate; to duplicate a bamboo steamer, cover the pan with a clean dishtowel or paper towels before putting on the lid)
- Roasting pan with rack set over two burners (use a tight-fitting lid or use heavy-duty aluminum foil)
- Rice cooker plus collapsible steamer basket or footed metal colander that fits
- Lidded canning kettle with a round rack, or the removable rim of a cheesecake pan, or three empty 2- to 3-inch-tall cans with both ends removed
- Slow cooker with accompanying tray or collapsible steamer basket (set cooker to High and adjust cooking time)
- Lidded wok with a trivet or two crossed chopsticks placed in the bottom
- Fish poacher with the rack elevated by two jar lids

### STEAMER BASKET, THAI *(woven basket; used for steaming sticky rice over water)*
- Colander or steamer insert lined with dampened muslin or cheesecloth
- Pasta pot insert lined with softened banana leaf, fresh corn husks, or softened dried corn husks sprayed with cooking spray

### STEAMER INSERT/RACK *(steel-footed wire rack; used for holding food in a skillet or saucepan by suspending it above simmering water)*
- Wok trivet or perforated trivet from a pressure cooker, propped up with custard cups, ramekins, or 3-inch-high empty food cans
- Small, footed, stainless-steel colander
- Pair of chopsticks crisscrossed (for balancing a plate in a wok)
- Inexpensive splatter screen with handle removed (for a large wok)

### STEAMER LINERS *(perforated paper disks for providing a nonstick surface)*
- Parchment paper cut to size with several small holes poked in it with a chopstick or skewer
- Lettuce leaves, cabbage leaves, mature spinach leaves, or softened banana leaf (for fish, rice, or Chinese buns and dumplings)

### STEAMER RACK; *see STEAMER INSERT/RACK*

### STEAMER, STACKABLE *(8- or 10 1/2-inch-round unit with two steamer baskets; used for steaming dumplings and vegetables)*
- Two disposable pie pans plus two clean empty tuna cans with both ends removed (perforate pie pans and then stack them in a saucepan with an empty can between each pie pan; bend the pie pans if necessary)

### STEAMER, TALL *(large steel pot with a perforated basket insert; used for moist heat cooking)*
- Double boiler plus improvised steamer rack (use inner pan, inverted, as the lid)

## STEAM-INJECTED OVEN/BREAD OVEN/COMBI OVEN (steam-infused oven for creating a moist environment when baking yeast bread)

* Regular oven plus cast-iron grill humidifier
* Regular oven plus heavy, shallow pan (such as an old cast-iron skillet or broiler pan) containing small stones, pebbles, or lava rocks placed on the oven floor or bottom rack while the oven is preheating (immediately after placing bread in the oven, throw a cup of ice cubes quickly over the hot stones/rocks and then immediately close the oven door)
* Convection oven plus heavy shallow pan containing small stones, pebbles, or lava rocks placed on the shelf near the blower while the oven is preheating (immediately after placing bread in the oven, use a watering can to add 1 cup boiling water to the hot stones/rocks and then immediately close the oven door)

## STEEL WOOL/SCOURING PAD (abrasive material for removing baked-on food from pots and pans)

* Crumpled-up plastic netting from fruit or vegetables
* Wadded-up ball of aluminum foil

## STERILIZING KETTLE (deep pot with rack; used for sterilizing canning jars before filling with jams, pickles, or preserves)

* Oven set at 225°F (place clean jars on a baking sheet, open end up and not touching; then heat for 30 minutes)
* Dishwasher set at high-temperature rinse cycle, or use the "sanitize" setting if the machine has one
* Large pot plus folded towel on the bottom (place clean jars in the pot, add water to cover, and boil for 10 minutes)

## STOCKPOT (tall, narrow, lidded pot for making stock)

* 10-quart pasta pot plus lid
* Large saucepan with a lid
* Pressure canner/cooker (use a different lid, such as a Universal lid)

**STONEWARE *(high-fired ceramic cookware and serveware)***
- High-fired earthenware
- Porcelain
- Pyrex glass


**STOVETOP *(gas or electric heating elements used for cooking)*;** see also
*OVEN*
- Two-burner camp stove using propane or liquid camping fuel (for use outdoors)
- Charcoal or gas grill, cast-iron hibachi, or earthenware *shichin* (for use outdoors)
- Electric hotplate (single or double)
- Butane brazier/little butane stove (in well-ventilated area)
- Alcohol burner and grill (preferably using Everclear or denatured alcohol)
- Sterno or gel-fueled burner
- Portable induction cooktop (for use with cast-iron or All-Clad steel)
- Oven (for most simmered, boiled, or braised items). For braising, brown meat under the broiler or in a 450°F oven, turning until all surfaces are brown and crusty before adding liquid and other ingredients. For making hard-boiled eggs, place a dozen in a 12-cup muffin tin and cook in a preheated 325°F oven for 30 minutes; cool immediately in iced water.
- Electric skillet (for most fried, sautéed, simmered, boiled, or braised items)
- Wood-burning fireplace (for use with cast-iron or oven-safe pans for braising, frying, searing, and most applications; to keep pans soot free, place on disposable pie pans or coat the pan's undersurface with a film of soap or detergent)
- Electric kettle (for cooking quick oatmeal, eggs in the shell, asparagus spears, instant noodles, instant rice [or regular rice presoaked 20-30 minutes], or quick soups [mince the vegetables finely; for heating canned soups, hot chocolate, and other liquids; or for blanching peaches and tomatoes for peeling)

- Electric rice cooker (for cooking grains, steaming vegetables, or poaching fruit)
- Electric coffee maker or inversion heater (for heating water, soup, or other liquids)

**STOVETOP PEPPER AND TORTILLA ROASTER/ASADOR; see** PEPPER AND TORTILLA ROASTER, STOVETOP

**STOVETOP SMOKER; see** SMOKER, STOVETOP/SMOKER COOKER

**STRAINER; see** CHINOIS/CHINA CAP/BOUILLON STRAINER; CHEESE BAG; COLANDER; HAWTHORNE STRAINER/COCKTAIL STRAINER; JELLY BAG/JELLY-STRAINING BAG; NUTMILK BAG; OIL STRAINER POT: SIEVE/STRAINER; TOMATO STRAINER

**STRAWBERRY HULLER (miniature tongs; used for removing the green stem and core from strawberries)**
- Pointed end of a stationary or swivel peeler
- Puncture-type can opener
- Grapefruit knife
- Paring knife with a pointy tip

**STRAWS, PAPER OR PLASTIC, DRINKING**
- Stainless-steel or glass reusable straws
- Trimmed lovage stems
- Sturdy, dry fennel stalks

**STRING DISPENSER; see** TWINE, KITCHEN, DISPENSER/STRING KEEPER

**STUFFED PEPPER PAN (baking pan with six indentations for holding peppers upright while baking)**
- Tube pan (place the peppers close together)
- Jumbo muffin pan (place each pepper in a muffin cup)

- Cake pan or ovenproof skillet (cut a small slice from the bottom of each pepper and then place them as close together as possible)

**STUFFING BAG/SAC (cheesecloth bag for holding stuffing in the poultry cavity while the bird is cooking)**
- Double thickness of folded cheesecloth (place inside the cavity before adding the stuffing; knot both ends together, trim the excess, and then leave the knot barely showing for easy removal)

**SUGAR BEAR; see** BROWN SUGAR SAVER/SUGAR BEAR

**SUGAR DUSTER (small tool with a fine-mesh screen and squeeze-action handle; used for sprinkling confectioners' sugar)**
- Chinois, tea or spice infuser, tea-straining ball, inverted rasp-type Microplane grater, or any fine-meshed sieve or strainer (gently tap the edge to disperse the sugar)

**SUNDAE DISH (small glass dish with pedestal base; used for holding ice cream and toppings)**
- Small wine glass or teacup

**SURIBACHI (Japanese ceramic mortar); see** MORTAR AND PESTLE/ MOLCAJETE Y TEJOLOTE/SURIBACHI & SURIKOGI

**SUSHI MAT/SUDARE (Japanese bamboo mat; used for assembling and rolling sushi)**
- Cheese mat
- Undyed bamboo placemat or placemat woven of colorfast plastic slats (line with plastic wrap to keep it clean and prevent sticking)
- Silicone mat
- Large, thick cloth napkin, preferably linen

**SUSHI MOLD/PUSH FRAME/OSHIWAKU/OSHIZUSHI (*Japanese three-piece sushi press*);** see also *TERRINE/PÂTÉ MOLD*

* Two small, same-size stackable loaf pans (line one pan with plastic wrap, leaving a 3-inch overhang, and weight the other with food cans; fill lined pan 1 1/2 inches deep with sushi mixture, cover with overhanging wrap, set the weighted pan on top, and firmly press down); in place of the second pan, use a piece of sturdy cardboard, cut to fit and then wrapped in plastic wrap

**SWEDISH PANCAKE PAN; *see*** *PLETT PAN/PLÄTT PAN/PLÄTTLAGG*

# T

## TABLECLOTH (*fabric or plastic table covering*)
- Clean cotton top sheet
- New hardware-store drop cloth

## TABLE MARKERS (*signage used for identifying dishes on a buffet table*)
- Chalk cloth runner (write with chalk directly on the runner)
- Plain umbrella picks plus pieces of colored foam as a base
- Folded 3-x-5-inch plain index cards
- Construction paper cut into 6-x-3/4-inch strips, folded in half, and glued to toothpicks
- Clean, used domino tiles, mah-jongg tiles, or cribbage tiles plus circular paper clips (use hot glue to attach the clips to the tiles)

## TABLE PAD, CUSTOM/SILENCE CLOTH (*thick felt protective pad*)
- Large terrycloth towels

## TABLE PLACE MATS; *see* PLACE MATS

## TACO SALAD BOWL FRYING BASKET; *see* TORTILLA FRY BASKET

## TACO SHELL HOLDER (*ridged metal rack for holding taco shells for filling*)
- Nonstick taco grill rack
- Toast rack
- Small slotted desk/letter organizer
- Empty, plastic-wrap-lined egg carton (can do four at a time)
- Dinner fork (for individual tacos; wedge the base of the taco shell between the tines to hold it upright while filling)

**TACO SHELL MAKER (metal mold for holding tortillas while they are being fried in hot oil);** see also *TORTILLA FRY BASKET*
- Metal spatula (when the tortilla floats to the top of the hot oil, push the edge of spatula into its center so it bends it in half, and then cook until golden)
- Oven rack (brush the tortillas lightly with oil and drape each one over two bars of the oven rack; bake at 375°F until crisp and lightly golden, 8 to 10 minutes)
- Toaster (microwave the tortillas for 15 seconds under a damp paper towel, and then crisp them, folded, in the toaster)

**TAGINE/TAJINE (North African, wide, shallow, earthenware vessel with a tall, cone-shaped lid; used for slow-cooked, stovetop stews)**
- Spanish cazuela plus parchment paper (wet a crumbled sheet of parchment and place it atop the food; then cover with a lid, preferably domed)
- Small covered stockpot plus heavy-duty foil (fashion a cone with the foil, and then tent it over the ingredients before putting on the lid; use a heat diffuser unless the pot is very heavy)
- Small Dutch oven
- Shallow, enameled cast-iron, lidded casserole
- Wide, heavy skillet with a lid, preferably domed

**TAGRA (Moroccan, deep, oval, unglazed earthenware pan; used for low-temperature cooking)**
- Spanish cazuela
- Deep tagine
- Straight-sided, flameware baking dish

**TAMALE/TAMAL STEAMER/TAMALERA/VAPORERAS PARA TAMALES (large aluminum pot with a steamer chamber and tight-fitting lid; used for steaming tamales)**
- Large pasta pot with the perforated insert set on upturned custard cups and the top tented with heavy-duty foil

* Large lidded stockpot plus a 12-inch metal colander (or small rack elevated with canning jar screw bands or balls of aluminum foil)
* Covered roaster plus collapsible vegetable steamer (or roasting rack set on clean empty tuna cans)
* Broiler pan and two dishtowels for steaming in the oven (use one dampened dishtowel for lining the broiler rack and one for covering tamales: place lined rack containing tamales on broiler pan filled with 2 cups hot water, cover with dishtowel and foil, and steam in a 450°F oven until done, about one hour)

**TAMIS/DRUM SIEVE (*flat, wire-mesh or cloth screen for sieving, sifting, or straining dry or liquid ingredients*)**
* Fine-mesh sieve

**TAMPER (*conical wooden pestle for pressing food through a sieve*);** see also *TART TAMPER*
* End of a French-type rolling pin
* Hardwood dowel
* Back of a wooden or silicone spoon

**TANDOOR OVEN; *see*** *BRICK OVEN/HEARTH OVEN/BREAD OVEN/PIZZA OVEN*

**TARTE TATIN PAN (*heavy tart pan; used for a French inverted apple tart of the same name*)**
* 8- or 9-inch ovenproof, nonstick sauté pan
* 9- or 10-inch flameware or cast-iron skillet, or any heavy-duty ovenproof skillet

**TART/GALETTE/CROSTATA TEMPLATE (*pattern or guide for cutting pastry into a large circle*); see also PASTRY TEMPLATE, LARGE (*stencil used as guide for cutting dough into a desired shape***
* 7- to 14-inch expandable flan ring
* Embroidery frame/hoop

* Pan lid
* Inverted bowl, plate, or saucer
(Cut around the template with the tip of a sharp knife.)

### TARTLET CASES (small individual pastry molds)
* Clean, empty 2-inch-deep food cans (PBA-free and not pop-top)
* 8-x-8-inch pieces of heavy-duty foil molded on the outside of a 4-inch ramekin or 29-ounce food can (fold the excess foil back on itself to make a sturdy rim). For a 2-inch tartlet case, use 5-x-5-inch pieces of foil molded on a tomato paste can, folding excess foil back onto itself into a 1/2- to 3/4-inch rim.

### TARTLET RINGS (shallow, bottomless frames for baking pastry directly on a baking sheet)
* Wide-mouth canning jar rings
* Pieces of heavy-duty foil folded lengthwise into thick 1/2- or 3/4-inch strips and then formed into 4-inch rings (overlap the ends and then staple or clip them together)
* Strips of heavy card stock (1/2 or 3/4 inches wide) formed into rings, ovals, rectangles, or squares (overlap the ends and then staple or clip them together)

### TART PAN, TWO-PIECE (fluted, straight-sided metal pan with removable rim)
* Flan ring set on a greased or parchment-lined baking sheet
* Cake pan (8- or 9-x-1 1/2-inch)
* Piece of heavy-duty foil folded lengthwise into a thick 1-inch strip and formed into a ring (overlap the ends and staple, pin, or clip them together, and then set the ring on a parchment-lined baking sheet)

### TART TAMPER (small wooden implement for pressing dough into tart shells)
* Fat end of a honey dipper

* Small, narrow jar, such as sauce, garlic, or spice
* End of a wooden spoon (for mini tarts)
* Narrow food jar, such as sauce, garlic, or spice jar

## TASTING SPOON/TESTING SPOON (long-handled porcelain spoon with a small bowl; used for tasting food as it cooks)

* Chinese white ceramic soup spoon (use the cooking/stirring spoon to deposit a sample in the ceramic tasting spoon)

## TAVA (flat, cast-iron pan; used for cooking Indian flatbreads)

* Indian cast-iron tawa
* Mexican metal comal
* Cast-iron griddle or sizzle plate

## TEA BALL/STRAINER/INFUSER (small perforated container with two halves that snap or slide together; used for brewing tea from loose tea leaves)

* Bouquet garni spice bag
* Piece of cheesecloth tied with kitchen twine or a leftover tea-bag string

## TEA COZY (knitted or padded cloth cover; used for keeping a teapot warm between servings)

* Woolen beanie
* Padded ski cap
* Kitchen towel or guest towel (to wrap around the teapot)

## TEAPOT (porcelain or ceramic vessel; used for brewing tea from loose tea leaves)

* Drip coffee-maker base
* Plunge-filter coffee maker/French press
* 1-quart Pyrex jug plus a saucer or small plate to serve as a cover

**TEAPOT SPOUT PROTECTOR** *(short, angled rubber cylinder; used to protect a porcelain spout during storage)*
- Empty toilet-paper tube, or section of a paper-towel tube
- Thumb cut from an old leather gardening or work glove

**TEGAME** *(heavy Sicilian skillet or casserole; used for cooking and serving one-dish meals)*
- Cazuela
- Large ovenproof skillet

**TEPPAN/IRON SHEET** *(Japanese large iron griddle; used for cooking food at the table)*
- Electric griddle or grill fully opened
- Electric skillet
- Heavy skillet set over an electric hotplate or tabletop butane burner

**TERRINE/PÂTÉ MOLD** *(narrow oval or rectangular, straight-sided dish with a vented or unvented lid; used for making pâté without a crust)*
- Small Pyrex or earthenware loaf pan covered with heavy-duty foil (for a vented lid, make a small hole in the foil for steam to escape; for an unbaked pâté, line the mold with plastic wrap, allowing a 3-inch overhang on each side to act as a cover; for a baked terrine, line the mold, bottom and sides, with parchment paper
- For an unbaked pâté: Two well-washed pint- or quart-size milk cartons (cut the top and one long side out of each carton, and then slide the sides of the two cartons onto one another to the desired length; tape the bottom to keep the mold straight, and then line the inside with plastic wrap

**TETSUNABE/SUKIYAKI-NABE** *(large shallow iron pan; used for cooking sukiyaki at the table)*
- Electric skillet
- Large cast-iron skillet set over a hotplate

**THALIS** *(large, rimmed metal platter from India; used for holding small food bowls); see SERVING PLATTER/BUFFET TRAY*

**THERMOMETER HOLDER** *(container for housing kitchen thermometer[s])*
- 8-x-4 1/2-inch clear plastic pencil case (for storing cooking thermometers flat)
- The center hole of a kitchen twine spool, or a toothbrush caddy (for storing cooking thermometers upright)
- Wooden knife block (for storing an instant-read thermometer; drill a small hole near the bottom of the block)

**THERMOMETER, CANDY** *(thermometer used for measuring the temperature of boiled sugar)*
- Google the Internet for the cold-water test for candy making (dropping a little into water and checking for the results) or visit whatscookingamerica.net

**THERMOMETER, CANDY/DEEP-FRY** *(thermometer that clips to the side of a cooking pot; used for measuring the temperature of boiled sugar or hot oil)*
- Digital, instant-read/probe thermometer plus small binder clip (attach the clip to the side of the pot and slide the thermometer through one of the clip's handles, making sure it clears the bottom of the pot)

**THERMOMETER, CHEESE** *(glass thermometer with a circular, flat dial top; used for measuring the temperature of milk for cheese making)*
- Instant-read thermometer
- Meat thermometer

**THERMOMETER, DEEP-FAT FRYER** *(thermometer used for measuring the temperature of hot fat for deep-frying: 350°F to 365°F)*
- Instant-read thermometer (insert thermometer through one hole of a slotted cooking spoon; then hold onto the spoon handle to dip the thermometer tip into the fat)

* Wooden skewer, tip of wooden chopstick, or handle end of a wooden spoon (bubbles form immediately around the wood when dipped in the hot oil)
* Drop of batter or small particle of food (food sizzles immediately or skitters on the surface when dropped in the hot oil)
* Few popcorn kernels (corn pops immediately at 360°F)

**THREE-CHANNEL PAN; see** LOAF PAN, THREE-PIECE/TRIO/THREE-IN-ONE/LINKED

**TIAN (glazed, shallow, earthenware baking dish from Provençe, usually square or rectangular)**
* Cazuela
* Terrine
* Rectangular ovenproof dish

**TIERED SERVER (two-tier stand for holding small sandwiches, hors d'oeuvres, or petit fours)**
* Two different-size cake decorating stands or pedestal servers (stack the smaller one on top of the larger one)

**TIMBALE MOLDS; see** DARIOLE/TIMBALE MOLDS

**TIMER/PORTABLE TIMER (small digital or wind-up gadget for monitoring cooking times)**
* Alarm clock or cell-phone alarm (set to go off at the designated time)

**TOASTER (small electrical appliance for toasting bread and bakery items)**
* Oven broiler (toast bread 4 inches from the heat until browned, 30 to 60 seconds each side)
* Convection oven on broil setting (preheat oven before toasting the bread)

- Stovetop and preheated, heavy-bottomed skillet (toast bread both sides)
- Fireplace embers (toast bread with a long-tined turning fork, barbecue/grill fork, or bent coat hanger)
- Gas or charcoal grill, preheated (toast bread on the rack or over low heat using a grill fork; grill tongs; or long, sturdy skewer)

**TOASTER OVEN BAKING STONE (*flat piece of unglazed clay or terra-cotta; used for producing a crustier finish on pizza and free-form breads*)**
- Inverted 9-inch unglazed terra-cotta dish
- Unglazed quarry tile

**TOASTER RACK (*small silver or stainless-steel 5- or 6-slot serving rack; used for holding dry toast to prevent it becoming soggy*)**
- Prop slices of toast up against a jar, mug, or something similar for about 1 minute

**TOASTER TONGS (*long silicone or bamboo tweezers; used for safely removing stuck toast*)**
- Bamboo chopsticks
- Unfinished wood mixing fork
- End of a wooden spoon
- Two plastic take-out knives

(Unplug the toaster before removing the toast)

**TOBAN/DONABE SKILLET (*Japanese earthenware/ceramic grilling plate for stovetop and oven cooking and serving*)**
- Japanese iron teppan
- Mexican comal
- Wide, shallow, cast-iron roaster

⦁ Shallow, stoneware, stovetop and oven-safe baking dish

**TOFU PRESS/TSUKURIKI (Japanese cypress press; used for extracting liquid from tofu)**
⦁ Small cutting board or plate plus weight, such as heavy skillet or food cans (gently press the tofu several times to extract the water)

**TOMATO DESEEDER (tool for removing seeds from halved tomatoes)**
⦁ Small end of a melon baller
⦁ Small scoop
⦁ Demitasse/espresso or baby spoon
⦁ Grapefruit spoon
⦁ Pointed end of a stationary or swivel peeler

**TOMATO KNIFE (small knife with sharp serrations and rounded tip)**
⦁ Serrated steak knife
⦁ Citrus knife

**TOMATO STRAINER (small electric appliance for separating skin and seeds from juice and pulp)**
⦁ Italian, hand-operated tomato press/*passapomodoro*
⦁ Food mill
⦁ Large holes of a box grater (deseed plum tomatoes and then grate, discarding skins)

**TONGS, CANNING; see** CANNING TONGS/JAR LIFTER

**TONGS, KITCHEN (12-inch-length tongs with scalloped-edged blades; used for picking up or turning food items)**
⦁ **For turning over crepes, tortillas, fish, meat, and poultry:** ice tongs, cooking chopsticks, long toaster tongs, or two flameproof spatulas
⦁ **For handling cold ingredients:** salad tongs
⦁ **For roasting fresh chiles over a stovetop gas flame:** long-handled fork

* **For dipping food in egg and coating mix, or for aligning garnishes:** strawberry huller, sugar-cube tongs, tea-bag squeezer, kitchen tweezers, or one's own hands

### TONGS, LOCKING SPRING-ACTION (long tongs with a small steel loop that locks tongs closed for storage)

* Non-locking tongs plus small rubber band or plastic ring from the screw top of a plastic food or juice container (place over the top when not in use)

### TOOL CADDY (countertop container for holding cooking utensils)

* Terra-cotta flowerpot
* Small galvanized bucket
* Wide-mouth, ceramic pitcher/jug
* Large, empty coffee can or 28-ounce tomato-juice can, with labels removed

### TOOTHPICKS/COCKTAIL STICKS; see also SKEWERS, APPETIZER/FOOD PICKS

* Small lengths of uncooked dried spaghetti (for serving bite-sized pieces of light food, for testing cakes for doneness, or for joining or holding ingredients together, such as stuffed cabbage, rollatini, or roulades)

### TORTILLA FRY BASKET (long-handled duel basket; used for frying soft tortillas into crisp basket shapes); see also TORTILLA PAN SET; TACO SHELL MAKER

* Potato bird nest maker
* Two strainers, one a little smaller so it fits into the larger one
* Wire spider or fry basket plus ladle (use the ladle to hold the tortilla in the spider or basket)
* Ladle (use the ladle to press into the tortilla to give it a bowl shape; then remove when tortilla is set and continue frying)

• Clean, empty, PBA-free food can with label and both ends removed (use tongs to gently press the can into the center of the tortilla; then remove when tortilla is set and continue frying)

**TORTILLA PAN SET (*small fluted pans; used for baking soft tortillas into crisp basket shapes in a preheated 450°F oven*)**
• Small Bundt pans, large empty food cans, or jumbo muffin cups set on a baking sheet (press warm greased tortillas over the backs of the pans or cups before baking)

**TORTILLA PRESS/TORTILLERA (*7-inch cast-iron, hard plastic, or wooden hinged press; used for flattening tortilla dough into disks*)**
• Rolling pin and two pieces of parchment paper (roll each piece of dough between the papers)
• Heavy skillet and two pieces of heavy plastic cut from a large freezer bag (place piece of dough between the pieces of plastic and then press down hard with the skillet)
• Empty coffee can and piece of plastic wrap or thin plastic cut from a produce bag (attach plastic to the bottom of the can and press down hard with the can)

**TORTILLA STEAMER (*shallow, terra-cotta pot with cover for warming tortillas*)**
• Two (8- or 9-inch) unglazed terra-cotta plant saucers—one for the base and the other, inverted, for the cover—(soak saucers in water 15 to 30 minutes before adding tortillas, placing in a cold oven, and heating to 400°F until hot; use for several tortillas at a time)
• Skillet plus splatter screen (place splatter screen over the skillet filled with an inch or so of simmering water; use for one tortilla at a time)

**TORTILLA WARMER/CHIQUIHUITE (*traditional woven basket lined with a towel; used for keeping tortillas warm while serving*)**
• Styrofoam tortilla warmer

- Heated 8- to 10-inch earthenware cake or pie pan plus a cover: dinner plate, pan lid, or aluminum foil
- Heated, cast-iron, lidded skillet
- Clean, non-terry dishtowel or linen napkin

## TRAY, CORK-LINED (*rectangular tray with cork base; used for transporting drinks*)
- Regular tray containing a silicone-baking sheet or piece of mesh shelf liner cut to size

## TRAY, SERVING; *see* SERVING PLATTER/BUFFET TRAY

## TRAY, SILVER OR GOLD; *see* SERVING PLATTER/BUFFET TRAY, SILVER OR GOLD

## TRIFLE BOWL; *see* DESSERT SERVING DISH, LARGE

## TRIVET (*small flat stand for protecting surfaces from hot serving dishes*)
- Ceramic tile or bread-warming tile
- Wok rest
- Small cooling rack
- Old wooden cutting board
- Heavy potholder
- Thick folded kitchen towel
- Inverted heatproof plate, or cover of a flat metal or earthenware casserole dish
- Inverted heavy baking sheet (for large pans)

## TRUFFLE SHAVER/SLICER (*small device with a razor-sharp blade; used for slicing white truffles*)
- Cheese plane/slicer with a 2- to 3-inch slot
- Chocolate shaver
- Mini mandoline
- Y-shaped vegetable peeler

**TRUSSING NEEDLE/BUTCHER'S NEEDLE (long metal needle; used for trussing/tying poultry or meat to keep its shape during cooking)**
  ● Large darning or upholstery needle

**TUBE PAN (deep baking pan with a hollow tube in the center, which allows for more uniform baking)**
  ● Bundt pan or angel food pan

**TUILES MOLD/MOULE À TUILES (pan with curved troughs; used to shape hot cookies as they cool)**
  ● Rolling pin, sturdy glass bottle, or clean broom handle

**TUREEN (deep, bulbous serving dish with domed lid; used for holding soup)**
  ● Covered bean pot
  ● Deep-lidded casserole dish
  ● Stoneware insert from a slow cooker
  ● Hollowed-out winter melon/wax gourd, winter squash, or sugar pumpkin (cut a small slice from the bottom to stabilize)
  ● Large jug (for pouring; use in place of tureen and ladle)
  ● Electric coffee maker (insides removed) or carafe (for pouring and keeping soup hot)

**TURKEY LIFTERS (small pitchfork-type utensils; used for moving the cooked turkey from roasting pan to carving board)**
  ● Long-handled wooden spoon (insert into the main cavity for lifting; use two spoons for a large bird—one in each cavity)
  ● Clean silicone oven mitts, or regular oven mitts covered with plastic produce bags
  ● Few layers of folded paper towels (one for each hand)
  ● Two long strips of folded cheesecloth (or heavy-duty foil) placed beneath the bird before cooking and then used to lift it when cooked

**TWEEZERS, KITCHEN (*long tweezer-type tool; used for picking up small food items and aligning tiny garnishes*)**
- Surgical tweezers
- Sugar-cube tongs or other small tongs
- Strawberry huller
- Tea-bag squeezer

**TWINE, KITCHEN, DISPENSER/STRING KEEPER (*storage holder for keeping kitchen twine clean*)**
- Sealable plastic bag with a small hole made near the bottom (feed the end of the twine through the hole)
- Glass sugar shaker, or lidded jar with a hole made in the center of the lid (feed the twine from the middle of the spool through the top of the container)
- Used 2- or 3-liter plastic bottle with the bottom half cut off (feed the end of the twine through the bottle's neck)

**TWINE, KITCHEN/WHITE KITCHEN STRING (*cotton, hemp, or linen twine; used for trussing poultry and securing various culinary items*)**
- Double strand of unflavored, unwaxed dental floss
- Untreated cotton string
- Heavy white cotton button or carpet thread (for light use)
- 15-inch paper-coated produce wire with paper stripped off (for a small amount)
- Leftover tea-bag string (for a bouquet garni or other small amounts of ingredients)
- Strong, sharp, uncolored toothpicks; skewers; or pieces of spaghetti (for holding food items together)
- Thawed frozen banana leaf softened over a flame (or in a steamer) and then cut into thin strips (or the banana leaf stem cut or torn in half)
- Fresh cornhusks or softened dried husks, cut into long thin strips
- Celery stalk strings peeled off with a vegetable peeler

* Plastic wrap torn into thin strips, or strips cut from a produce bag (for sealing microwave cooking bags)
* Japanese 8-inch dried gourd strips/*kampyo* soaked in water until softened, 10 to 15 minutes (edible food ties)
* Long, fresh chives blanched in boiling water for 1 or 2 seconds, cooled in ice water, and then patted dry (edible food ties)
* Long, fresh green onion blades, blanched in boiling water for 20 seconds, cooled in iced water, and then split lengthwise and patted dry (edible food ties)

## TWIST TIES, METAL (*paper-coated wire for closing produce bags*)
* 15-inch paper-coated produce ties cut into segments
* Plastic bread-wrapper tabs (can be used in the microwave)
* Plastic strips cut from the produce bag

# V

**VACUUM SEALER (*appliance for removing the air from plastic food bags*)**
- Heavy-duty freezer bag (with a pressable, non-zipper top) and pot of water (partly seal bag, leaving small opening; immerse bag nearly to the top edge, and then seal after air escapes)
- Heavy-duty freezer bag (with a pressable, non-zipper top) and straw (pack food flat; press air out of the bag by hand; close zipper, leaving small opening at the end; insert straw 1/2 inch and suck out any remaining air; remove straw; and seal bag)

**VEGETABLE BRUSH/VEGETABLE SCRUBBER (*small brush for cleaning sturdy raw vegetables*)**
- New large nailbrush
- Japanese natural-coconut-fiber vegetable brush/*tawashi* (from an Asian market)
- New bath/exfoliating mitt (from a dollar store)
- Scrunched-up plastic netting (from fruit or vegetables)

**VEGETABLE CHOPPER; *see* CHOPPER, SPRING ACTION/SPRING LOADED**

**VEGETABLE PEELER, SERRATED (*small tool for removing fruit and vegetable skins, especially tomatoes, plums, and peaches*)**
- Small, serrated knife

**VEGETABLE SPIRAL SLICER; *see* SPIRAL SLICER, VEGETABLE/SPIRALING MACHINE**

**VERTICAL ROASTER; *see* CHICKEN ROASTER, VERTICAL**

## VOL-AU-VENT CUTTER *(metal cutter for forming puff-pastry cases)*

* **For square or rectangular vol-au-vents:** cut pastry to size; then, using a sharp knife, make a 1/4- or 1/2-inch-deep incision, 1 to 1 1/2 inches from the edge, continuing all the way around
* **For round vol-au-vents:** cut pastry into 4-inch rounds; then, using a 2 1/2-inch cutter, press down two-thirds of the way into the pastry
* **For hors d'oeuvre vol-au-vents:** cut pastry into 1 1/2-inch rounds; cut a 3/4-inch hole in half of the rounds, and then lay the doughnut-shaped rounds on top of the whole ones

# W

### WAFFLE IRON (small lidded appliance for cooking waffles)
- Countertop grill/griddle (prop up the lid, if necessary, with a piece of crushed foil placed on each side of the grill surface; and then press down slightly when flipping the waffles so as to create ridges)

### WARMING DRAWER (small appliance with a temperature range of 80°F to 120°F; used for warming dishes and keeping food warm)
**For warming serveware and dishes:**
- Dishwasher set on waterless "preheat" setting or on dry cycle (for warming oven-safe plates and platters)
- Microwave set on Medium or High for 60 to 90 seconds (for warming microwavable-safe plates and platters; sprinkle them with a little water beforehand)
- Toaster oven set to 200°F for a minute, or regular oven preheated to 175°F
- Covered electric skillet set on warm (for warming a few plates)

**For keeping food warm:**
- Gas or electric oven set at 175°F to 200°F (if heating elements are located at the top, place a wire cooling rack on the floor of the oven to create extra space)
- Slow cooker or electric roaster set on warm or low (for keeping stew and soup warm)
- Seasoned earthenware container, cast-iron pot, or heavy granite/stone bowl such as a Korean dolsot/*dolsotsi* (for cooking in and then keeping food warm; these containers absorb heat and stay hot for a long time)
- Insulated ice cooler or microwave oven plus a hot water bottle or a hot pack heated in the microwave (wrap the dish in foil and a kitchen towel; for longer duration in a cooler, add a blanket or towels)

**WASABI GRATER; see** *GINGER GRATER/OROSHIGANE*

**WATERMELON KNIFE** *(long, perforated knife for slicing and cubing watermelon)*
* Serrated bread knife

**WAXED PAPER** *(thin, waxed-coated paper for wrapping food plus other culinary applications)*
* **For lining baking pans:** parchment paper (can be reused), foil, or salt-free butter wrappers
* **For placing between raw hamburgers or flattened meat or chicken for freezing:** flattened cupcake liners/papers, or saved plastic lids from food or coffee cans
* **For laying on top of custard to prevent a skin from forming:** greased parchment paper
* **For pounding meat or chicken; crushing bread, crackers, or spices; or for holding flour or crumbs for breading/dredging:** opened-up cereal box liner or produce bag, parchment paper, plastic wrap, or sheet of printer paper
* **For lining the food scale:** parchment paper, sheet of printer paper, or interior page of a newspaper
* **For separating baked cookies for storage/shipping:** flattened basket-type coffee filters
* **For covering food being heated in the microwave:** microwave cooking lid/vented plastic dome, microwave steamer lid, or inverted microwave-safe bowl

**WHISK/WHIP, BALLOON** *(stainless-steel looped wires joined to a handle; used for blending, whipping, and incorporating air into a batter)*
* Whip attachment from an immersion blender
* One of the beaters from a handheld electric mixer
* Two dinner forks held together facing inward

* Beverage frother
* Wire-type pastry blender

**WHISK/WHIP, FLAT (*semi-flat whisk for getting into the corners of a saucepan or skillet*)**
* Slotted fish spatula

**WHISK/WHIP, PLASTIC-COATED (*whisk used for nonstick cookware*)**
* Plastic fork

**WHOOPIE PIE PAN (*nonstick pan with 12 shallow indentations for making cake-like cookies*)**
* Muffin-top pan
* Ice-cream sandwich pan
* Cast-iron silver dollar pan
* Tart pan with 2 1/2-inch-wide shallow cups (for smaller versions)
* Parchment-lined baking sheet (pipe mounds with a plain tip, 2 inches apart and 2 inches in diameter, pressing down the point made by the pastry bag tip; or drop the batter in 2- to 3-tablespoon mounds, 3 inches apart)

**WINDSOR PAN (*saucepan with a narrow base, wide top, and deep flared sides; used for reducing sauces efficiently*)**
* Chef's pan/multi-function pan/*fait-tout* pan
* Sauté pan/*sauteuse*

**WINE AERATOR (*handheld gadget used for quickly decanting wine by introducing air/oxygen*)**
* Two large pitchers (pour the just-opened wine from one pitcher to another about 15 times)
* Freestanding or immersion blender (blend the just-opened wine on high speed for 20 to 30 seconds)

### WINE COOLER/BUCKET (container for chilling wine or keeping it chilled at the table)
* Plastic bucket, stainless-steel stockpot, or hibachi lined with plastic wrap (for chilling wine, use 4 parts ice, preferably crushed, 1 part water, and 1 part salt)
* Large cast-iron pot chilled several hours in the refrigerator (for keeping wine chilled)
* Chilled ice-cream freezer canister from a freezer-stored ice-cream maker (for keeping wine chilled)
* Bubble wrap, or thin flexible ice pack/Cryopak blanket wrapped around the wine bottle and held in place with tape or kitchen twine (for keeping wine chilled)
* Wet and wrung out linen dishtowel, or dampened paper towels, wrapped around the bottle before placing it in the freezer for 15 minutes (for quick chilling)
* Picnic cooler filled half-full with cold water and ice (for chilling several bottles)
* Clay pot cooler/Zeer pot (for keeping wine chilled while outdoors)

### WINE DECANTER/CARAFE (glass or crystal ornamental vessel for serving decanted wine)
* Tall glass or Borosilicate vessel or plastic pitcher (decant/aerate young wine by pouring it from one vessel to another several times; decant old wine with sediment by slowly pouring it into the decanter along the side, stopping when the sediment gets to the top of the bottle or when 1 inch remains in the bottle)

### WINE DRIP COLLAR/DRIP RING (felt-lined ring for absorbing any drips as wine is poured)
* Napkin (held under the neck of the bottle)
* Dab of butter (rubbed around the top of the bottle)

### WINE SAVER/STOPPER/VACUUM-PUMP KIT (system for vacuuming air from an opened bottle of wine); see also CHAMPAGNE SAVER

* Exhaling into the bottle so carbon dioxide forces the oxygen out (inhale deeply and hold the breath a few seconds before exhaling deeply)
* Smallest container possible with an airtight lid, such as an empty water or soda bottle (fill bottle to the very top to exclude air or squeeze bottle until the wine comes as close to the top as possible, and then quickly tighten the cap and refrigerate; use within three or four days if possible)
* Heavy-duty freezer bag (freeze wine for future use in sauces, stews, and marinades, or freeze in ice-cube trays to chill sangrias or wine spritzers and then transfer to a freezer bag when frozen; alternatively, simmer the wine until reduced to 1/4 of the volume and then freeze—the alcohol will be mostly boiled out and the flavor intensified)

    Boxed wine (lasts up to four weeks after opening; as wine is used, the inner bag deflates, preventing exposure to air). Or consider canned wine (no leftover to cope with)

### WINE SLEEVE (padded sleeve for safely transporting a wine bottle)

* Bubble wrap plus duct tape or a rubber band

### WOK (large, wide, bowl-shaped carbon steel, flat-bottomed pan; used for high-temperature stir-frying)

* Round-bottomed wok plus wok ring (place wok ring over the burner with the grate removed)
* Large, high-sided sauté pan; wide cast-iron skillet; or large nonstick skillet made without PTFE and PFOA coatings, which break down over high heat
* Roasting pan set over two burners (for a large amount of ingredients)

**WOK RACK (*metal rack that fits inside the wok; used for supporting a dish or bowl of food for steaming*)**
- 7- or 8-inch cake-cooling rack
- Four wooden chopsticks, flat metal skewers, or knives (place two length-wise and two crosswise)

**WOK SPATULA (*shovel-type tool; used for stirring and flipping ingredients being cooked/stir-fried*)**
- Long-handled metal stirring spoon
- Wooden spoon for a nonstick wok

**WOOD CHIP BOX; *see* GRILL SMOKER BOX**

**WOOD CHIPS (*hardwood slivers; used to impart a smoky flavor to grilled food*)**
- Shavings or sawdust from deciduous trees, not pine, softwood, or treated wood (for gas grills; soak like wood chips)
- Black or green dried tea leaves (for gas grills; soak like wood chips)
- Hardwood chunks; wood pellets; coconut-shell discs; dried sticks; or cut-up, dried, trimmed tree prunings (for charcoal grills; soak or place directly on the hot coals)
- Woody herbs, such as fennel, lemon verbena, rosemary, or sage; or dried bay, basil, or chervil stems (for charcoal grills; dampen and scatter directly on the hot coals)
- Chopped-up dead stalks from the garden (for charcoal grills; soak like wood chips and throw directly on the hot coals)
- Nut shells, such as walnut, preferably crushed (for charcoal grills; soak and scatter directly on the hot coals)
- Cedar paper wraps (soak wrap and then place food directly on the wrap, parallel to the grain; fold over the edges and secure with kitchen twine; grill on all sides for a light, smoky taste)

**WOOD CHIPS, FRUITWOOD (*apple, cherry, peach, and other fruitwood slivers; used to impart a smoky fruitwood flavor to grilled food*)**
- Prunings from fruit trees, trimmed into small pieces and soaked in water overnight
- Regular wood shavings or sawdust soaked at least 30 minutes in unsweetened fruit juice (for wine-infused chips or wine barrel staves, soak applewood chips in equal parts red wine and water; for whiskey barrel staves, soak chips in equal parts whiskey and water)

# Y

**YOGURT CHEESE BAG (12-x-12-inch cotton drawstring bag for draining yogurt); see** *CHEESE BAG; NUTMILK BAG*

**YOGURT INCUBATOR (controlled environment for keeping milk and starter at the proper temperature for bacteria growth)**
- Dehydrator set at 115°F for 3 1/2 to 4 hours (place the yogurt on the bottom of the dehydrator after removing some of the shelves)
- Preheated electric bread-proofing box
- Gas or electric oven heated to 200°F and then immediately turned off
- Unlit gas oven with a pilot light
- Gas or electric oven with the oven light on (switch the light on 30 minutes before putting in the yogurt)
- Microwave oven or dishwasher containing a large jug of hot water
- Preheated, insulated picnic cooler containing crumpled newspaper, hot water bottle, or jars of hot water

**YOGURT MAKER/YAOURTIÈRE or ELECTRIC PRESSURE COOKER WITH A YOGURT SETTING (machine for keeping milk and starter at the proper temperature for bacteria growth)**
- Large, wide-mouth vacuum bottle/jug
- Small slow cooker preheated to warm, unplugged, and then wrapped in a blanket or terry towels (use 1-cup or pint-size canning jars for the yogurt)
- Heatkeeper Food Jar, such as Stanley
  (Scald vacuum bottle or jars with boiling water and then let cool slightly before adding warm milk-yogurt mixture; cover and leave, undisturbed, until slightly thickened, 8 to 12 hours.)

### YOGURT STRAINER/SOFT CHEESE MAKER/YOGURT CHEESE FUNNEL (mesh-lined, wedge-shaped sieve for draining whey from yogurt)

- Fine-mesh sieve, or strainer from a drip coffee maker, lined with a double layer of dampened cheesecloth (or a rinsed cotton napkin, or two paper coffee filters)

### YONANAS (small electric frozen fruit dessert maker; used for turning frozen fruits into instant dessert)

- Food processor or high-speed blender (process or blend the frozen chopped fruit until smooth, adding 1 or 2 tablespoons liquid (fruit juice, coconut water, or water), if necessary
- Juicer (juice the frozen fruit with the blank plate in position)

# Z

**ZESTER/CANELLE KNIFE/LEMON ZESTER** *(hand-held device with an etched, stainless steel grating surface; used for shaving the peel without the pith)*
- Microplane rasp grater
- Channel knife (slice the strips into tiny slivers)
- Smallest holes on a box grater
- Vegetable peeler or paring knife (remove citrus peel in lengthwise strips, scrape away any white pith, and then slice into tiny slivers)

**ZUCCHINI CORER** *(tool with a long, narrow, trough-shaped blade; used for hollowing out the cores of zucchini or cucumbers)*
- Apple corer
- Grapefruit knife
- Sharp-tipped vegetable peeler, stationary or swivel

## BAKING DISH EQUIVALENTS

When substituting one dish for another use the following guidelines:

Soufflés and casseroles: fill dishes up to 3/4 to 1-inch below the top

Ovenproof glass pan: reduce oven temperature by 25°F

Deeper pans or square pans: increase baking time by one-eighth to one-quarter, although same depth as original is best

Shallower pan: reduce baking time by one-eighth to one-quarter, although same depth as original is best

**1 pint (2-cup)**

5" x 2" soufflé dish

5" x 2 1/2" baking dish

**3/4 quart (3-cup)**

5 3/4" x 2 3/4" baking dish

**1 quart (4-cup)**

6" x 3" soufflé dish

8" x 3" bowl

8" x 6" x 1 1/2" baking dish

6 1/2" x 6 1/2" x 2" Corning casserole dish

**1 1/4 quart (5-cup)**

6 1/2" x 3" soufflé dish

**1 1/2 quart (6-cup)**

7" x 3" soufflé dish

8" x 8" x 1 1/2" square pan

10" x 6" x 1 1/2" baking dish

**1 3/4 quart (7-cup)**

8 1/2" x 2 1/2" soufflé dish

**2 quart (8-cup)**

7" x 3 1/2" soufflé dish

8" x 3" soufflé dish

8" x 8" x 2" square pan

8" x 8" x 2 1/2" Corning casserole dish

8" x 10" gratin dish

9" x 2" round pan

9" x 9" x 1 1/2" square pan

9" or 10" cast-iron skillet

11" x 7" x 2" rectangular pan

12 1/4" x 8 3/4" x 2 1/2" oval baking dish

## 2 1/2 quart (10-cup)

9" soufflé dish

10" x 10" x 1 1/2" baking dish

10" x 10" x 2" Corning casserole dish

11 3/4" x 7 1/2" x 1 3/4" Pyrex baking dish

## 3 quart (12-cup)

9" x 12" gratin dish

10" x 10" x 2" square pan

13 1/2" x 8 1/2" x 2" glass baking dish

13" x 9" x 2" glass baking dish

15" x 10" x 2" oval gratin dish

## 3 1/2 quart (14-cup)

13" x 9" x 3" Le Creuset baking dish

16" x 10" oval gratin dish

## 4 quart (16-cup)

12" x 12" x 2" square

## BAKING PAN EQUIVALENTS

When substituting one pan for another use the following guidelines:

Bread: fill pans half full

Cakes: fill round pans half full, loaf and tube pans two-thirds full, fluted pans three-quarters full

Ovenproof glass pan: reduce oven temperature by 25°F

Deeper pans or square pans: increase baking time by one-eighth to one-quarter, although same depth as original is best

Shallower pan: reduce baking time by one-eighth to one-quarter, although same depth as original is best

### 2 tablespoons (1/8 cup)

1 3/4" x 3/4" mini muffin cup or madeleine cup

1 7/8" x 3 3/4" barquette mold

2 1/2" scallop shell

### 3 tablespoons

1 7/8" x 2 3/4" financier mold

### 4 tablespoons (1/4 cup)

2 3/4" x 1 1/8" muffin cup

### 6 tablespoons

4" x 3/4" two-piece tart

### 1/2 cup

2 1/2" high *baba au rhum* mold

2 2/3" x 1 3/8" muffin cup

3" x 1 1/2" ramekin

4" x 1" fluted round tartlet

4" x 1 1/4" round tart

3 1/4" x 2" x 1 1/4" mini loaf

### 2/3 to 3/4 cup

2 1/4" x 1 3/4" x 1/2" madeleine cup

3" x 1 1/4" jumbo muffin cup

3" x 2 1/2" popover cup

3 1/8" x 1 3/8" (5 fluid-ounce) ovenproof ramekin

3 1/2" x 1 1/4" jumbo muffin cup

3 1/2" x 1 3/4" (6 fluid-ounce) ovenproof ramekin

3 7/8" x 2 1/2" x 5/8" mini loaf

4 3/4" x 3/4" two-piece tart

**1 cup**

6" x 3 1/2" x 1 3/4" mini angel food cake

**1 1/2 cups**

4 1/2" deep-dish mini pie

5 1/2" x 1" two-piece tart

**1 3/4 cups**

5 3/4" x 3 1/4" x 2" mini disposable loaf

5 3/4" x 3 1/4" x 2 1/4" mini loaf

**2 cups**

5" x 3" x 2" loaf

5 1/2" x 3" x 2 1/2" loaf

5 3/4" x 3 1/4" x 2 1/2" loaf

5 5/8" x 3 1/8" x 2 1/4" loaf

7" x 1" pie

7" x 1 1/2" round cake

**2 1/4 cups**

5 3/4" x 3 1/2" x 2 1/4" loaf

**3 to 3 1/2 cups**

6" sapphire-style Bundt

6" x 1 3/4" heart-shaped cake

6" x 2" petal- or heart-shaped cake

6" x 3 1/2" x 2" loaf

6" x 4 1/2" x 3" loaf

6 1/4" x 2 1/2" ring mold

7 3/4" x 1" two-piece tart

8" x 1 1/4" pie

**3 3/4 cups**

6" x 1 1/2" round cake

**4 to 4 1/2 cups**

    6" x 2" round cake

    5 1/2" (12-ounce) coffee can

    6" x 3" springform

    7 1/2" x 3 3/4" x 2 1/4" loaf

    7 3/4" x 3 5/8" x 2 1/4" loaf

    8" x 1 1/2" pie

    8 "x 1 1/2" round cake

    8" x 4" x 2 1/2" loaf

    8 1/4" x 2 1/4" ring mold

    8 1/2" x 2 1/4" ring mold

    9" x 1 1/4" pie

    9 1/2" x 1" two-piece tart

    9 1/2" x 4 1/2" x 2 1/2" stoneware loaf

    10 1/4" x 1 1/4" fluted obsttortenform

    1-quart casserole dish

**5 to 5 1/2 cups**

    6 1/2" x 3" Turk's head

    6 1/2" x 3 1/2" small Bundt

    7" x 2" round cake

    7" x 2 1/2" springform

    8" x 3 3/4" x 2" disposable loaf

    8" x 3 3/4" x 2 3/4" brioche

    8" x 4" x 2" loaf

    8 1/4" x 4 1/4" x 2 1/2" ceramic savarin mold

    9" x 1 1/2" pie

    9" x 1 1/2" heart-shaped cake

    9 1/2" x 1" tart

    10" x 1" two-piece tart

    10" x 1 1/2" fluted quiche mold

**6 to 6 1/2 cups**

    7" x 3" brioche mold

    7" x 5 1/2" x 4" oval melon mold

7 1/2" x 3" Bundt

8" bevel/fluted tube

8" x 2" round cake

8" x 3 1/4" Bundt

8" x 3" x 2" loaf

8" x 8" x 1 1/2" square

8 1/2" x 3 5/8" x 2" loaf

8 1/2" x 4 1/2" x 2 1/2" loaf

8 1/2" x 4 1/2" x 2 5/8" loaf

9" x 1 1/2" round cake

9" x 2" ceramic pie

9 1/4" x 8 1/2" x 2" heart-shaped cake

10" x 1 1/2" pie

10" x 6" x 1 3/4" rectangular

1 1/2" quart casserole

## 7 cups

8 1/2" x 3 1/2" Kugelhopf mold

8 1/2" x 4 1/4" x 3 1/8" seamless loaf

9 1/2" Pyrex deep-dish pie

11" x 1" two-piece tart

## 7 1/2 cups

6" x 4 1/4" Charlotte mold

8 1/2" x 2 1/2" springform

9" x 2 3/4" ring mold

## 8 to 8 3/4 cups

8" x 8" x 2" square

9" x 2" deep-dish pie

9" x 2" round cake

9" x 3" fluted brioche

9" x 4" x 4" lidded /Pullman/*pain de mie* loaf

9" x 5" x 2 5/8" loaf

9" x 5" x 3" loaf

9" x 9" x 1 1/2" square

9 1/4" x 2 3/4" ring mold
9 1/2" x 3 1/4" glass Kugelhopf mold
9 1/2" x 3 1/4" fluted brioche
9 5/8" x 5 1/2" x 2 3/4" loaf
10" x 2" two-piece tart
10" x 4" x 3" loaf
10" x 5" x 2 5/8" loaf
11" x 7" x 1 1/2" rectangular
11" x 7" x 2" rectangular (2 quarts)
12" x 4" x 2 1/2" tea loaf
13" x 4" x 4" lidded Pullman/*pain de mie* loaf
13 3/4" x 4 1/2" rectangular two-piece tart
14" x 4 1/2" rectangular two-piece tart
2-quart casserole

## 9 cups

8" x 3" tube
8" x 3 1/4" professional tube
9" x 3" Bundt
9" x 3 1/2" Bundt
12 1/2" x 1" two-piece tart

## 10 cups

8" x 3" round cake
8" x 3 1/4" round cake
9" x 2 1/2" springform
9" x 2 3/4" springform
9" x 3" tube
9" x 9" x 2" square
9 1/2" x 2 1/2" springform
11" x 6 1/2" x 3 1/4" baking pan
11 3/4" x 7 3/4" x 1 3/4" Pyrex baking dish
12" x 7 1/2" x 1" baking pan
15" x 10" x 1" jellyroll

**10 3/4 to 11 cups**

    9" x 3" round cake

    9" x 4" Kugelhopf mold

    9" x 4 1/2" Fluted tube

    15 1/2" x 10 1/2" x 1" jellyroll

**12 cups**

    9" x 3 1/2" angel cake or tube

    9 1/2" x 2 1/2" three-in-one springform

    9 3/4" x 4 1/4" Kugelhopf mold

    10" x 2 1/4" springform

    10" x 2 1/2" springform

    10" x 3 1/4" Kugelhopf mold

    10" x 3 1/2" Bundt

    10" x 10" x 2" square

    13 1/2" x 8 1/2" x 2" glass baking dish

**12 to 13 cups**

    10" x 4 1/4" Kugelhopf mold

    12" x 2 1/2" Bundt

**15 cups**

    10" x 4 1/4" Bundt

    12 1/4" x 8 1/4" x 2" rectangular

    13" x 9" x 2" rectangular

    14" x 11" x 2" baking dish

**16 cups**

    9 1/2" x 4" tube

    9 1/2" x 13" x 2 1/2" rectangular

    10" x 4" tube

    10" x 5" nonstick tube

    10" x 3" round cake

    12" x 2" round cake

**18 cups**

    17" x 12" x 1" rectangle

    14" x 10 1/2" x 2 1/2" roasting pan

# U.S. VOLUME AND LIQUID EQUIVALENTS

| Volume Measure | | Liquid Measure |
|---|---|---|
| **Teaspoon** | | |
| 1/16 teaspoon | Pinch/dash | 6 drops |
| 1/8 teaspoon | 1/2 of 1/4 teaspoon | 10 drops |
| 1/4 teaspoon | 1/12 tablespoon | 20 drops |
| 1/2 teaspoon | 1/6 tablespoon | 40 drops |
| 3/4 teaspoon | 1/4 tablespoon | 1/8 fluid ounce |
| | | 1 fluid dram |
| 1 teaspoon | 1/3 tablespoon | 1/6 fluid ounce |
| | | 1 1/3 fluid drams |
| **Tablespoon** | | |
| 1/4 tablespoon | 3/4 teaspoon | 1/8 fluid ounce |
| 1/3 tablespoon | 1 teaspoon | 1/6 fluid ounce |
| 1/2 tablespoon | 1 1/2 teaspoons | 1/4 fluid ounce |
| 2/3 tablespoon | 2 teaspoons | 1/3 fluid ounce |
| 1 tablespoon | 3 teaspoons | 1/2 fluid ounce |
| | | 4 fluid drams |
| **Cup** | | |
| 1/16 cup | 1 tablespoon | 1/2 fluid ounce |
| | | 4 fluid drams |
| 1/8 cup | 2 tablespoons | 1 fluid ounce |
| | | 8 fluid drams |
| 1 jigger | 3 tablespoons | 1 1/2 fluid ounces |
| 1/4 cup | 4 tablespoons | 2 fluid ounces |
| | | 1/2 gill |
| | | 16 fluid drams |
| 1/3 cup | 5 tablespoons+1 teaspoon | 2 2/3 fluid ounces |

| | | |
|---|---|---|
| 3/8 cup | 6 tablespoons | 3 fluid ounces |
| | | 1/4 cup + 2 tablespoons |
| 1/2 cup | 8 tablespoons | 4 fluid ounces |
| | | 1 gill |
| | | 32 fluid drams |
| 5/8 cup | 10 tablespoons | 5 fluid ounces |
| | | 1/2 cup + 2 table-spoons |
| 2/3 cup | 10 tablespoons+2 teaspoons | 5 1/3 fluid ounces |
| 3/4 cup | 12 tablespoons | 6 fluid ounces |
| 7/8 cup | 14 tablespoons | 7 fluid ounces |
| | | 3/4 cup + 2 tablespoons |
| 1 cup | 16 tablespoons | 8 fluid ounces |
| | | 1/2 pint |

**Pint**

| | | |
|---|---|---|
| 1/16 pint | 1/8 cup | 1 fluid ounce |
| | | 2 tablespoons |
| 1/8 pint | 1/4 cup | 2 fluid ounces |
| | | 4 tablespoons |
| 1/4 pint | 1/2 cup | 4 fluid ounces |
| 1/3 pint | 2/3 cup | 5 1/3 fluid ounces |
| 3/8 pint | 3/4 cup | 6 fluid ounces |
| 1/2 pint | 1 cup | 8 fluid ounces |
| 5/8 pint | 1 1/4 cups | 10 fluid ounces |
| 2/3 pint | 1 1/3 cups | 10 2/3 fluid ounces |
| 3/4 pint | 1 1/2 cups | 12 fluid ounces |
| 7/8 pint | 1 3/4 cups | 14 fluid ounces |
| 1 pint | 2 cups | 16 fluid ounces |

## Quart

| 1/16 quart | 1/4 cup | 2 fluid ounces<br>1/8 pint |
| 1/8 quart | 1/2 cup | 4 fluid ounces<br>1/4 pint |
| 1/4-quart | 1 cup | 8 fluid ounces<br>1/2 pint |
| 1/3 quart | 1 1/3 cups | 10 2/3 fluid ounces |
| 3/8 quart | 1 1/2 cups | 12 fluid ounces<br>3/4 pint |
| 1/2 quart | 2 cups | 16 fluid ounces<br>1 pint |
| 5/8 quart | 2 1/2 cups | 20 fluid ounces |
| 2/3 quart | 2 2/3 cups | 21 1/3 fluid ounces |
| 3/4 quart | 3 cups | 24 fluid ounces<br>1 1/2 pints |
| 7/8 quart | 3 1/2 cups | 28 fluid ounces |
| 1 quart | 4 cups | 32 fluid ounces<br>2 pints |

## Gallon

| 1/16 gallon | 1 cup | 8 fluid ounces<br>1/2 pint |
| 1/8 gallon | 2 cups | 16 fluid ounces<br>1 pint |
| 1/4 gallon | 4 cups | 32 fluid ounces<br>2 pints<br>1 quart |
| 1/3 gallon | 5 1/3 cups | 42 2/3 fluid ounces<br>2.66 pints |
| 3/8 gallon | 6 cups | 48 fluid ounces<br>3 pints |

| 1/2 gallon | 8 cups | 64 fluid ounces |
| | | 2 quarts |
| 5/8 gallon | 10 cups | 80 fluid ounces |
| | | 5 pints |
| 2/3 gallon | 10 2/3 cups | 85 1/3 fluid ounces |
| | | 2 2/3 quarts |
| 3/4 gallon | 12 cups | 96 fluid ounces |
| | | 3 quarts |
| 7/8 gallon | 14 cups | 1 12 fluid ounces |
| | | 3 1/2 quarts |
| One gallon | 16 cups | 128 fluid ounces |
| | | 8 pints |
| | | 4 quarts |

# BIBLIOGRAPHY

Allen, Darina. *Forgotten Skills of Cooking.* London: Kyle Books, 2009.

America's Test Kitchen eds. *The America's Test Kitchen Do-It-Yourself Cookbook: 100+ Foolproof Kitchen Projects for the Adventurous Home Cook.* Brookline, MA: America's Test Kitchen, 2012.

America's Test Kitchen eds., and Guy Crosby. *The Science of Good Cooking: Master 50 Simple Concepts to Enjoy a Lifetime of Success in the Kitchen.* Brookline, MA: America's Test Kitchen, 2012.

Anderson, Jean. *1,001 Secrets of Great Cooks.* New York: Berkley Publishing Group, 1995.

_____. *Process This: New Recipes for the New Generation of Food Processors Plus Dozens of Timesaving Tips.* New York: William Morrow, 2002.

Arkin, Frieda. *Kitchen Wisdom.* New York: Holt, Rinehart & Winston, 1977.

_____. *More Kitchen Wisdom.* New York: Holt, Rinehart & Winston, 1982.

Aronson, Emily, Florence Fabricant, and Burt Wolf, eds. *The New Cooks' Catalogue.* New York: Alfred A. Knopf, 2000.

Bader, Myles H. *Grandmother's Kitchen Basics & Solutions.* Philadelphia: Creative Product Concepts, 2002.

_____. *10,000 Food Facts, Chefs' Secrets, & Household Hints.* New York: Metro Books, 2001.

Bader, Myles H., and Deborah Rose Peek. *Grandmother's Kitchen Wisdom.* Las Vegas: Northstar Publishing, 1998.

Bader, Dr. Myles H., and Tony Notaro. *Grandma Knows Best: Great Kitchen Secrets.* Fairfield, NJ: Telebrands Press, 2012.

Bayless, Rick. *Rick Bayless's Mexican Kitchen.* New York: Scribner, 1996.

Beard, James. *The Cooks' Catalogue.* New York: Avon Books, 1975.

Bernard, Ruth M. *Recipes and Instructions for Vita Mix 3600 Model.* Cleveland: Vitamix Corp., 1978.

Bluestein, Barry, and Kevin Morrissey. *Home Made in the Kitchen: Traditional Recipes and Household Projects Updated and Made Easy.* New York: Viking Studio Books, 1995.

Bradley, Fern Marshall, and eds. of Yankee Magazine. *Shameless Shortcuts; 1,027 Tips and Techniques That Help You Save Time, Save Money, and Save Work Every Day!* Dublin, NH: Yankee Publishing, 2004.

Brody, Lora. *The Kitchen Survival Guide.* New York: William Morrow, 1992.

Brown, Alton. *Gear for Your Kitchen.* New York: Stewart, Tabori & Chang, 2003.

_____. *Good Eats 2: The Middle Years.* New York: Stewart, Tabori & Chang, 2010.

_____. *I'm Just Here for More Food.* New York: Stewart, Tabori & Chang, 2004.

_____. *I'm Just Here for the Food,* Version 2. New York: Stewart, Tabori & Chang, 2006.

Brown, Rosemary Carleton. *Rosemary Brown's Big Kitchen Instruction Book.* Kansas City, MO: Andrews McMeel Publishing, 1998.

Cadwallader, Sharon. *The Living Kitchen.* San Francisco: Sierra Club Books, 1983.

Campbell, Susan. *Cooks' Tools.* New York: Bantam Books, 1980.

Carter, Noelle. "Great Indoors." *Los Angeles Times*, March 4, 2010, sec. E.

Chase, Andrew, and Nicole Young. *The Blender Bible.* Toronto: Robert Rose, 2005.

Cook's Illustrated, eds. *834 Kitchen Quick Tips: Techniques and Shortcuts for the Curious Cook.* Brookline, MA: America's Test Kitchen, 2006.

_____. *Inside American's Test Kitchen: New Recipes and Products.* Brookline, MA: America's Test Kitchen, 2001; 2003; 2005; 2006.

Cottrell, Annette, and Joshua McNichols. *The Urban Farm Handbook: City-Slicker Resources for Growing, Raising, Sourcing, Trading, and Preparing What You Eat.* Seattle, WA: Skipstone, 2011.

Craig, Elizabeth. *Cookery Illustrated and Household Management.* London: Odhams Press, 1938.

Darling, Benjamin. *Helpful Hints for Housewives.* San Francisco: Chronicle Books, 1992.

Doerfer, Jane. *Going Solo in the Kitchen.* New York: Alfred A. Knopf, 1995.

Douglas, Erika, ed. *The Family Circle Hints Book*. New York: Times Books, 1982.

Davis, Jenni. *The Cook's Compendium: 265 Essential Tips, Techniques, Trade Secrets and Tasty Recipes*. Buffalo, NY: Firefly Books, 2014.

Emery, Carla. *The Encyclopedia of Country Living: An Old-Fashioned Recipe Book*, Updated 9th ed. Seattle: Sasquatch Books, 2003.

Ettlinger, Steve. *The Complete Illustrated Guide to Everything Sold in Hardware Stores*. New York: Collier Books, 1988.

_____. *The Kitchenware Book*. New York: Barnes & Noble Books, 2001.

FC&A eds. *Uncommon Uses for Common Household Products*. Peachtree City, GA: Frank W. Cawood and Associates, 1999.

Ferriss, Timothy. *The 4-Hour Chef: The Simple Path to Cooking Like a Pro, Learning Anything, and Living the Good Life*. New York: New Harvest/ Houghton Mifflin Harcourt, 2012.

Fine Cooking Magazine eds, contributors, and readers. *How to Break an Egg*. Newtown, CT: Taunton Press, 2005.

France, Christine. *Cooking Hints & Tips*. New York: DK Publishing, 1997.

Goulding, Matt, and David Zinczenko. *Grill This, Not That: Backyard Survival Guide*. New York: Rodale Press, 2012.

Hamelman, Jeffrey. *Bread: A Baker's Book of Techniques and Recipes*, 2nd ed. Hoboken, NJ: John Wiley & Sons, 2013.

Hamilton, Leslie. *The Cheapskate's Guide to Living Cheaper and Better*. Secaucus, NJ: Carol Publishing Group, 1996.

Heloise. *Handy Household Hints from Heloise*. New York: Rodale Press, 2010.

Henry, Diana. *Salt Sugar Smoke: How to Preserve Fruit, Vegetables, Meat, and Fish*. London: Mitchell Beazley, 2012.

Hensperger, Beth. *Not Your Mother's Microwave Cookbook*. Boston: The Harvard Common Press, 2010.

Hériteau, Jacqueline. *The Best of Electric Crockery Cooking*. New York: Grosset & Dunlap, 1976.

Hill, Barbara. *The Cook's Book of Essential Information*. Kennewick, WA: Sumner House Press, 1987.

Hillman, Howard. *The New Kitchen Science*. Boston: Houghton Mifflin, 2003.

Hornby, Jane. *What to Cook and How to Cook it: Fresh and Easy*. New York: Phaidon Press, 2012.

Huck, Sarah, and Jaimee Young. *Campfire Cookery Adventuresome Recipes and Other Curiosities for the Great Outdoors*. New York: Stewart Tabori & Chang, 2010.

Hudges, Tom. *The Commonsense Kitchen: 500 Recipes + Lessons for a Hand-crafted Life*. San Francisco: Chronicle Books, 2010.

Hunt, Mary. *Cheaper, Better, Faster: Over 2,000 Tips and Tricks to Save You Time and Money Every Day*. Grand Rapids, MI: Revell, 2013.

Hupping, Carol, Cheryl Winters Tetreau, and Roger B. Yepsen, Jr., eds. *Rodale's Book of Hints, Tips and Everyday Wisdom*. Emmaus, PA: Rodale Press, 1985.

Jacobs, Carole, and Patrice Johnson. *The Complete Idiot's Guide to Pressure Cooking*. New York: Alpha Books, 2011.

Janjigian, Andrew, and Dan Souza. "Kitchen Notes." *Cook's Illustrated*. Jan-Feb 2012, 30-31.

Joachim, David, and Andrew Schloss, with A. Philip Handel. *The Science of Good Food: The Ultimate Reference on How Cooking Works*. Toronto: Robert Rose, 2008.

Kafka, Barbara. *Microwave Gourmet*. New York: William Morrow, 1987.

Keller, Thomas. "*Sous-vide* Comes Home." *Los Angeles Times*, September 8, 2011, sec. E.

Kesselheim, Alan S. *The Lightweight Gourmet: Drying and Cooking Food for the Outdoor Life*. Camden, ME: Rugged Mountain Press, 1994.

Klippensteen, Kate. *Cool Tools: Cooking Utensils from the Japanese Kitchen*. New York: Kodansha International, 2006.

Lampe, Ray. *Slow Fire: A Beginner's Guide to Barbecue*. San Francisco: Chronicle Books, 2012.

MacLeod, Jean B. *If I'd Only Listened to My Mom, I'd Know How to Do This*. New York: St. Martin's Griffin, 1997.

Martha Stewart Living, eds. *Simple Home Solutions*. New York: Clarkson Potter, 2004.

McCarthy, Bonnie. "Raise a glass to smart ideas." *Los Angeles Times*, December 16, 2017, sec. F.

Myhrvold, Nathan. *Modernist Cuisine: The Art and Science of Cooking*. Bellevue, WA: The Cooking Lab, 2011.

Nowak, Barbara. *Cook it Right*. South Pasadena, CA: Sandcastle Publishing, 1995.

Panati, Charles. *Extraordinary Origins of Everyday Things*. New York: Harper & Row, 1987.

Paskett, Angela. *Food Storage for Self-Sufficiency and Survival*. Iola, WI: Living Ready Books, 2014.

Reiman, Roy, ed. *1,628 Country Shortcuts from 1,628 Country People*. Greendale, WI: Reiman Publications, 1995.

Richardson, Alan, and Grace Young. *The Breath of a Wok: Unlocking the Spirit of Chinese Wok Cooking through Recipes and Lore*. New York: Simon & Schuster, 2004.

Sales, Georgia MacLeod, and Grover Sales. *The Clay-Pot Cookbook: A New Way of Cooking in an Ancient Pot*. New York: Atheneum Books, 1974.

Sass, Lorna. *Recipes from an Ecological Kitchen*. New York: William Morrow, 1992.

_____. *The Pressured Cook: Over 75 One-Pot Meals in Minutes Made in Today's 100% Safe Pressure Cookers*. New York: William Morrow, 1999.

Simmons, Marie. *Things Cooks Love: Implements, Ingredients, and Recipes*. Kansas City, MO: Andrews McMeel Publishing, 2008.

Sinclair, Charles G. *International Dictionary of Food & Cooking*. Chicago: Fitzroy Dearborn Publishers, 1998.

Stancil, Rosemary Dunn, and Lorela Nichols Wilkins. *The Microwave Cook's Complete Companion*. New York: Fawcett Columbine, 1990.

Stobart, Tom. *The Cook's Encyclopedia*. New York: Harper & Row, 1980.

Terry, Beth. *Plastic Free: How I Kicked the Plastic Habit and How You Can Too.* New York: Skyhorse Publishing, 2012.

Wolfert, Paula. *Mediterranean Clay Pot Cooking.* Hoboken, NJ: John Wiley & Sons, 2009.

Wolke, Robert L. *What Einstein Told His Cook 2: The Sequel: Further Adventures in Kitchen Science.* New York: W. W. Norton, 2005.

Zilkia, Janet. *Latin Food Culture.* Westport, CT: Greenwood Press, 2008.